Southern Biography Series

William J. Cooper, Jr., Editor

Alton Ochsner, Surgeon of the South

Alton Ochsner

Surgeon of the South

John Wilds *and* Ira Harkey

NIVERSITY PRESS

Baton Rouge and London

Copyright © 1990 by Louisiana State University Press
Manufactured in the United States of America
First printing
99 98 97 96 95 94 93 92 91 90   5 4 3 2 1
Designer: Laura Roubique Gleason
Typeface: Sabon
Typesetter: The Composing Room of Michigan, Inc.
Printer and binder: Thomson-Shore, Inc.

Frontispiece: Alton Ochsner at middle age. Courtesy Isabel Ochsner Mann.

LIBRARY OF CONGRESS CATALOGING-IN-PUBLICATION DATA

Wilds, John.
    Alton Ochsner, surgeon of the South / John Wilds and Ira Harkey.
        p.   cm.
    Includes bibliographical references.
    ISBN 0-8071-1564-9
        1. Ochsner, Alton, 1896–   .   2. Surgeons—Louisiana—Biography.
    3. Ochsner, Alton, 1896–   .   I. Harkey, Ira, 1918–   .   II. Title.
        [DNLM: 1. Physicians—biography.   WZ 100 0165w]
    RD27.35.O24W55   1990
    617'.092—dc20
    [B]
    DNLM/DLC
    for Library of Congress   89-13524
                                                                            CIP

The paper in this book meets the guidelines for permanence and durability of
the Committee on Production Guidelines for Book Longevity of the Council
on Library Resources. ∞

For Virgia Quin Harkey *and* Tommie Pittman Wilds

Contents

Illustrations

Preface

W hy don't you write the biography of Dr. Ochsner?" The question was put to one of the authors by Dr. Merrill O. Hines, then president of the Alton Ochsner Medical Foundation. The doctor brushed aside his patient's explanation about already being committed to other projects.

"You're a native of New Orleans. You've known Dr. Ochsner all your life. You understand New Orleans and the South. The Ochsner facilities are great southern institutions that have grown into international status."

Little more persuasion was needed. By the time the author left Dr. Hines's office, he had said he would write the book.

But it didn't turn out exactly that way.

Dr. Alton Ochsner, master surgeon and teacher known worldwide, was then eighty-one years old. His practice had occupied up to twenty hours of his every day for nearly sixty years. His career produced pioneering operations, important experiments, hundreds of students, nearly six hundred articles and books, scores of speeches made round the world. When the writer asked Dr. Ochsner's secretary for a list of people who knew him well, she handed him a catalog of 632 names. More than 500 of them responded with reminiscences of Dr. Ochsner.

Hundreds more—from persons of global reputation to typists and student nurses—responded to letters-to-the-editor that were printed in several dozen medical and medically related publications. Scores of persons—a college classmate, a fellow intern of the 1920s, surviving relatives, former students, eminent scientists and politicians, business and social acquaintances, current associates—were interviewed, supplying more than twelve hundred single-spaced sheets of anecdote, history, critique, accolades, and slurs. Perhaps the most notable words came in a letter from Dr. Michael E. DeBakey, coronary surgeon and Dr. Ochsner's most outstanding protégé.

I was privileged to come under his influence early in my life, first as a medical student and graduate trainee, and later as a surgical associate and friend. His keen intellect, creative imagination, and dynamic personality left an indelible imprint on me.

As my mentor, he imparted his phenomenal knowledge of surgery to me, as he has done to untold numbers of medical students and residents through the years. As co-investigator and colleague, he inspired astute observations and persevering research for the solutions to yet unsolved surgical problems. As devoted friend, he offered counsel, encouragement, support, and comfort when they were needed.

His long, fearless fight against lung cancer, undaunted by his critics who attacked his belief that smoking causes this dreaded disease, inspired an enduring reverence for this man, who stood by his convictions. His scholarly contributions to the surgical literature serve as an objective toward which the surgical student should strive. His Clinic is one of the finest examples of the group medical practice concept.

His extensive travels to lecture in clinics, hospitals, and medical schools around the world have made him an American ambassador of goodwill in a world plagued with strife and dissension. His sparkling personality and warm, friendly demeanor have endeared him to all who know him, especially the citizens of his adopted city—New Orleans—who showed their affection and esteem by bestowing on him their greatest honor when they designated him Rex, the King of Carnival.

Dr. Ochsner will leave his mark in surgical history as a brilliant surgeon, incomparable teacher, ingenious researcher, and beloved clinician.

The coauthor, John Wilds, was completing a history of the Ochsner Medical Institutions when the original writer, Ira Harkey, was forced by circumstances to set the biography aside. Wilds is a news reporter who had known and written about Dr. Ochsner over a period of some thirty years. Dr. George H. Porter III, president of the Alton Ochsner Medical Foundation, and Dr. Frank A. Riddick, Jr., medical director of the Ochsner Clinic, commissioned him to pick up where the work had ceased and put the biography together. The second phase began with digesting the mountain of research done by Harkey, a meticulous doctor of philosophy and Pulitzer Prize winner, who had taken the trouble himself to transcribe the tapes of many hours of interviews, and who provided all of the material, the result of many hundreds of hours of effort, as a contribution to the Ochsner Foundation. The material is a resource that will be available to future biographers and medical historians in the archives of the Historic New Orleans Collection. It is an irreplaceable asset because many of the interviews, including those with Dr. Ochsner himself, were given by men and women in the last years of their lives.

As a contemporary biography, this volume is largely a product of the spoken word. Dr. Ochsner was the principal contributor because he was patently pleased to have his life story published and responded cheerfully to all of the interviewer's demands. As noted, the collaborators divided the labors, the research mostly being Harkey's and the writing Wilds's.

Alton Ochsner, Surgeon of the South

I Growing Up on Main Street

Alton Ochsner's roots stretched back into Germany, Switzerland, Alsatian France, perhaps Holland. The name is German, meaning "herder of oxen."[1] A bull's head is featured in an Ochsner coat of arms borne by a Sir Knight of the name in the First Crusade, in A.D. 1096.

On the basis of a passage in Will Durant's *The Story of Civilization*, Ochsner liked to speculate that he might have been of the same blood as Paracelsus, the Swiss physician and alchemist whose activities in the early sixteenth century won him the appellation "father of pharmacology." Durant wrote that Paracelsus, whose real name was Theophrastus Bombastus von Hohenheim, was the son of Wilhelm Bombast von Hohenheim and Elsa Ochsner, an innkeeper's daughter in Einsiedeln, Switzerland. Durant's report that she developed a manic depressive condition brought a quip from Alton that this may explain "some of the peculiarities of the Ochsner clan." Paracelsus had no children.[2]

Ochsner's paternal grandfather, Joseph Philip Ochsner, who was born in Blicheim Benteingen County, Baden, Germany, on May 5, 1817, emigrated to the United States in the 1840s, and lived in Troy, New York.[3] Alton's paternal grandmother, Mary Ann Rothmund, was born in Geubweiler, Alsace, France, on February 21, 1821. She came to America in 1848, making her home with a sister at Utica, New York. She and Joseph were married at Utica on July 4, 1848. With their six children, they moved

1. New Orleans *Times-Picayune*, January 22, 1978, Sec. 3, p. 4.
2. Will Durant, *The Reformation* (New York, 1957), 875, Vol. VI of Durant, *The Story of Civilization*.
3. Genealogical data provided by Ochsner and Shontz families, in Alton Ochsner Papers, Historic New Orleans Collection. Unless otherwise noted, all unpublished materials—typescripts of interviews, letters, speeches, memos, clippings, dictated recollections, and genealogical data hereinafter cited—are on deposit in Alton Ochsner Papers, Historic New Orleans Collection. Most interviews were conducted by Ira Harkey, the rest by John Wilds.

in 1856 to Sextonville, Wisconsin. At about the time the Civil War began, Joseph built a flour mill in Bear Valley, Wisconsin. Eleven children in all were born to the Ochsners. Those who made the move to Wisconsin were Joseph, Charles, Edward Philip (Alton's father), Margaretta, William Henry, and Benjamin. Born in Wisconsin were Mary Ann, Louise, Louis, Arthur, and Fannie. Grandfather Joseph died on February 22, 1893, in Bear Valley, and Grandmother Mary Ann on December 26, 1906, at Lone Rock, Wisconsin.

The first Doctor Ochsner to become prominent in the United States was Albert John, the son of Joseph Philip Ochsner's brother, William Henry. Born on April 3, 1858, at Honey Creek, Wisconsin, Albert John practiced surgery in Chicago for thirty-six years. He won a place among the influential surgeons of his generation and contributed greatly to the development of the cousin who followed him into the profession.

The Shontz family of which Alton Ochsner's mother was a member has been traced to thirteenth-century Germany. Alton's ancestor Jacob Shontz was born in Switzerland in about 1710 and settled in Pennsylvania in 1737. He may have come to America to escape religious persecution as a member of the Mennonite sect. Some members of the Shontz family fled to Holland, an oasis for religious dissidents. Whether these included direct ancestors of Alton is not clear. His great-grandparents were John Shontz, born in Pennsylvania on September 7, 1797, and Martha Schoonmaker, born in Ulster County, New York, on April 3, 1799. His grandparents were John Alexander Shontz, born at Evansville, Pennsylvania, on January 25, 1828, and Rebecca Keziah McFadden, born at Cambridge Coro, Pennsylvania, on November 2, 1832. Alton's mother, Clara Leda Shontz, who married Edward Philip Ochsner, was their second daughter. Her older sister, Lola Kathryn, married Edward Ochsner's brother William Henry. The other children of John and Rebecca were Florence, who married Charles Brainard, and George McFadden Shontz. Rebecca Shontz died on March 24, 1904; John Alexander Shontz on November 19, 1913.

Clara Leda Shontz Ochsner's most prominent relative was a cousin, Theodore, who changed the spelling of his name to Shonts. Born in Pennsylvania in 1856, he became an accountant and lawyer and was appointed by President Theodore Roosevelt as chairman of the Isthmian Canal Commission, which began the planning for the Panama Canal. Shonts organized the Panama Canal Commission, from which he resigned in 1907 to become president of the Interborough Rapid Transit Company of New York, at the princely salary of $50,000 a year. When he died in 1919, the New York subway trains came to a halt for one minute to honor his memory.

Anybody wondering from whom Alton Ochsner inherited the intrepidity that marked his career as a surgeon need search back no further than his father and mother. The winning of the West, one of the bright periods of American history, was under way after the Civil War, and an optimistic generation was fired with a desire to make dreams come true. It took more than ambition in late 1879 and early 1880 to impel the twenty-eight-year-old Edward Philip Ochsner and his twenty-year-old wife to give up their security in Bear Valley, Wisconsin, in quest of greener pastures. It also required courage and a willingness to take a chance. For the couple elected to homestead in the prairie of the Dakota Territory, just beginning to be settled as the Chicago, Milwaukee and St. Paul Railroad extended its tracks westward. They had no illusions about the country: they knew about the fearsome blizzards, the frequent droughts, the occasional tornadoes, and the backbreaking work needed to wrest a living from a treeless plain. They might even have been warned that a plague of locusts could destroy the results of a year's labors. Certainly they were aware that the possibility still existed of having a tomahawk embedded in one's skull, for this was territory roamed by the Sioux tribes, among the most belligerent of the Indians resisting the white man's intrusion. Barely three years earlier the Sioux, Crows, and Cheyenne had slaughtered George A. Custer and his troopers at Little Bighorn. Gradually, however, the Indians were retreating; many had been forced into reservations west of the Missouri River. Now a migration of Europeans—Germans, Scandinavians, and Russians—was creating the great Dakota land boom of 1878–1886.

The Ochsners packed their belongings in a covered wagon, one of the prairie schooners of the Wild West era, and turned the noses of a team of oxen toward an area that now is part of the state of South Dakota. They took with them their infant daughter, Edna Pearl, and her two-year-old sister, Elizabeth. No details of their trek survive, but they crossed the Mississippi River and, five hundred miles from Bear Valley, reached the site on which they established a homestead claim. They stopped some twenty miles short of the Missouri River. Other migrants pushed on across the Missouri and through the Badlands to the Black Hills gold rush, but a search for nuggets and quick riches had no appeal for the straightforward E. P. Ochsner.[4]

He and Clara Leda chose a spot about two miles west of Stake No. 48, a milepost on the Milwaukee railroad line being constructed beyond Mitchell. There Ochsner built a dwelling suited to the extreme climate, a sod-roofed structure two-thirds underground, insulated against cold and heat. Even so, the Great October Blizzard of 1880 tested the determination of the newcomers.

At Stake No. 48, shanties had been built and occupied by Joseph Bird and a few others as the new rail lines reached a point a mile or so in the direction of the Ochsner claim. In the unforested prairie there was no ready source of fuel for fires that could keep people alive when the temperature dropped, as it sometimes did, to forty degrees below zero. Bird and the others at Stake No. 48 were unprepared when the early blizzard struck. In desperation, they pried up the newly laid railroad tracks and hauled the cross-ties away to burn in their shelters. They were marooned for weeks by ten-foot drifts during the severe winter that followed the blizzard.

In the spring of 1881 the lifesaving cross-ties were replaced, and construction gangs resumed the westward progress of the tracks, opening up a virgin territory for those who would farm or operate cattle or sheep ranches. Stake No. 48 became a center of activity. The settlement was given the name Kimball in honor of Edmund P. D. Kimball, father of railroad surveyor Frank W. Kimball.[5]

Among those who moved to the community in 1881 were E. P. Ochsner and his brother Benjamin. For the next four decades the Ochsner family would be prominent in the business, political, religious, and social life of Kimball, which was organized as a village in 1883 and incorporated as a city on April 4, 1889. The state of South Dakota was admitted to the Union on November 2, 1889.

One of the first community projects in Kimball was the building of a schoolhouse, measuring twelve by twelve feet. The first classes were conducted on December 19, 1881, by Benjamin Ochsner.[6] The Ochsner brothers erected the first general merchandise store in Kimball. It opened in August, 1882, offering implements, seeds, harnesses, groceries, and drugs. "Small profits, quick sales, and fair dealing" was the motto. For

4. Autobiography and Childhood in AO Recollection Folders.
5. Brule County (Kimball, S.D.) *News*, July 3, 1980, Sec. A, p. 1.
6. *Ibid.*

several years, as a growing enrollment made the original school building inadequate, some of the teaching was done in a room of the Ochsner store. The family and other residents responded with joy on December 7, 1886, when C. R. Tinan rushed out to announce that artesian water was flowing from a 1,048-foot well drilled by the village. Shallower wells drilled earlier had not remained productive, and for years water had been brought in and peddled at five cents a pail.

E. P. Ochsner became the first sheriff of the newly organized Brule County in 1887. In the early 1890s the brothers built the two-story Ochsner Mercantile Building on South Main Street. The upper floor became the "opera house," where traveling shows were staged and dances and meetings held. Ochsners were among the first communicants to be baptized in the Presbyterian church, built in 1882. E. P. erected and expanded a home that offered the first gaslighting, indoor bathrooms, central heating, and circulating hot water in Kimball. The Ochsner daughters attracted numerous suitors. If Kimball, which barely reached the thousand mark in population, was a small pond, Alton Ochsner was born a not insignificant frog.

Although Sheriff Ochsner had to deal with an occasional Indian who wandered into Kimball in quest of whiskey, the town was spared tribal forays or other incidents of unsettled times. The resistance of the Sioux to white encroachment gradually ended with the extinction of the buffalo herds, the death of the great chief Sitting Bull in 1890, and the massacre of squaws as well as braves at Wounded Knee Creek on December 29 of the same year.

The Ochsners' third daughter, Mabel Claire, was born on March 24, 1881, about the time the family moved to Kimball. She died of diphtheria at the age of four. The other girls born at Kimball were Genevieve May, April 10, 1884; Ava Marie, April 30, 1887; and Marguerite, July 27, 1889. The eldest daughter, Elizabeth, was married to W. W. Orcutt, her father's partner in a hardware store at Sioux City. Edna Pearl became the wife of Burton Colby, Genevieve of Fred Griswold, Ava Marie of William Kaynor, and Marguerite of Frank Huelsman.[7]

Edward Philip Ochsner set an example of industry that served his only son well. He also passed along a heritage of honesty and compassion that played no small role in the successes of the surgeon and medical teacher. Others, notably Alton's cousin A. J., helped shape the young man's char-

7. Ochsner family data.

acter and philosophy, but by his own account the person who most influenced his life was his father. A by-product of Alton's early training was his indifference to the accumulation of wealth, an attitude shared with E. P., and one that resulted in major career decisions. There is no indication that E. P.'s intellectual gifts approached those of his son, yet by the standards of his times he led a productive and satisfying existence— all ninety-three years of it. Alton once remarked on the difference between his father's life and his own: "His was more of a humdrum thing, the same thing every day; whereas mine is a different challenge every hour." Nevertheless, the elder man had a zest for living, enhanced by a fine sense of humor.

Born at Troy, New York, on November 7, 1851, E. P. was one of the children his father moved to Bear Valley, Wisconsin. E. P. learned to be a miller, an able one according to family legend. Apparently he had a minimum of formal schooling, but he enjoyed reading newspapers and was interested in history. Stocky and muscular, E. P. was about five feet, three or four inches in height, an inch or two shorter than his son would grow to be. The two men resembled each other in their build and facial features.

Alton and his sisters recalled that E. P. could not refuse a request for credit and that he shrank from demanding payment when it was due. Apparently nobody who was hungry ever left his store without food, even if there was no money to pay for it. Alton remembered his father as "the hardest-working man I ever knew."

In 1916 or 1917 E. P. sold his interest in the store and also the homesteaded land outside of Kimball. He bought a citrus grove in Sherryland, Texas, in the Rio Grande valley near McAllen, and he and Mrs. Ochsner spent the winters there, returning to South Dakota each summer. "He worked so hard that he would come back having lost a great deal of weight," Alton said. After about six years the couple went to live with their daughter Edna Pearl, now Mrs. B. E. Colby, at her home in St. Onge, South Dakota. E. P. died of pneumonia at St. Onge on March 24, 1945. He left little money; his legacy was character and a spotless reputation.

Clara Leda was born to John Alexander and Rebecca Shontz at Erie, Pennsylvania, on April 16, 1859. Her family migrated to Wisconsin, where she met Edward Philip Ochsner. Early marriages were the custom, and Clara was barely seventeen years old when on July 11, 1876, at Bear Creek, she became the bride of the man to whom she would be wed for nearly sixty-seven years.

Like her husband, she was disappointed not to have had a son among six children. Childbearing in primitive conditions took a toll, and after the birth of the sixth daughter, E. P. wrote to his first cousin, Dr. A. J. Ochsner in Chicago, and said he wanted his wife to undergo reparative surgery. She went to Chicago. After examining her, A. J. said, "You need this operation, and I don't want you to have any more children. You've had your last child."

"But, Doctor," Clara Leda responded. "We still haven't had our boy."

"How do you know you'll have a boy?" A. J. countered. "You've had six girls. How do you know?"

"Well," she replied, "we just have a feeling." She refused the procedure that would have prevented more children and returned to South Dakota. In due course she became pregnant again, and at term the future surgeon was born. Alton Ochsner owed his very existence to the determination of his mother to try one more time for the boy for whom she and her husband yearned.[8]

Clara's physical problems reappeared after her son's birth, which occurred when she was thirty-seven years old, and once again she went to Chicago to Dr. Ochsner.

"Well, this will end it," he told her. "This will complete your family."[9]

"That's all right, Doctor, because we have our boy now, and it's a wonderful thing to have him."

Clara brought into the union with E. P. Ochsner a sweet disposition. "She never said anything bad about anybody," her son recalled. "She gave people the benefit of the doubt, and always could find excuses for others' shortcomings." Alton believed his own interest in medicine might have been stirred by the stories he heard about her illnesses and the beneficial treatment she received from A. J. Ochsner. "I loved my mother," Alton said simply.

She was deeply religious, and one of the mainstays of the Presbyterian church at Kimball. On Sundays the Ochsner family attended Sunday school and morning church services, then the children went to the Christian Endeavor meeting and joined their parents at evening services. Prayer meeting was obligatory on Thursday evenings. When revival services were held, once or twice a year, the visiting minister was a house guest of the Ochsners and took precedence over all others during his stay.

8. Ava Marie Kaynor, interview, September 2, 1976.
9. *Ibid.*

Clara was the same height as her husband, as energetic as he, and nearly as long-lived. She was eighty-eight when she died at St. Onge on May 23, 1947, two years after E. P.'s death at ninety-three, and fifty-one years after Alton's birth.[10]

It was Monday, May 4, 1896, when E. P. and Clara Ochsner finally got their boy, almost seven years after the birth of the last of their daughters. E. P., who had been storing up boys' names through six births, settled for three: Edward, after himself; William, honoring his brother; and Alton, reflecting E. P.'s admiration for Alton Brooks Parker, a New York state supreme court justice who in 1904 was the presidential nominee of the Democratic party against Republican Theodore Roosevelt. There is irony in the choice of the one given name that the surgeon would use exclusively once he began medical practice. By the standards of the day, Parker was liberal in his politics. He represented the American Federation of Labor in the landmark Danbury Hatters' Case of 1902, in which the United States Supreme Court issued a ruling about boycotts that affected labor relations for years. A strong Populist movement developed in South Dakota in the middle 1890s, and E. P.'s philosophy apparently leaned toward the liberal side. Nevertheless, Alton Ochsner grew up to have conservative views—and availed himself of opportunities to express them.

The birth of a first son to a prominent family in a town the size of Kimball naturally created a stir, and the beaming father saw to it that the news was spread around. His efforts, of course, did not suffice to carry the tidings a thousand miles to the south, to an environment strikingly different from the raw, stark landscape of a one-main-street pioneer settlement. There was no omen in mature, cosmopolitan New Orleans to herald the birth of the surgeon-to-be who three decades later would make the city his base for an extraordinary career. It was, in fact, a rather humdrum late spring day in the bustling port on the Mississippi River. Lilly Forsher, eight years old, was bitten on the foot by a dog. Eighteen-month-old Sara Martino was scalded when she overturned a pot of boiling soup. Police nabbed John Bridges for stealing ten barrels of flour from a railroad depot. The Mississippi Packet Company's steamboat, the *Paul Tulane*, arrived from Bayou Sara. There was one rather ominous development: at Baton Rouge, Governor Murphy J. Foster ordered the inspection of crews and cargoes of ships arriving at New Orleans from foreign ports known to be infected with yellow fever or cholera. Both diseases had dealt devas-

10. AO Recollection, Childhood.

tating blows to the city in the past, and the threat of yellow fever still was an annual source of great worry.[11]

May 4 also was a routine day at the New Orleans Charity Hospital, the state-operated institution at which Alton Ochsner's operating-room accomplishments one day would begin to win recognition. In addition to the usual outpatients treated for wounds, broken bones, and fevers, the staff admitted thirty-one persons with such complaints as mumps, rheumatism, cholera, diarrhea, syphilis, acute indigestion, pleurisy, alcoholism, variola, lipoma, and sarcoma. The international character of the port city was underlined by the fact that Germans, Italians, Irish, and French were among those assigned to beds.[12]

At another New Orleans institution where Ochsner was destined to leave his footprints, the Tulane University School of Medicine, the 1895–1896 term had ended three weeks earlier with the graduation of sixty-eight doctors of medicine and nine pharmacists. The enrollment for the term had been 336 students.[13]

If E. P. Ochsner had gone twenty miles to the western boundary of Brule County and tossed a corked bottle into the Missouri River, it could have floated all the way down to the Mississippi River and on to New Orleans. Alton Ochsner would reach that destination ultimately, but he took a much more circuitous course. And one thing he never did was to drift with the current.

There were times during the first two years when Clara despaired of her son's survival. "Father, we'll never raise this baby," she moaned. "He's just too delicate." He was laid low by attacks of asthma, complicated, it appears, by his father's habit of wrapping him in warm clothing and taking him outside to the yard where chickens, cows, and Shetland ponies were kept. E. P. had no way of knowing that Alton was allergic to the animals. One of sister Marie's memories was of her mother administering pills to Alton. At about the age of two years, however, he outgrew the ailment. Long afterward, his own eldest son was a victim of asthma, and when the child's Aunt Marie suggested that he would get well, as his father had, she discovered that Alton did not even remember his bouts of wheezing and difficulty in breathing.[14]

11. New Orleans *Daily States,* May 4, 1896.
12. New Orleans Charity Hospital Admission Records, May 4, 1896.
13. Tulane University School of Medicine, 1904, student records.
14. Kaynor, interview, September 2, 1976.

In fact, Alton developed into a bright, attractive youngster, full of life and full of the dickens. Naturally the whole household revolved around him, the baby of the family and the only son. He was affectionate, hugging and kissing the sisters who took turns playing horsey by pulling him around the big home in his wagon. He followed his father's every step. "Suh-papa" (say, Papa) was his introduction to an endless barrage of questions that reflected his early curiosity. Out in the barn, he watched E. P. milk the two cows, chuckling in glee when his father directed a squirt into the open mouth of the cat. Carrying the child, E. P. would climb the ladder to the loft to toss down hay for the cows. At the age of ninety-four, Etta Dorwart of Kimball could recall a small-framed boy who usually wore a cap pulled far down over his eyes yet "always seemed to be looking for something."[15]

Some elders in Kimball opined that Alton never would amount to anything because his parents and doting sisters were spoiling him, but this outlook ignored another possibility. As the center of attention in a close-knit family, Alton was acquiring self-confidence—an indispensable attribute for a surgeon. His was no calling for one with an inferiority complex, and there is no evidence that Ochsner ever was handicapped by a feeling of inadequacy. Probably it was inevitable that the object of all the devotion would become self-centered, as those who had doubts about his upbringing expected. He could not have achieved all that he did without a single-minded devotion to his own aims. In his productive years, his career came first—before marriage, parenthood, recreation, hobbies, reading for the broadening of his philosophic outlook, or anything else. A day was not long enough to allow diversions or interruptions. The cause of humanity was well served by his treatment of a horde of patients, and he was delighted when he could effect a cure or at least slow the onslaught of disease. He devoutly hoped that the people who came to him would get well, and he unhesitatingly devoted all the time and effort needed if there was a chance of reaching that goal. It would take a paragon with the unselfishness of an angel to take a purely impersonal view of operating-room triumphs—and whatever else might be said about him, Ochsner was human. He courted recognition. He savored his successes. And from each one became more confident and proficient in his handling of his next case.

Aside from the fact that the school was primitive—although Alton's

15. Mrs. George Fousek to Ira Harkey, July 8, 1977.

records in college and medical school indicate that his preparation was not inadequate—his rearing in Kimball may have been as good early training as he could have obtained for the career that lay ahead. There was one significant side effect—the harsh climate. It was one of the factors that caused him to settle in a city where palm trees grow, where there are many winter days when an overcoat can be left at home. Sometimes when a blizzard would surprise Kimball, his father would go to the school, tie Alton and his sisters to himself with a rope, and lead them home through the blinding snow. For one period in his youth, Alton insisted on sleeping on a screened porch in subzero cold, and for the rest of his life he had difficulty when his cheeks and nose became chilled. The cold was not all. Like others in the town, he learned to run to a basement whenever a funnel-shaped cloud appeared on the horizon. Kimball was spared damage by a tornado while he lived there, however.

From birth through high school, Alton led the secure, busy existence that E. P. could offer his children. The father provided all the comforts available to small-town American families at the turn of the century. Until electricity was provided, the Ochsner home had gas illumination generated by mixing carbide and water. The Ochsners had the first indoor plumbing in Kimball, the pipes draining into a septic pool. The family also had the first residential furnace for central heat. Alton remembered turning the crank of a big freezer, then eating heaping bowlsful of his mother's rich ice cream as he sat on the steam radiator in the dining room to keep warm. E. P. kept adding rooms until the home was the town's largest and most comfortable. It was demolished after the family moved away.

Before Alton was born, E. P. had acquired Shetland ponies for his daughters. When Alton was old enough he became responsible for a herd of ten or more. He found them to be fractious creatures, but he asserted his mastery until he could ride every one. He insisted on learning to milk the family's cows by the time he was seven or eight years old, but regretted it when the milking became his daily chore. The work left him with unusually strong hands and forearms, an asset for a surgeon.

School lessons were easy for Alton. In the early grades he finished his assignments before anyone else, then mischievously looked around for something to do, often ending up in trouble. The problem was solved by his mother, who told the teacher to have him do extra reading. His favorite outside reading was the Horatio Alger books, then at the peak of their popularity. "I was interested in success stories," he explained. His lifetime basic philosophy was about as complicated as Alger's poor-boy-makes-good plots. He believed in hard work and discipline. He had little patience with welfare programs. Above all, communism was anathema, a source of most of the world's troubles.

E. P. occasionally administered spankings, but was not the stern father that Alton turned out to be. Alton did not resent the punishment. "I deserved it," he said. Actually, most of his transgressions were trivial. Even so, the man who would live to apply "the fastest belt in New Orleans" to his offspring could not trace the practice to his own childhood.

His prodigious work habits were acquired early. Everybody in the family had jobs to do. While the sisters made beds and dried dishes, the only boy was busy outside. In the wintertime he shoveled snow; in the summer he mowed the big yard; in all seasons he looked after the animals and the milking. Pumping out the septic pool was an almost weekly task. He also helped out at the store. Farmers brought in many dozens of eggs to exchange for goods, and one of Alton's tasks was to check every egg for freshness by candling. At first this was a tiresomely slow process, but he soon developed an idea that made it easier and speedier. He rigged up a contraption using a light bulb and battery. When an egg was pressed against the rim of a hole, the bulb would go on, and then turn off when the egg was removed.

Obviously good with his hands, Alton regularly took his bicycle apart and reassembled it. His mechanical talents deserted him on one occasion, however: As a teenager he used his savings to buy the first vacuum cleaner seen in Kimball. It worked with a hand-operated pump. Employing a friend to man the pump, Alton expected to make money by hiring out to clean carpets for housewives. The enterprise was off to a good start until he decided to take the cleaner apart and reassemble it. He found himself with leftover parts, and the machine never worked again. In another money-making endeavor, he worked all one summer from early morning until dark helping a cement gang lay sidewalks. His wage was a dollar a day.

His duties in the store included changing scenery and doing other jobs in the "opera house" on the second floor. He set out the chairs for meetings, swept out the next day, and otherwise made himself useful. Traveling troupes that played in a town as small as Kimball were not sophisticated and needed no expert stagehands for such productions as *East Lynn.* The hall also was used for other types of gatherings, and for a time masses were said there after the Catholic church was destroyed by fire. The Ochsners sometimes went by train to Mitchell to see chautauqua shows and other entertainments. Alton attended a concert by the John Philip Sousa Band in the Corn Palace. He marveled at the elaborate designs, made with dried corn of different colors, that adorned the building's exterior.

Against the wishes of his mother, Alton tried out for the high school football team and received a knee injury that occasionally bothered him in later years. He played the cornet well enough to be a member of the town band. The Fourth of July celebration was a highlight of the Kimball year. More than sixty years later, Alton's boyhood friend Harry Bray told about spending the night of July 3 at the Ochsner home. "We got up early in the morning, walked down to where Oscar Upshal lived, opened the screen over his bedroom window, and threw a lighted firecracker into his room."

As an Ochsner, Alton had an assured place in the Kimball community and was under no pressure to prove himself. He was shorter than most of the boys of his age, yet had no recollection of the lack of height ever being a problem. His father advised him not to be belligerent, but to fight when he had to. He curbed a temper that otherwise might have caused problems, but he was not of a quarrelsome nature, and the occasions when he had to use his fists were rare.

The urge to excel, the ambition that drove him to prodigious efforts in his career, apparently remained latent until he entered college. Nevertheless, as a boy he was conscientious, eager to do his homework when the family settled down for a long winter's evening after supper. E. P. kept a barrel of apples in the cellar; everybody liked a snack of popcorn and milk, and Clara's luscious ice cream was a frequent treat. Sometimes Alton and his sisters went on sleigh rides when the thermometer stood at twenty-five below. In high school Alton kept company with Elizabeth Smith. He was the only boy, along with eleven girls, in the class of 1914.[16]

One thing was certain: Kimball could not hold the boy whose superior intellect is shown in his school record. Some of his age group would be content to settle down to a comfortable lifetime in the prairie town. Not Alton. Apparently neither E. P. nor Alton—nor Uncle Ben, for that matter—ever counted on a continuation of the family business by a new generation. Although later in life Alton would demonstrate remarkable salesmanship, everyone seems to have known early that he was not cut from the cloth of which local merchants are made.

16. AO Recollection, Childhood.

Presbyterian luck—Ochsner never doubted that he was the benefici-
ary of chance that favored him in climactic situations throughout his
life—launched him into a career in medicine under circumstances that
hardly could have been more propitious. He became the protégé of a
sponsor who was in a unique position to speed him along the road to
achievement and fame.

As a youth, E. P. Ochsner saw his cousin Albert John frequently, and
the boys became attached to each other. But their paths diverged, E. P.
winding up in the mercantile business at Kimball, whereas A. J. cut short
a career as a schoolteacher, entered medical school, and eventually practiced surgery. If Alton never had entered medicine, the Ochsner name still
would be printed in big letters in the annals of the profession, because A. J.
was a superlative and innovative surgeon as well as a great-hearted human
being who influenced the lives of his colleagues.

From 1889 until his death in 1925, A. J. was a member of a select
handful of Chicago practitioners who made their impact on medical
practice and surgical techniques. In the number were Christian Fenger,
cited as the father of modern surgery in the West; Nicholas Senn, who
proved to be jealous of Ochsner's brilliance; and John B. Murphy, the
most flamboyant and the most famous trail-blazing surgeon of the generation. A. J. also was the closest friend of William J. Mayo of the Mayo
Clinic, who wrote of him: "A fearless crusader for the truth, he was so far
in advance of his time and so little interested in attracting attention to
himself, that his name is not associated with many of his great contributions." He was a founder and later president of the American College of
Surgeons, president of the American Surgical Association, president of
the Clinical Congress of Surgeons of North America. He was chief surgeon at the Augustana and St. Mary's hospitals in Chicago and the chairman of clinical surgery at the University of Illinois School of Medicine.
A. J. was a pioneer in microscopy. He made advances in the treatment of
hernias. His advocacy of conservative treatment of acute appendicitis was
controversial, but it saved lives. "Ochsner was a man without vanity,"
said Will Mayo.[17]

Because of A. J.'s regard for E. P., he became interested in the future of
his cousin's son. Alton Ochsner was uncertain as to when he first met the
man who would be his benefactor. In one interview, he said that he could
remember from his young boyhood A. J. coming to South Dakota to hunt

17. Ralph H. Major, *A History of Medicine* (2 vols; Springfield, Ill., 1954), II, 950–51.

prairie chickens. In a later discussion Alton said, "He was very close to my father when they were young, but I never knew him until I was in medical school." That was when A. J. called him to Chicago to work in the summers at Augustana Hospital. No matter when, at some point the magnanimous A. J. formed an attachment to the young kinsman in whom he recognized potential greatness. A. J.'s only son, Albert Henry, did not choose a career in medicine, and A. J. transferred his hopes to Alton. Long afterward, Alton gave jobs to A. J.'s two grandsons, A. J. II and Seymour Ochsner, both of whom were doctors. Edward Ochsner, A. J.'s brother, also practiced surgery in Chicago.

A. J.'s kindnesses never were forgotten by Alton, and once he reached a place in his career where he was in a position to be helpful to others he went out of his way to give a boost to students, trainees, or young doctors. His door always was open to anyone seeking aid or advice, and frequently he did not wait to be asked: he would initiate a recommendation for a coveted membership in a medical society, or tip off a resident to the existence of an attractive opening. He was popular with succeeding classes of fellows who trained in the Ochsner Medical Institutions. A regular feature was meetings at which he sat with the young doctors and invited questions and frank discussions about the problems of medicine and its practice.

Above all, despite the vaguenesses of memory, Alton must surely have been following his prominent cousin's star when, in the late summer of 1914, at eighteen years of age, he left the childhood and adolescent phases of his life behind and took the first long stride toward the man he would become.

2 Making the Grade

On September 15, 1914, Alton Ochsner, by now aspiring to a surgeon's career, began a ten-year period of preparation that may have been equaled by a lucky handful of his contemporaries but hardly could have been surpassed in its breadth and thoroughness. The smiling eighteen-year-old from Kimball matriculated at the University of South Dakota at Vermillion, in the southeastern corner of the state 125 miles from home. If there were fears that coddling by his sisters might have resulted in a youth who expected success to be handed to him on a tray, those fears soon vanished. He was endowed with exceptional intelligence, and somewhere in his upbringing had acquired not only an urge to excel but also the energy and willingness to work. The result was a record at the university that still gives gifted students a standard for which to aim. The university at the time offered two years of premedical courses and a two-year medical school. In his freshman year Ochsner had grades of A in botany, Latin, and drawing, A minus in zoology, and B in chemistry and English. As a sophomore he scored A or A minus in zoology, physics, analytical and organic chemistry, and economics, rating a B only in Latin. He hit his stride in the first year of medical school, his junior year, with straight A's in five anatomy courses and chemistry, A minus in embryology and bio-chemistry and physiology, and a B in histology. Only one B, in philosophy, and one A minus, in bacteriology, spoiled a perfect A record in the two semesters of his last year. His overall average for four years was 3.87 on a scale of 4.[1]

In college Ochsner discovered that he could thrive on as little as four or five hours' sleep, and for the rest of his active years he gladly sacrificed slumber for accomplishment. Long past middle age, he still had a ready reply for friends who told him he was staying up too late and working too hard: "It's not work. I am enjoying myself." His long hours at the univer-

1. University of South Dakota, registrar's records, 1915–18.

sity were necessary because he largely supported himself during the four years he was there. "Father did not have much money," he explained. He waited tables at the house of the Phi Delta Theta social fraternity, of which he was a member. He also was responsible for tending the furnaces at the Phi Delt residence and at a sorority house. In the winter he set his alarm clock to ring at 3 A.M. in order to open up the fires in the furnaces. Then he would serve his brothers breakfast before banking the fires at both houses. The fires had to be opened up again before he served lunch, then banked. He followed the same routine in the evening, finally banking the fires for the night at ten or eleven o'clock.[2]

One of the secrets of Ochsner's success in college and in his career was his ability to concentrate. He could do his homework, oblivious to the noise in a boisterous fraternity house. Later the bedlam created by his four children failed to distract him from writing papers at home. Once his daughter Isabel, his beloved "Sis," was asked how he coped. Did he go off to a private room and close the door? "No, he just closes his ears," she explained. Somewhat shy in his student days and slow in developing friendships, he was no scholastic grind, and he willingly gave time to other students who asked his help. He was well liked at the university, and it came as a surprise some sixty years later when he learned that he had been blackballed by Sigma Alpha Epsilon before he joined the Phi Delts. The disclosure was made by one of his college friends, Dr. J. Douglas Alway. "He was terrific mentally and not pledged," Alway wrote. "Got busy and had him over to our house, but when he was voted on, to my surprise and chagrin he was blackballed." Ochsner was amused by the rejection.[3] "I can understand why," he told Alway.

For as long as he lived, Alton liked parties and never turned down an invitation unless there was a conflict with his professional duties. At the university he enthusiastically joined in fraternity functions. He especially enjoyed picnics. The brothers would buy steaks or wieners, arrange for the housemother to make potato salad, pick up their girls, and paddle canoes up the Vermillion River to a spot where they could build a fire and barbecue. The lively Ochsner had no difficulty in getting dates for these outings, but he never asked a girl who was taller than he. Before long his attention and affections were settled on Neva Streeter of Canton, South Dakota. They probably were introduced by Ochsner's roommate and

2. AO Recollection, Childhood.
3. J. Douglas Alway to Geoffrey I. W. Cottam, February 22, 1974.

fellow medical student, Royal (Roy) Rudolph, who also lived in Canton. By the senior year Neva was wearing Ochsner's Phi Delt pin, and their friends assumed that they would be married as soon as Ochsner could support her.[4] She was the first of three women who would figure romantically in his life.

Ochsner was nearing the end of his junior year at the University of South Dakota when the United States entered World War I on April 6, 1917. He was two weeks past his twenty-first birthday when the conscription law, requiring all men between the ages of twenty-one and thirty to register for the draft, went into effect on May 18. He was not called into the service, but the next year, after graduating from South Dakota and enrolling at Washington University, he entered the nation's officer training program for students. The war ended before he completed his training. He was entering middle age by the time of World War II, and the armed services were inducting mostly younger doctors. As a result, he never saw active duty, although he later played an advisory role for the military.

When Ochsner received his bachelor of arts degree from the University of South Dakota on June 3, 1918, he still had to prove that he possessed the qualifications needed by a practicing medical doctor, especially a surgeon. His record made it clear that he could master the intricacies of anatomy, physiology, chemistry, and other subjects concerning the human body. Intellectually, he could make the grade. But the university provided almost no clinical training. Could he develop the manual dexterity required to insert a catheter? Could his ears pick up telltale noises through a stethoscope? Were his hands sensitive enough to detect abnormalities when he palpated the stomach or back? Could experience provide him with the intuition to interpret symptoms? Could he relate to sick people, knowing when to be stern and when to be gentle? Was he driven by an urge to heal? The answers soon would begin to emerge.

It was at this time that Albert John Ochsner became the dominating force in Alton's development. As noted, the earlier meetings between the two cousins, if indeed there had been any, were fleeting. Now the older man arranged for Alton and Roy Rudolph to spend the summer of 1918 as externs at Chicago's Augustana Hospital, where A. J. was chief surgeon. A kindly man who enjoyed helping to shape the career of many a neophyte, A. J. became fond of Alton, to whom he referred as "my nephew." Alton was the type of young man in whom an older benefactor

4. Cottam, in cassette sent to Ira Harkey, August, 1977.

easily could take pride. His black hair topped a slightly stocky but trim physique. His black eyebrows arched over dark, alert eyes that locked in on the person to whom he was talking and reflected unfeigned interest in what the other had to say. He had the distinctive Ochsner nose, which began high between the eyebrows and dominated the face. He was quick to pick up the medical lore imparted by A. J. and his other teachers, and he had little difficulty mastering the profession's scientific vocabulary.

To fellow student Geoffrey I. W. Cottam's suggestion that he was blessed with a photographic memory, Ochsner responded, "No, I have a good, retentive memory and a pigeonhole memory. I put certain things here and there and then relate them to other things."[5] By a more up-to-date comparison he had a computer memory: data were stored away and would come pouring forth at rapid printout speed when the code was fed into the equipment. The computer analogy was especially apt in his old age. In widely spaced interviews, the same questions would elicit almost identically phrased answers. For a born teacher such as A. J., working with Alton was a rewarding experience.

Alton's personality, a lifelong asset, smoothed his relationships with A. J. and the others who showed him how to be a doctor. In his twenty-two years he had developed a dignity and a sense of self-worth that facilitated his dealings with more mature, distinguished men. He was respectful without being fawning, reasonable without yielding his right to his own opinions—although he could admit it when he was wrong. Later, when he was the expert, the one with authority, he could handle encounters with patients or medical students with the same ease. From the beginning his manner inspired confidence and hope.

On June 29, 1918, Ochsner mailed to Geoff Cottam at Sioux Falls, South Dakota, a letter in which he told of his activities since the commencement exercises the month before. He had visited his sister, Elizabeth Orcutt, in Sioux City, then had spent a few days at Canton, where he could be with Neva. Then Neva had spent a week with the Ochsner family at Kimball. "I certainly did have a wonderful time," the smitten young swain related. "There was absolutely nothing to do but ride but that didn't make any difference. We wished several times that we might have some of our old picnics—but no chance. I'm afraid that it will be a long time before we can get the gang together again. I certainly do hate the thots [sic] of not going back to old S.D. next fall and I surely will miss

5. Cottam, interview, November 5, 1976.

you fellows." He said he would leave soon to work in the Chicago hospital. "Sincerely yours in the bond" was his sign-off to his fraternity brother. Cottam also was the recipient of Ochsner's July 17 account of his initiation into operating room activities:

> I am crazy about my new work and will try to tell you in a way what it consists of. In the morning from 7:30 until noon (or whenever the operating is over) I assist in the operating room. I even gave the anesthesia for a hernia operation this morning, but was scared stiff for fear I would kill the patient. After lunch until about three I assist in changing the dressings on the wounds—and then from 3 to 5 or 6 I go into the laboratory and work there.
>
> You can see it makes a pretty full day. Monday we were in the operating room from 7:30 in the morning until 2:30 in the afternoon.[6]

In keeping with his cheerful, positive approach to life, Ochsner did not mention to Cottam whatever difficulties he may have had in adjusting to his new environment. His sister Marie Kaynor said in an interview in old age that "he fainted dead away, they had to take him out" when he witnessed his first operation. "I think that happened two or three times," she added. She quoted A. J. as asking, "You do want to be a surgeon, don't you, Alton?" Alton replied, "Yes, I do," whereupon A. J. said, "You'll have to get a hold of yourself."[7]

Mrs. Kaynor's account is the only known indication that Alton reacted as hundreds of medical students have done before and since to their early close-up experiences with surgical invasion of the body. Years later, in an article about Rudolph Matas (whose name will be encountered frequently in the pages to follow), Ochsner quoted from a discussion by Matas of the medical student who faints when he witnesses his first operation: "The youth, who feels deeply, and struggles at his first surgical experience shows that he is physically and physiologically sound. He shows that he has feeling. . . . that he has human quality which will make him a humane surgeon. He is a man who will worry, and who will, through his very sensibility, feel most keenly the burden of his responsibility when it will be his turn to be a leader and a master. . . . It is all wrong for people to believe that the sight of blood is indifferent to the surgeon."[8]

6. Alton Ochsner to Cottam, June 29, 1918.

7. Kaynor, interview, September 2, 1976.

8. Alton Ochsner, "Rudolph Matas: Scientist, Scholar and Humanist," *Journal of Cardiovascular Surgery*, III (1962), 3–11.

Mrs. Kaynor also recalled that, accustomed as he was to long hours of work at the University of South Dakota, Alton nevertheless found it difficult to keep up with A. J.'s strenuous schedule. "He's going to kill me before we get through," she quoted Alton as telling his family. A. J., who rode horseback almost every morning of his adult lifetime, wanted Alton to get up early and accompany him in order that they could discuss medicine. "I'll be too tired," Alton demurred. "You're an Ochsner and you can take it," said A. J. If Mrs. Kaynor's memory was accurate and her youthful brother did indeed complain about A. J.'s demands upon his time, he soon changed his tune. No one ever heard the mature Ochsner express any reluctance about working long and hard.

Whatever Alton's private grousing, he quickly impressed A. J. to the extent that the latter took over the planning of the young man's training for a career in surgery. The first decision was the choice of a school at which Alton would obtain his doctor of medicine degree. A. J. selected the Washington University Medical School, which had been reorganized and renamed from the Medical College of St. Louis. In A. J.'s opinion, it and Johns Hopkins University were the best places in the United States for studying medicine.

Alton applied during the summer for admission into the third year of the four-year course. A recommendation from the University of South Dakota called him "one of the best students we have had in our medical courses. He will be a credit to any institution which may confer upon him the M.D." A memorandum attached to his application file noted "a remarkable record at high school, college and medical school." Nevertheless, he had to pass an entrance test in written German before he was admitted.[9]

On September 24, 1918, Ochsner and Roy Rudolph, also under the aegis of A. J., matriculated in the junior year at the Washington medical school. Both were inducted into the Nu Sigma Nu medical fraternity. Fellow members recall how Alton spent time every day writing to Neva. He also served as an unofficial conscience for the brothers. When a bridge game developed after dinner, Alton would let the play continue for forty-five minutes or so, then come down from the room where he was studying and send the participants off to begin their homework.

Ochsner's aptitude for medicine grew in the demanding environment of a highly rated professional school. His grade average for his junior year

9. Washington University Medical School, student records, 1919–20.

was 88.16. Some of his marks included clinical chemistry and microscopy, 85; medicine, 90; dietetics, 80; neurology, 80; surgery, 90; surgical
pathology, 90; obstetrics, 92; obstetrics and gynecology, 92; pediatrics,
85; preventive medicine, 82. His performance was good enough that
when a shortage of interns brought a crisis at Barnes Hospital during his
senior year, he was appointed an intern in medicine while continuing his
studies at the school. The class of interns had been reduced because
several of the doctors had left to accompany Herbert Hoover's food
commission, which went to Europe when widespread starvation threatened there. While carrying on his hospital duties, Ochsner scored an
average grade of 90 for his senior year, in courses that included medicine,
neurology, psychiatry, surgery, G-U surgery, orthopedic surgery, ophthalmology, otology, laryngology and rhinology, and obstetrics.[10]

The internship in medicine dovetailed with A. J.'s grand design for
making his protégé a highly trained surgeon. A. J. insisted that Alton be
grounded in internal medicine, and after graduating with his M.D. degree
on June 10, 1920, Alton served a term as an assistant resident in medicine
at Barnes Hospital under internist George Dock. Even then, in a period
when many doctors leaped directly into practice without serving even one
year of internship, Ochsner was not finished with his training.

In St. Louis, Ochsner came under the tutelage of three professors who
influenced his medical thinking. One was Dock, a professor of medicine
who had trained under William Osler and had taught at Tulane University at one time. "He was a most stimulating man," Ochsner recalled.

When one of our patients on the medicine service was operated
upon, we always went—he and the residents—to see what he
called *living pathology*. This is true. It's entirely different for a
gastroenterologist to *envision* an ulcer of the stomach than it is to
see it. Or to make a diagnosis of an infection of the gall bladder and
to see it. So we'd go to the operating room, and the surgeons would
show us what they had found. I was impressed by Dr. Dock's
thoroughness, and he was a man who emphasized the making of
medicine as exact as possible.

He had a clinic for the students, and you'd be called in and there
would be a patient on the table. You couldn't say a word to the
patient or touch him. You would just look. What do you see? What

10. *Ibid.*

else? What else? And it is surprising what you can see if you'll just look. And we all had to make a diagnosis. It was a very good pedagogic exercise.

Ochsner said Dock was not only an expert internist, but a marvelous pathologist. As a student Ochsner did not realize how profound Dock's thinking was, but later, as assistant resident, he came to appreciate the older man's intellect.

The acting head of surgery during Ochsner's first year was Ernest Sachs, a neurosurgeon whose teaching method involved the demonstration of patients followed by a quiz of students. This technique was the basis for Ochsner's celebrated "bull pen" at Tulane; Dock's clinic apparently also was a model. The head of surgery in Ochsner's senior year was Evarts A. Graham, an innovator whose tragic and ironic ending make up part of another chapter of Ochsner's life and of this account.

A fourth figure in Ochsner's St. Louis days was George Herrmann, the chief resident in medicine when Ochsner was assistant. It was he who later made the suggestion that started Ochsner on the road to New Orleans.[11]

Upon the completion of Alton's junior year at Washington, A. J. brought him back to Chicago for another summer as an extern at Augustana. By now the chief of surgery had enough faith in Alton's ability to put him in charge of the laboratory during the absence of the director. Some of A. J.'s interest in microscopy was transmitted to Alton, who became a regular at his cousin's "Sunday school." Each Sunday morning he and the residents joined A. J. in the laboratory, where they went over all of the specimens removed during the previous week. With A. J.'s guidance they reviewed the clinical history, examined the gross specimens, and then studied the microscopic sections. This was scientific medicine at its best.[12]

A chance encounter that would change the course of Alton's life occurred in June, 1921, just at the beginning of a sixteen-month surgical residency under A. J. He had completed his year's internal medicine training under George Dock and was ready to concentrate on preparing for his chosen career in surgery. On his very first day, June 30, he visited the operating area at Augustana, familiar territory because of his two summers there as an extern. "I walked into the anesthesia room, and a young girl was about to be operated upon for a thyroid enlargement," he

11. AO, interview, March, 1981.
12. *Ibid.*

recalled. "She was about to be put to sleep and asked me to hold her hand, which I did. I subsequently went down to see her when she was convalescing from her operation." The girl was Charlotte Lockwood, member of a Chicago family. "I met her sister, Isabel, when she came to visit Charlotte, and I liked her very much," Alton related. His frequent references to his Presbyterian luck could have added, "And the luckiest day of my life was the one when I met Isabel."

Ochsner's long romance with Neva Streeter did not survive his newfound interest. The details of their breakup have been forgotten, but Neva married Herbert Rudolph, Roy's elder brother, who became a justice of South Dakota's supreme court. It was a happy ending all around. Toward the close of Ochsner's residency he and Isabel became engaged. But A. J. had more immediate plans for Alton.

A. J.'s own training had included a stint in Europe, notably with Theodorus Billroth in Vienna, and he wanted Alton to top off his long preparation with two years of work under outstanding surgeons abroad. Despite its defeat in World War I, Germany still was a center of medical excellence, with Switzerland and Austria also ranking among the world's best. Because of his international connections, A. J. was able to arrange exchange surgical residences with Professor Paul Clairmont at the Kantonsspital, University of Zurich, in Switzerland, and with Professor Victor Schmieden at the Staedtisches Krankenhaus, University of Frankfurt, Frankfurt-am-Main, Germany.

A. J. believed that marriage would be a distraction from Alton's training, but finally agreed to a compromise. Alton would spend a year alone in Switzerland, after which Isabel could join him for a wedding ceremony and the assignment in Germany.

In spite of what must have been an almost painful mixture of joy and frustration, Alton was able to concentrate on his career. Marvin G. Peterson of Lake Mills, Wisconsin, then a medical student, spent the summer of 1922 under A. J. Ochsner's tutelage. He recalled how eager Alton, in the final phases of his residency, was for surgical experience. "Another resident, Joseph Laibe, whose father was a well-known Chicago physician, and Alton somehow found dogs, from where I do not know, in order to practice surgical techniques," Peterson related. "This extracurricular activity was conducted in an outbuilding behind Augustana Hospital." There, under anesthesia, the dogs were subjected to various procedures. "On at least one occasion I was invited to participate," Peterson remembered. "The project that day was intestinal anastomosis [the operative reconnection of bowel or blood vessel that has been severed]. After the suturing was completed, the segment used was excised and tested for leaks under pressure from a water faucet. How extensive this outside activity was, I do not know."[13]

In the last weeks of his residency under A. J.'s tutelage, Alton finally had the opportunity to do his first unsupervised surgery, to take responsibility for making the decision to operate, and to carry out the procedure on his own. A. J. arranged for him to go to Sioux City, Iowa, to fill in for a vacationing doctor. Herbert Schmitts, an extern at Augustana, went with Alton. A. J. sent Alton off with an admonition: "Don't operate on anybody who is not going to get well." Alton understood that there was a double purpose in the statement. A. J. wanted to caution against any rash acts by an eager youth. He also was emphasizing his basic conservative philosophy.

A. J.'s words were fresh in Alton's mind when he was presented with a dilemma that challenged his judgment and his faith in himself. He was called to see a young man in the country near Sioux City who had a ruptured appendix. "He was just as sick as hell," Alton related. "Well, all I could think of was what A. J. had said. I was scared to death the patient wasn't going to get well. I knew if I didn't operate he had no chance, even though he might not get well if I did operate. So I took the bull by the horns, and operated upon him and stayed right with him, and he did get well. I remember how scared I was."[14]

13. Marvin G. Peterson to Harkey, February 3, 1977.
14. AO Recollection, Career.

3   A European Polish

Alton Ochsner set out for Europe alone in the fall of 1922. The next two years would complete the decade-long transformation from a small-town high school graduate to a skillful, innovative surgeon, a self-assured cosmopolite ready to make his mark in medicine. In Switzerland and Germany, Ochsner began to fulfill the promise of his student days. He demonstrated his proficiency in the operating rooms of prestigious hospitals, published the results of trail-blazing research, and cemented friendships in international professional circles. By the time he next set foot on the shores of the United States, bringing with him a wife and newborn son, he was one of the best-trained surgeons of his day.

During his residency at Chicago, Alton had gained experience with blood transfusions, helping Nelson Percy, A. J.'s associate, in treating pernicious anemia. The transfusion method was to draw blood from a vein of the donor into a glass tube, then introduce it directly into a vein of the recipient. The tube was coated with paraffin to prevent damage to the blood. A. J. knew that the early development of transfusions had taken place in Europe, but that they were not as widely used in the Germanic countries as they were in the United States. He suggested that Alton take transfusion equipment with him. Alton later was thankful for the idea, although he had difficulty explaining to a customs agent at Hamburg what was in the case containing the big tube. He reached Zurich by train on a Sunday and was met at the station by Oscar Winterstein, a resident who became one of his close friends. Winterstein, too, was puzzled by the case that Ochsner handled with such care.

Language was the first difficulty. Ochsner knew almost no spoken German. He attacked the problem by refusing to answer associates at the Kantonsspital who addressed him in English, and also devoted all of his free time to developing a German vocabulary. He was rewarded after about two months, when he began dreaming in German. At first he had an arrangement with another resident, Albert Perrola, who took the histories and made the physical examinations in two wards while Ochsner did the other work. It wasn't long, however, before Alton could communicate directly with the patients.

A. J. wanted Alton to begin his European training under Professor Clairmont, an Austrian who had done his own residency at Vienna with the renowned Anton Freiherr von Eiselsberg. A vascular surgeon of note, Clairmont had performed numerous gastrectomies for ulcers. He was the most meticulous worker Ochsner ever knew. He required those who operated with him to wear white cotton gloves over their rubber gloves. At the first spot of blood, the cotton gloves had to be changed. Sometimes a surgeon would use fifty pairs during an operation. "What a consumption of time!" Ochsner thought, but the Germanic attention to detail did not fail to register. "Although at first it seemed clumsy using the cotton gloves over the rubber gloves," he recalled, "one became used to it and actually it helped a lot because they did not slip as rubber sometimes does." In his late years Ochsner developed an allergy to rubber, and as a result wore plastic gloves in the operating room.

The chief surgical resident, Karl Nather, had come from Vienna with Clairmont. He and Ochsner became friends and collaborated on research projects. It disturbed Ochsner when patients died who he thought might have been saved by blood transfusions. He asked Nather why transfusions were being avoided. Nather explained that five transfusions had been done at the Kantonsspital in the previous years; three of the patients had died. In Switzerland and Germany blood typing was not done. The custom was to test by giving a tiny injection of donor blood. If there was no reaction, it was assumed that the blood was compatible and the transfusion would proceed. Ochsner pointed out that with his test sera he could make sure that donor blood would be compatible, and he kept pressing for an opportunity to demonstrate the lifesaving possibilities of the equipment he had brought from Chicago.

At last his chance came. A notorious criminal who was bleeding to death from a gunshot wound was admitted to the hospital. His only hope of survival was blood. Nather told Ochsner that, in view of the circumstances, he could transfuse the patient. The American already had arranged for a suitable donor and did the procedure immediately. The criminal rallied and lived. Professor Clairmont still was not convinced. But the same afternoon a prominent banker, a friend of his, was about to die from the bleeding of a duodenal ulcer. "Professor Clairmont came to me with tears in his eyes and asked me if I could give blood safely,"

Ochsner related. "I told him he would not die as a result of blood, but I was sure he was going to die without it." Clairmont gave the go-ahead, and Ochsner's transfusions enabled the banker to undergo lifesaving surgery. Resistance melted, and Ochsner recalled, "I went all over Switzerland giving transfusions and became *the* blood specialist." It was, at the least, an eye-catching performance by a young doctor.[1]

Professor Clairmont's eagerness for Ochsner to learn everything his clinic had to teach resulted in some three months of early-morning rising for the resident. Splanchnic analgesia—performed by putting needles into the retroperitoneal space and injecting a local anesthetic agent—was widely used in Europe at a time when inhalation anesthesia was not so safe. The injections had to be made half an hour before an operation was started. Since the rule at the hospital was that the incision was to be made at seven o'clock in the morning, Ochsner was required to get up at five in order to handle all the preliminaries in time.

His blood transfusion experience provided Ochsner with subject matter for his first scientific paper, written in German and published in the September, 1923, issue of a Viennese journal. Not many doctors have had publications only three years after medical school. There followed a series of papers, in German or English, in which he was joined by Karl Nather in reporting a sophisticated new surgical technique for draining subphrenic abscesses. Clairmont was alarmed over the high mortality of the pus-forming abscess that develops in the area of the liver and right kidney between the peritonium (the abdominal sac that contains the intestines) and the pleural diaphragm (the membrane that envelops the lungs). While not common, the abscess was by no means rare in Switzerland, because it often was a sequel to peritonitis. In hospitals where the policy was to operate at once for acute appendicitis, the danger of peritonitis always was present. The subphrenic abscess, situated as it was in an inaccessible area, was difficult to diagnose and difficult to treat. Surgical intervention, which was a last resort after conservative treatment failed, consisted of making an incision in the side and draining the pus through the pleural space. As Ochsner noted, consequent infection of the pleural space was almost ubiquitous, and the death rate was about 50 percent.

Clairmont himself had devised a technique for draining other types of abscesses, and he proposed to Ochsner and Nather that they join together

1. Alton Ochsner, "My Experience in Introducing Blood Transfusions into Europe," *Medical Tribune*, August 28, 1974, p. 19.

in an effort to find a means of letting pus out of a subphrenic abscess without bringing it through the pleural cavity. Working with cadavers, the two found a solution. They showed that by resecting the twelfth rib and incising through the bed of the rib, a surgeon could reach the abscess, lodged as it was between lung and liver. The method requires a delicate touch because the operator is working in close quarters, navigating between diaphragm and peritoneum. To puncture either is to invite disaster. But Ochsner had a sensitive hand, as did Nather, and they demonstrated that the abscess cavity could be opened and drainage tubes installed to carry the pus from the body without contamination. Usually the patient's condition improved rapidly, and the mortality rate plummeted.[2] Once antibiotics came into general use, there was less need for surgery in cases of subphrenic abscess, although the method has not been abandoned. Ochsner remained proud of his work. "It was away ahead of its time," he remarked in his old age. "It's a classic."

Along with a White Russian doctor, Fraulein M. Meyer, Ochsner and Nather also devised a valve that would relieve the usually fatal tension that developed in the thorax when there were accidental injuries to the throat made during blind operations for cancer of the esophagus.[3]

The kindly Clairmont was one of the important persons in Ochsner's life. "He was a great teacher," Ochsner said. "He would inquire, 'Why? Why?' He would shake his finger in the faces of students as he walked around the room." From Clairmont, and to some extent from Nather, Ochsner said he learned techniques "and also an appreciation of the necessity of treating tissue very kindly."

All in all, the young American was too busy to mope over the five-thousand-mile distance that separated him from his fiancée. He soon was friendly with other residents at the Kantonsspital, where he had a private room and where every morning he was served a breakfast of hot chocolate, rolls, and cheese. Weekends were special.

As soon as twelve o'clock on Saturday came, we would put on our hiking clothes, take a train to the foot of the Alps in some area, start climbing and continue until around midnight, and spend the

2. Alton Ochsner and Karl Nather, "Retroperitoneal Operation for Subphrenic Abscess," *Surgery, Gynecology and Obstetrics,* XXXVII (1923), 94–99.

3. Alton Ochsner, M. Meyer, and Karl Nather, "Der Parietale Inspiratorische Ventilpneumothorax, Der Exspirations-Ventiltroikart," *Deutsche Ztschr. f. Chir.,* CLXXXVIII (1924), 13–75.

night in an Alpine hut. Then we would start out around three in the morning and climb until about eight, when we would reach the summit. The sight was unbelievable. We would open our rations and eat a light breakfast, and then spend the rest of the day coming down, getting back to the railroad station about late afternoon, and then would take the train home to Zurich. We would arrive completely exhausted but feeling very fit.[4]

The prospects of his first Christmas abroad, separated from his family, apparently did not bother him. On December 3, 1922, he wrote a cheerful note to "My Dear Ones in Kimball," saying it seemed funny to be writing a Christmas letter three weeks early, but he wanted it to arrive in time.[5] His holiday turned out to be a memorable one. He and another resident spent ten days at the Suvrette House in St. Moritz as guests of one of the owners, a patient. "We had a delightful time learning to ski," Ochsner reported. "At this time there were very few injuries because there were no such things as ski lifts. We spent all day climbing the slope and usually made only one run. We were so tired when we came down that, if we did fall, it didn't do much harm."

Skiing injuries were rare, but in Zurich, Ochsner gained experience in setting broken legs of sledders. "Every Saturday night during the winter there would be sled injuries," he related. "There would be half a dozen to a dozen broken legs due to the fact that they would sit on those small sleds, steering by sticking out their legs and digging their feet into the snow. This was all right unless the foot happened to hit an immovable object, then usually the lower portion of the leg gave 'way."[6]

As valuable as his medical training in Europe would prove to be, Ochsner's greatest gain during his stay abroad was a wife, an ideal mate for the exciting years that lay ahead. Isabel Kathryn Lockwood had the qualities needed by the spouse of a practitioner. She was bright, said to be the first woman to be able to win a scholarship in mathematics to Carnegie Tech, and possessed of acumen that enabled her to handle the family financial affairs without bothering her busy husband about details. "I never knew whether we had a cent in the bank or whether we had $50,000. She handled everything, did all the investments. She was the smart one," Ochsner would recall after her death.

4. AO Recollection, Career.
5. Alton Ochsner to family, December 3, 1922.
6. AO Recollection, Career.

Isabel had the tact to smooth relations with patients and with Ochsner's colleagues and their wives. A sense of humor helped her shrug off the inevitable conflicts between professional demands and family needs. It was not her nature to nag or grouse when a patient emergency called Ochsner away from a dinner party and left her to play hostess alone. Most of all she was ambitious, loyal, and willing to take the responsibility for the upbringing of four children in order that Ochsner could devote all of his energy and attention to the advancement of his career. At times she could be a bit snobbish and indifferent to the feelings of those with whom her husband worked, but overall she was a model doctor's wife.

Isabel was born at Chicago on November 8, 1900, the daughter of Mr. and Mrs. Ozro John Lockwood. Her father operated a German bakery that had been established by her grandfather. The family was in comfortable circumstances, although not wealthy. Ochsner could not be accused of fortune hunting when he broke off his long romance with Neva Streeter in favor of Isabel. He said he was attracted by her good looks and her kind, sweet nature. He especially noted her deep affection for her younger sister, Charlotte. On the other hand, by the time he was serving his surgical residency under A. J., Alton clearly was a young doctor with a future, a good matrimonial prospect for any young woman and an obvious prize for one with Isabel's ambitions. After a few months' courtship they became engaged.

Alton was in no position to defy A. J.'s dictum that he complete his exchange residency in Switzerland before marriage, and Isabel was willing to wait. The ensuing eleven months must have seemed an age to her, and Alton counted the days, busy though he was. At last, in September, 1923, Isabel set sail for Europe, accompanied by her younger brother, Ozro. Long afterward, Isabel confided that she met an attractive man on the ship and began to have qualms about a union with the young doctor from whom she had been separated so long.[7] After two days in Paris, Isabel's group reached Zurich on September 12. "It was a real occasion meeting them again," Ochsner commented with his sometimes deadpan humor. The wedding took place the very next day. First there was a civil ceremony in the Zurich courthouse, and then rites in a small church. Among the attendants were Isabel's brother, residents from the Kantonsspital, and a distant cousin of Alton's, Dr. Erwin Schmidt, with his

7. Alton Ochsner, Jr., interview, June 16, 1977.

wife, Mary. Professor Clairmont and his wife were among the guests. The party had the wedding breakfast at the Bauerlach Hotel, on the shore of Lake Zurich. The couple honeymooned in the Alps, spending the first night in the Hotel National at Lucerne.

Isabel found out that she was wed to a foreigner, who for months had spoken only German and who, in communicating with her, had to think in German and translate his thoughts into English. It did not take long, however, for the flame to be rekindled.

The wedding was noted back in South Dakota by the Kimball *Star*: "Dr. Ochsner made many friends here during his boyhood and school-days who will rejoice over the happy event culminating in Switzerland. Miss Lockwood is to be complimented upon her choice of a husband and lifelong companion. Dr. Ochsner, 'Alton' as Kimball knows him, is kind hearted, good natured, pleasant and industrious, along with being loving and affectionate, fulfilling the requirements for a perfect husband, and from reports from the Lockwood household, Isabel Kathryn is as grand a woman as Dr. Ochsner is a man, and a union has been formed where discord will never enter."[8]

The second and more exciting phase of Alton's European training now began. Although the couple experienced the woes of runaway German postwar inflation, Alton had the opportunity of working with some of the foremost surgeons of the day, and of visiting clinics in Munich, Vienna, Rome, and Bologna. He also formed some lasting friendships. Isabel took it all in stride.

The Staedtisches Krankenhaus of the University of Frankfurt, the institution at which Ochsner served his second exchange residency, was the place where in 1909 Paul Ehrlich demonstrated the usefulness of arsphenamine in treating syphilis and the yaws, an important break-through in chemotherapy. The first successful cardiac suture also was done there. Ochsner came under the tutelage of Victor Schmieden, who completed the American's indoctrination in the German school that stressed the value of pathology in surgery. Schmieden, one of the leading gastric surgeons in Europe, also was the ranking authority on adherent pericarditis, and Ochsner picked up considerable experience in the treatment of the condition. "Although his movements during an operation seemed slow and deliberate," said Ochsner of Schmieden, "there was

8. Kimball (S.D.) *Star*, undated clipping.

never a wasted motion and the rapidity with which he completed an operation of considerable magnitude was astounding."[9] Schmieden was a stern Prussian type, hard to get to know, but the cheerful, competent Ochsner soon won him over.

Postwar inflation in Germany was reaching its dizzying heights. Alton and Isabel occupied a bedroom, small dining room, and bath in the home of Bernhard Fischer, professor of pathology at the University of Frankfurt. They paid $125 a month in American currency. The Fischer family lived on this payment, because the plunge in the value of the mark had destroyed the purchasing power of salaries. The Ochsners ate breakfast and the noon main meal with the Fischers. They had a toaster and a hot plate in their tiny apartment, on which Isabel prepared creamed eggs on toast for the evening meal, keeping the hard-boiled eggs warm by wrapping them in a down comforter. They could not afford to eat out often, and only sparingly accepted dinner invitations to homes of other residents, where tips were expected by maids.

Alton and Isabel never forgot their experiences with inflation. One day they took a two-hour train ride from Frankfurt to Marburg. At the Frankfurt station they received ten thousand marks to the dollar. Upon their arrival at Marburg they found that the exchange had gone to fifty thousand. "I used to go down to the bank in the morning with a doctor's bag and for five dollars [American] get the bag filled with bills, which were printed on only one side and the ink wasn't dry," Ochsner related. "The bills were done up in packets, and nobody took the trouble to break the packets but would simply hand over packets to pay for purchases."

Once they went with a knowledgeable friend to spend several days visiting a clinic at Heidelberg. The friend found that he could return to Frankfurt each evening, exchange dollars for marks on the black market, go back to Heidelberg, and make more than enough money to pay for the round trip. But one day he telephoned Alton to say that the mark had not gone down enough for him to go back to Heidelberg. He promised instead to wire Alton's money to him. Alton and Isabel sneaked out of the hotel that morning because their bill had to be paid daily. They waited at the post office until just before closing time that evening, and their money came. They paid their hotel bill, put aside train fare to Frankfurt, and spent the rest on a big dinner because it was Isabel's birthday. But they had

9. AO Recollection, Autobiography.

forgotten that the Frankfurt streetcars stopped running at midnight, and upon arrival had to walk four miles carrying their bags to the Fischer home because they lacked taxi fare.

The collapse of the German financial structure jarred Ochsner's sense of discipline and order. His later analysis of the situation, however, is perhaps less revealing as history than as an example of the kind of thinking into which Ochsner could fall when he stepped beyond his own field of expertise: "There was a great deal of speculation at the time, much of which was some manipulation of the finances, much of which was by the Jews. In fact, the Jews had become prominent in Germany and, because of the speculation and almost stranglehold on the universities and the economy and everything else, the anti-Semitic feeling was beginning. It is easy for us to understand why Hitler, who I am sure was just a symbol and a rabblerouser, was able to accomplish what he did. Inflation became so bad that no one was interested in doing any work."

In the fall of 1923, inflation brought normal activities almost to a standstill. "How does the dollar stand today?" was the first comment Ochsner heard upon his arrival at the hospital. Before long the hospital was almost empty, and Ochsner's training was handicapped by a lack of patients. He decided to make better use of the time by visiting Eiselsberg's clinic in Vienna. As he and Isabel were leaving Frankfurt, he received four million marks for one dollar, a million times the normal rate and, as it happened, the high point (or perhaps low point) of the inflation. Ochsner knew he had entered a different—sane—world when, upon arrival at Vienna, he handed a taxicab driver a dollar bill and was told that it was not enough to cover the fare. Even so, the exchange rate was favorable for Americans, and it was a period when doctors from the United States were crowding into Vienna to seek training in what was then the medical center of the world. Some lectures were given in English to accommodate free-spending Americans whose dollars helped bolster the Austrian economy.

While Alton was at the clinic, Isabel went hunting for a reasonable *pension* because they could not afford to continue in their hotel. In what appeared to be a settled, affluent neighborhood, she went into a building that had rooms for rent. She was shown a tiny room furnished with a small bed and a table over which hung a light. She explained that her husband was a doctor who was doing much studying, and wondered whether a better light could be provided. "I don't think you want to stay here," the landlady told her. "Why not?" Isabel demanded. "This is a place where the boys bring their girl friends," the woman replied. Only then did Isabel realize she was about to move them into a house of assignation. The Ochsners found another place to live, and Alton was able to continue to train under the great Eiselsberg.[10]

Alton continually saw that A. J. Ochsner's influence extended into Europe. He was especially eager to visit the Munich clinic of Professor Ferdinand Sauerbruch, who had left Zurich not long before Alton went there. It was Sauerbruch's work that had aroused Alton's interest in thoracic surgery. But Alton learned that the intensely nationalistic Sauerbruch blamed the United States for Germany's defeat in World War I. He would not admit American doctors to his clinic unless they signed a statement to the effect that Germany was not responsible for the war. Alton knew he would not sign such a statement. When he told A. J. of his wish to meet Sauerbruch, his mentor suggested that he write to the professor. When he did, he was surprised not only to receive a warm invitation to the clinic, but also to be told that he and his wife would be house guests of the Sauerbruchs. He eventually learned that A. J. had taken Sauerbruch in charge in 1912 when the German visited the United States to present his work on negative pressure. A. J. had translated his papers and accompanied him on a tour of American clinics. "I was probably the only American who was welcome at his clinic," Alton said.[11]

Upon his return to Frankfurt, Alton found that the German minister of finance, Haljmar Schacht, had worked out a solution to the chaotic inflation problem by introducing a new mark based on the value of land. Ochsner was impressed when stability was achieved at an exchange of four marks for a dollar.

The medical highlight of Ochsner's European training period, one of the unforgettable events of his career, occurred in March, 1924, when he joined some of his Frankfurt colleagues at a meeting of the German Surgical Congress in Munich. Professor Martin Kirschner of Königsberg presented a woman who, several weeks earlier, in effect had died and been brought back to life. She had suffered a pulmonary embolus—a blood clot in the lung. For the first time in history, Kirschner had performed a successful pulmonary embolectomy—surgical removal of the clot. The procedure first was described by Professor Freidrich Trendelenburg in 1908, and had been attempted unsuccessfully several times in Europe.

10. AO Recollection, Career.
11. *Ibid.*

Ochsner never forgot the excitement that greeted Kirschner's revelation. "It was electric," he said. And the experience influenced his important contributions in the diagnosis and treatment of blood clots throughout his career.

Some sleepless nights followed for Ochsner because Professor Schmieden was determined to duplicate Kirschner's feat, and the key to Kirschner's success was speed. The embolectomy had to be done at the first indication that a clot had broken loose in the bloodstream and had been carried to the lung, or it would be too late.

Whenever a patient who was a candidate for a blood clot entered the Frankfurt hospital, the so-called Trendelenburg set, including the sterile instruments needed for an embolectomy, was placed beside his bed, and a doctor assigned to "sit there like a wake waiting for the patient to die," Ochsner related. As the youngest resident, he frequently drew the night-long assignment. "Most of the time they didn't die," he related. "I used to think, my God, there must be a better way to do this." He could not read because that would put him to sleep, "so I just sat there for hours watching the patient." At the first sign of trouble, usually a gasp, he had to send out a call for help and make the incision. Most often the patient was unconscious, and Ochsner could cut without waiting for anesthesia. "I used to think as I sat there, if we just knew where those damned things came from, we could put a ligature on the vein and prevent the clots from reaching the lungs."[12]

Ochsner never forgot the frustration of those vigils, and the time came when he and an associate, Michael E. DeBakey, found a better solution.

In the spring of 1924 Professor Clairmont asked Professor Schmieden to allow Ochsner to return to Zurich to serve as interpreter during a visit of a British surgical travel club that later became the Moynihan Surgical Society. The leader of the group was Sir Berkeley Moynihan, later Lord Moynihan, one of Britain's distinguished practitioners, with whom Ochsner became friendly. The party was made up largely of young, promising surgeons who practiced in provincial areas. Ochsner's task was complicated because the Britishers tried to communicate in their limited German, and Clairmont used his inadequate English. But Alton did so well that he was invited to bring Isabel and accompany the club on a visit to Italy. There he met Italian surgeons and inspected clinics in Bologna and Rome.

12. *Ibid.*

Fifty years later a photograph of the group made in Italy was published in the *British Surgical Journal*. The caption identified everyone shown except a young man in the back row. Ochsner promptly wrote to the journal to set the record straight: the young man was he. Ochsner was invited to Leeds in 1965 to give the principal address upon the observance of the centennial of Berkeley Lord Moynihan's birth. He was one of only a handful of doctors at the banquet who had known the great man personally.

The travel club episode rounded out Ochsner's intensive two-year experience of training in Europe. Now the time had come to put the schooling phase of his career behind him and use his knowledge and skills to treat his own patients. Isabel was nearing her ninth month of pregnancy in November, 1924, when the couple sailed for the United States.

4 The Urge to Teach

B lessed with exceptional medical intelligence and surgical skill, Alton Ochsner also had the good fortune to be born at the right time. He completed the European phase of his training at the age of twenty-eight and headed back to the United States in 1924 to begin practice in a profession that was at a turning point. He was early enough to establish himself in time to take full advantage of the dawning of the golden age of medicine, late enough to benefit from the scientific advances of the early twentieth century. He moved into an environment that was made-to-order for an energetic, ambitious, visionary surgeon, one who would be willing to flout convention on occasion but always stay well within the bounds of professional respectability.[1]

The revolution that has transformed the delivery of health care since the 1930s has been so recent and so complete it is easy to forget that, by modern standards, medicine a decade earlier was in a primitive state. The great epidemics—yellow fever, cholera, typhus—were history, partly because of higher living standards and improved sanitation, partly because science was making strides. The discovery that the mosquito caused the spread of yellow fever is an example. Vaccination had almost eliminated the threat of smallpox. The death rate from tuberculosis was down. But syphilis, typhoid, poliomyelitis, measles, and dysenteries still took their toll, and a diagnosis of pneumonia could be a death sentence. Ochsner had learned in the course of his training that neither he nor any other physician could cure a disease. That ability would come in the 1940s with the advent of the antibiotics. He was well into his career before Alexander Fleming in 1929 discovered penicillin, the active substance of which was

---

1. Sources for state of medical practice in the 1920s and later included Albert S. Lyons and R. Joseph Petrucelli II, *Medicine: An Illustrated History* (New York, 1978); Major, *A History of Medicine*, II; Paul Gray, "In Celebration of Life," *Time*, May 14, 1979, pp. 86–94, a review of Dr. Lewis Thomas' *The Medusa and the Snail* (New York, 1979); John H. Knowles, "The Struggle to Stay Healthy," *Time*, August 9, 1976, pp. 60–62.

not isolated for another decade and not used clinically in the United States until 1942.

In 1924 surgery had outstripped general medicine in effective treatment, although surgery's own golden age was yet to come. The development of aseptic procedures and the use of anesthesia had begun late in the nineteenth century, and by Ochsner's time surgeons had improved techniques for taking out an appendix or gall bladder, repairing a hernia, or making an open reduction of a fracture. Yet they were only barely beginning to invade the chest. The heart was completely off limits, and the use of blood-vessel grafts a project for the future.

Most of the innovators who spearheaded the progress of surgery in the early twentieth century still were alive and active when Ochsner began practicing. The giants of the period included Alexis Carrel, George W. Crile, Harvey Cushing, Walter Edward Dandy, John B. Murphy, Albert John Ochsner, William Osler, William S. Halsted, Anton Freiherr von Eiselsberg, Nicholas Senn, Frank Lahey, Rudolph Matas, William J. and Charles H. Mayo, Paul Clairmont, Victor Schmieden, and Ferdinand Sauerbruch. A measure of the breadth of Ochsner's training is the fact that he came under the influence of so many of the men on the list.

The trend toward specialization also was under way, although the general practitioner remained predominant. Indeed, except for the ophthalmologist, the specialist was a self-anointed expert. The board of ophthalmology, established in 1916, was the only agency that gave examinations and certified proficiency. Other boards came into being in the 1930s and later. Meanwhile, some of the self-proclaimed specialists thrived because they demonstrated their skills to their colleagues, who referred patients to them. Others, with minimal training, set themselves up as specialists and tried to confine their work to their chosen areas. Yet the departmentalization of medicine was inevitable as the accumulation of knowledge became overwhelming, and specialization was one major development of the golden age of medicine.

Medicine in the 1920s continued to be mainly the province of the solo practitioner. The Mayo Clinic at Rochester, Minnesota, was associated in the public mind with remarkable cures, and the clinics established at Cleveland by George Crile and at Boston by Frank Lahey also were beginning to win favor for the concept of group practice—one-stop shopping for patients in quest of diagnosis and treatment. But in 1922 only 139 clinics in the United States were recognized by the American Medical Association. By comparison, in the late 1980s a quarter of all American practitioners were affiliated with clinics—and Alton Ochsner had been a major influence in the phenomenal proliferation.

In 1924 doctors still made house calls—as Ochsner would learn—although the automobile had replaced the horse and buggy. The hospital was a refuge mainly for the seriously ill or for patients who entered for surgery, although some institutions provided outpatient clinics. Only when government subsidies were offered, after World War II, did a multiplication of hospital beds begin.

The plight of destitute doctors was a problem that concerned medical societies, for the fact was that it was not easy to make a living in practice. A large proportion of the population could not afford a doctor's services. Private health-care insurance did not begin to be available until the 1930s, and some three decades would pass after that before the federal government stepped in with Medicare. The very poor had to seek free treatment at clinics operated as charities or by a city or state. For the merely poor, an illness could mean bankruptcy. The doctor, trained to be a Good Samaritan, faced a moral dilemma in choosing to allow a sick person to go untreated or to use up valuable hours, when he might be making a living, in taking care of a patient who could not pay him. A practitioner who collected more than two-thirds of the money owed him was doing very well. But with his connections and his extensive preparation, Alton Ochsner probably was not worrying about earning money when he escorted his pregnant wife aboard a steamship in November, 1924, and headed for his homeland.

Two days out of New York the liner *America* ran into a severe storm, and the roughness caused Isabel to go into labor prematurely. On November 16—eight days after her twenty-fourth birthday—she was delivered of a son, who was named Alton, Jr., and who came to be called Akky. (That is the family's way of spelling the name, which rhymes with *hockey*.) In a letter to "Our Dear Ones" Alton wrote: "We then took Isabel down to the ship's hospital which was empty and Dr. Stewart (the ship's physician) together with Miss Quaim, the ship's trained nurse, took charge of affairs and at exactly 6:40 a.m. Edward William Alton Ochsner, Jr., was born at 41–38 latitude North and 61–38 W longitude West. . . . Everything went off just like a million dollars, the delivery was perfectly normal and Isabel wasn't torn at all."[2] While in Frankfurt the Ochsners had become friendly with a visiting American, surgeon Joseph King of New York, and

2. Alton Ochsner to family, November 18, 1924.

his wife. Alton sent a radio message to King, who met the ship on arrival, along with an obstetrician and pediatrician. Isabel and the baby were taken by ambulance to the Prince George Hotel, where the new mother spent ten days in bed, in accordance with the medical custom of the time. Her parents came from Chicago to be with her.

Alton was on his own. He filled up on American ice cream—"best in the world," he said—and enjoyed selecting his meals at the Automat, which was new to him. There was an opportunity to visit hospitals, and one morning he went to the New York Hospital to see Eugene Pool, chairman of surgery at Cornell University. Pool welcomed him as a kinsman of his friend A. J. "Do you treat appendicitis as your distinguished cousin does?" Pool asked. He was referring to A. J.'s reluctance to operate when an appendix had ruptured. Alton explained that A. J. was willing to operate except when he felt that to do so might spread infection and cause peritonitis to develop. Pool had a different opinion. "When you get older and have had enough experience, you'll realize that the only time to operate upon appendicitis is as soon as you see it," he said. Alton replied that he would not think of questioning Pool's judgment, but added that he had observed the results of A. J.'s conservatism in Chicago, as opposed to the immediate operation approach in Zurich and Frankfurt, and was convinced of the merit of A. J.'s handling of such cases.

The two made the rounds of Pool's patients, then went to an evaluation conference at which recent deaths in the hospital were discussed. One of the patients was a woman about thirty with a classic case of acute appendicitis that had lasted for four or five days. She was not seriously ill when she entered the hospital—her temperature was ninety-nine degrees—but she did have a swelling in the region of the appendix. One of Pool's associates operated and found a walled-off mass. In removing the ruptured appendix he broke down the adhesions, releasing the fluid from the abscess into the peritoneum. The patient became critically ill and died three or four days later. "Dr. Pool turned to me and said, 'I think we killed her,'" Ochsner related. "I said, 'Yes, professor, I think you did.' I'm sure that if Dr. Pool and I had not engaged in the little argument earlier he would not have been impressed by the relationship of the operation and the death."[3] Pool became convinced of the validity of A. J.'s treatment and afterward was an outspoken advocate. Throughout his own career Alton seconded A. J.'s belief on the subject.

3. AO Recollection, Career.

Mrs. Lockwood and Alton bought a large clothes basket and made it into a bassinet, in which Akky was taken to Chicago after two weeks in New York. Alton and Isabel found a small apartment on Fullerton Parkway, near the Lockwoods. On January 1, 1925, Ochsner went to work as an associate of Daniel A. Orth, chief surgeon at Columbus Hospital, and George Muller, chief surgeon at St. Mary's Hospital. A. J., of course, had made the arrangements. There were some disappointments in Alton's early days in practice. Earl Garside, friend and later colleague, tells about it:

> He wasn't doing any surgery. We were as busy as we could be, but no surgery. One afternoon we saw a sixteen-year-old boy who had acute appendicitis. We were very proud of ourselves over making the diagnosis, and started taking the boy to the hospital. On the way Alton was saying he was going to make a McBurney's incision and do this and that, and he had the whole treatment outlined before he got to the hospital. Dr. Orth saw the boy. He was sure Alton didn't know enough to take out this kid's appendix, so we were dismissed and sent out to make more house calls and Orth took the kid's appendix out. Alton accepted it. He was not much of a grumbler.[4]

It must have been one of the last times, if not the last, that Ochsner had an operation taken away from him by a surgeon who thought he could do better. Within a few weeks he proved to Orth and Muller that he was competent, and afterwards found himself with all the work he wanted.

On three mornings each week he assisted in operations at Columbus Hospital, on the North Side of Chicago, and three mornings at St. Mary's, on the West Side. There were office hours every weekday afternoon and two evenings a week. In the afternoons Ochsner made hospital rounds and went to see patients who had gone home. He said he felt like a taxicab driver because he averaged something like a hundred miles a day in the Buick that Orth had bought for him.

On Thursday afternoons he visited the Northwestern University Medical School, on the South Side, to teach a class in surgical pathology—an assignment made available, once again, through A. J.'s good offices. He took laboratory specimens from the two hospitals to demonstrate in his two-hour sessions. He had to work overtime to take care of his regular

4. Earl Garside, interview, April 19, 1977.

assignments, and sometimes did not get home before one o'clock Friday morning.

There was little time for his family. "As a matter of fact, the only time I saw Akky at all, he was asleep. He was always asleep when I left and always asleep when I got back," he recalled. "The name he knew me by was 'Bye Bye.'" Ochsner's income was $10,000 a year, an enviable sum, and he was doing the clinical work for which he had trained so long. But within a year he realized he was unhappy. The highlight of his week was the class at Northwestern, and he came to understand that what he missed was teaching and research. Surgery alone was not enough. His life had come to a turning point—and again, out of the blue, came a fortuitous circumstance.

Erwin Schmidt, the cousin who had attended Alton and Isabel's wedding, was in the last phases of his European training at that time. Another of A. J.'s kinsman-protégés, Schmidt also had served a residency in internal medicine under George Dock in St. Louis, then been an exchange fellow under Victor Schmieden at Frankfurt, and finally a resident under Einar Key at Stockholm. When Carl Arthur Hedblom moved to the chairmanship of surgery at the University of Illinois, the chair of surgery at the University of Wisconsin opened up, and Schmidt, a Wisconsin alumnus, was appointed to the post in January, 1926. Impressed by Ochsner's potential, Schmidt invited him to come to Madison as assistant professor of surgery.

It was time for soul searching. "I was thrilled, of course, at the offer, but it was a full-time job, it paid only $5,000, and I was making twice that much in Chicago," Ochsner related. "I thought I would like to go, and when I would talk to anyone about it, everyone said I would be crazy to leave Chicago because anyone with the name of Ochsner could make a 'killing' in Chicago since A. J. had been so prominent, and it would be a shame for me to leave." He vacillated. "I would tell everyone that I wouldn't go to Wisconsin. After this had gone on for a number of months, it was obvious that I was unhappy, and Isabel said to me one day that I should make up my mind. 'You do what you want to do,' she said. 'Don't pay any attention to Akky and me, we'll be happy wherever you are.' That was all I needed, so I told Dr. Orth and Dr. Muller I was leaving, and I went to Wisconsin as a full-time teacher."[5]

Isabel's decision set her on a path from which she never strayed. In a

5. AO Recollection, Chicago.

way, she sacrificed more than Alton did in leaving Chicago. It was her hometown. Her parents, built-in babysitters for the family that would follow, were there. Alton's bright prospects assured her of an enviable standing among her friends. But she established once and for all the principle that her husband's happiness and career came first. Alton had his helpmate.

They drove to Madison in April, 1926, in the Buick given by Orth, and settled into a rented home. "The experience of Wisconsin was extremely pleasant," Ochsner said. "It was a new school, and all of the clinical faculty were relatively young and very enthusiastic. I fit in with it very well and had a delightful time." As assistant visiting surgeon at the State of Wisconsin General Hospital in Madison, Ochsner performed the thoracic surgery because Schmidt was interested in other types of operations. There was a steady flow of thoracic patients: Hedblom had been one of the leaders in that field. At the time, thoracic surgery was largely limited to a collapse of a lung in treating tuberculosis, to drainage of empyema, and to drainage of lung abscesses. The prohibitively high operative mortality rate pretty much ruled out surgery in treatment of bronchiectasis. Ochsner found Schmidt to be a meticulous surgeon and a hard worker with whom he got along well even though Schmidt "didn't have much sense of humor."

It was not in the operating room, however, that young Professor Ochsner gave the University of Wisconsin something to remember him by. His fascination for research resulted in a discovery that facilitated the diagnosis and treatment of bronchiectasis, a disease occurring mostly in cold climates. The bronchial tubes become dilated, and large quantities of foul-smelling sputum are produced in the lungs. The condition could be crippling, even fatal, and in the 1920s the only treatment was postural drainage—that is, placing the patient in a position with his head lowered so that the sputum would seep out of the lungs and through the throat.

From his early days in medicine Ochsner was fascinated by the idea of serendipity, defined as "a gift for discovering valuable or agreeable things by accident." His personal experience with serendipity began in the Kantonsspital in Zurich. He was attempting one day to perform esophagoscopy—radiologic examination of the esophagus—in a patient with carcinoma. The patient, whose pharynx had been anesthetized, was given barium to swallow as the contrast medium in preparation for the fluoroscopy. To Ochsner's amazement, all of the barium went into the trachea and bronchi instead of the esophagus. The next day, without anesthesia, that patient was able to swallow the barium normally, and Ochsner believed the previous failure resulted from the anesthetized condition of the pharynx. At Wisconsin he had time for research on the mechanism of swallowing. He found it to be a dual process, partly voluntary and partly involuntary. When part of the pharynx is anesthetized, any substance taken into the mouth is aspirated through the trachea into the lungs instead of swallowed through the esophagus into the stomach.

This knowledge enabled Ochsner to devise a passive method of bronchography allowing easy fluoroscopy of the chest. He learned to apply cocaine through the mouth, anesthetizing the pharynx for a few minutes. Then the patient was given a drink of lipiodol, a 40 percent solution of iodine in poppyseed oil, which went into the trachea and into the bronchi and lungs, providing a contrast medium for fluoroscopy. Afterward, the patient coughed up the lipiodol, and the effect of the cocaine disappeared. Ochsner made bronchography possible on a sort of assembly-line basis.

In chilly Madison the university's student health service was kept busy with young men and women who had recurrent colds and coughs. Ochsner persuaded officials to allow him to do bronchographies on these students, and he found that a surprising number showed bronchial dilatation, a manifestation of bronchiectasis. Most had histories of severe pneumonitis in early childhood.

The development of the easy bronchography was serendipitous, of course, and then there was a sequel. Upon follow-up visits to the clinic, many of the students who had submitted to bronchoscopy remarked that they had benefited from the "treatment." Ochsner first thought this was a psychological effect, but then tests showed measurable reductions of sputum in some students, and some subsequent bronchographies showed normal bronchial trees. Some gained weight. Alton attributed the improvement to the therapeutic properties of the iodine.

Ochsner was able to differentiate between functional bronchiectasis, a temporary dilatation caused by infection, and organic bronchiectasis, in which the damage is permanent. In his fifteen months at Wisconsin, the energetic professor examined more than seven hundred students with his new technique.[6] He was proving himself to be the type of researcher who wasted no time when he was in the laboratory. Since antibiotics have been available, bronchiectasis no longer is a major health problem.

6. Alton Ochsner, "Bronchography Following the 'Passive' Introduction of Contrast Media into the Tracheo-Bronchial Tree," *Wisconsin Medical Journal*, XXV (1926) 544–55.

Even while Ochsner was settling in at Wisconsin, events were occurring in New Orleans that would shape his future. Rudolph Matas was about to retire from his long-time position as chairman of surgery at the Tulane University School of Medicine. A lengthy search had begun for a worthy successor to a man who for three decades had dominated the medical scene in New Orleans, and whose exploits in vascular surgery and innovations in anesthesia and shock treatment won him international stature. He was regarded by some as the father of vascular surgery.

As the hunt went on, there were echoes from the 1890s, when Matas, a New Orleanian, had been appointed chairman upon the death of A. B. Miles. The Tulane trustees had debated whether to give the job to Matas or to bring in an outsider. Even the daily newspapers were involved, printing editorials supporting Matas and greeting his selection with front-page headlines.

Now, more than thirty years later, there were followers of Matas on the Tulane clinical faculty (those who practiced privately but also lectured to classes and instructed students in hospital rounds) who aspired to the honor of succeeding him. Among the contenders were Urban Maes, a distinguished surgeon in his own right; Isidore Cohn, Matas' confidant and later his biographer; and Lucien Landry, Matas' adopted son. Dean C. C. Bass and others advocated bringing in somebody from outside who would devote all of his attention to his Tulane duties and forego income from private patients. A year earlier John H. Musser had become chairman of the Department of Medicine under this kind of arrangement, and Bass, as well as some trustees, believed a full-time chairman of surgery would best serve the school. Maes took himself out of consideration for the Matas post because he did not want to give up his private practice.[7]

Jockeying continued for months. After the university administration decided not to name a member of the faculty, some of the staff doctors nominated outside friends. Invariably, these were scuttled by others who had their own favorites. Matas himself reportedly came to the conclusion that he wanted William F. Reinhoff, Jr., of the Johns Hopkins faculty, and Reinhoff traveled to New Orleans for interviews. Matas was host at a dinner for him, and his introduction gave the impression that Reinhoff was his choice. But the next morning somebody telephoned Reinhoff at his hotel and explained the difficulties that would confront the new chairman. As a result Reinhoff called Matas and withdrew his candidacy.[8] Obvi-

7. AO Recollection, Tulane.
8. Frank L. Loria, interview, May 17, 1978.

ously, the doctor who took the job would have to beware of ambushes.

In one of his early moves at Tulane, Musser had hired George Herr-mann as a member of the Department of Medicine faculty. Herrmann, it will be remembered, had worked with Ochsner for two years at Barnes Hospital in St. Louis. He was the assistant resident for the year during which Ochsner was a medical intern, and then the resident for the period when Ochsner was assistant resident. Because Herrmann regarded him as a talented practitioner who would become outstanding, he submitted Ochsner's name.

Thus, in January, 1927, at the age of thirty, Ochsner received a letter from Dean Bass inviting him to come down to Tulane to be sized up as a possible chairman of surgery.

Of literally thousands of photos
taken of Ochsner, this was the first.
He was eighteen months old.
Courtesy Isabel Ochsner Mann

Not looking particularly avuncular at twenty-seven months, Ochsner poses
with his niece Ester Pearl Orcutt.
Courtesy Isabel Ochsner Mann

Ochsner shows off his Sunday best.

Courtesy Isabel Ochsner Mann

The Ochsners' comfortable home in Kimball was a far cry from the sodbuster's dugout in which E. P. and Clara endured their first South Dakota winter.
Courtesy Isabel Ochsner Mann

E. P. and his brother Benjamin's store, with its second-floor "opera house," functioned as Kimball's commercial and entertainment hub. Note the hitching post.
Courtesy Isabel Ochsner Mann

Ochsner, a member of the Kimball Cornet Band, stands third from left, second row from top. The bass drummer is Harry Bray, Ochsner's childhood friend and accomplice in small-town pranks.

Courtesy Alton Ochsner

Ochsner as a fresh-faced and confident young man.
Courtesy Alton Ochsner

Albert John Ochsner—A. J.—an eminent and beloved physician in his own right, strongly influenced and aided his young cousin.

Courtesy Isabel Ochsner Mann

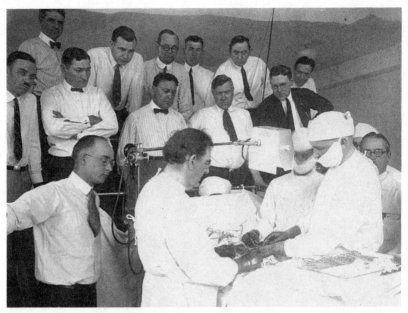

Before a group of attentive residents, A. J. operates in Augustana Hospital in 1924, just a year before his death.
Courtesy Isabel Ochsner Mann

Residents and doctors at Barnes Hospital. Ochsner, *third from left, standing,* developed a great respect for the director of medicine, George Dock, *seated on left.*
Courtesy Alton Ochsner

Ochsner treks the Swiss Alps with a companion during his two years of training in Zurich and Frankfurt.
Courtesy Alton Ochsner

Alton and Isabel's wedding day, September 13, 1923, in Zurich.
Courtesy Alton Ochsner

Around the time of his appointment as chairman of surgery at Tulane in 1927, Ochsner cultivated a moustache in the hope of appearing older than his thirty-one years.

Photograph by Frank Moore, courtesy Alton Ochsner

The house on Exposition Boulevard provided the setting for this formal portrait, *ca.* 1940, of Alton, John, Isabel, Sis, Mims, and Akky.

Courtesy Alton Ochsner

Sis as a young woman, savoring a New Orleans social event with her father.
Courtesy Isabel Ochsner Mann

Ochsner and his sons, all of whom were attached to the Clinic at one time or another. Eventually, rivalry between Akky, *second from left,* and John, *far right,* caused a major rift in the family.

Courtesy Ochsner Medical Foundation

Three generations of Ochsner doctors: Alton, John, and "Lock"—John Lockwood Ochsner, Jr.

Courtesy Isabel Ochsner Mann

The Ochsner and Sturdy clans gather, united by Ochsner's marriage late in his life to Jane Kellogg Sturdy.

Courtesy Isabel Ochsner Mann

5 Destiny Leads South

Alton Ochsner's own account was to the effect that he was happy at Wisconsin and did not take seriously the invitation to be looked over for the Tulane chairmanship. At thirty, he was unlikely to be chosen to pick up Rudolph Matas' scalpel. The later evidences of his ambition suggest that he actually was intrigued by the idea, and not at all averse to submitting himself to the scrutiny of university officials.

In any event, when word got around Madison that Dean Bass had written, Ochsner had a telephone call from William Stovall, professor of public health at Wisconsin and an alumnus of the Tulane medical school. Stovall said he and his wife wanted to come to the Ochsner home that evening. Stovall urged his colleague to take advantage of an expenses-paid trip to New Orleans. He told Ochsner about the wealth of clinical material at Charity Hospital, about the sunshine, about the beauties of Audubon Park, about Sazerac cocktails.

Ochsner left Madison in a blizzard and boarded the deluxe Panama Limited at Chicago. He stepped off the next morning in New Orleans to be greeted by a beautiful sunny day, and to be impressed by the first palm trees he ever had seen. "It seemed to be as much like heaven as anything could be," he said. Meanwhile, Stovall had written to some of his Tulane classmates who were practicing in New Orleans asking them to welcome Ochsner. Several prominent local doctors telephoned the dean's office asking how they could get in touch with the visitor, causing Bass to wonder at the popularity of the young professor, of whom he personally had little knowledge.[1]

During his visit Ochsner saw an exhibition that made him realize he would be entering the surgical big leagues if he were offered the Tulane job. He witnessed an operation so unusual that he would recall it fifty years afterward. He went to Touro Infirmary to make rounds with Matas,

1 AO Recollection, Tulane.

who showed him an elderly woman with a neurofibroma emanating from her lower back that weighed more than she: the tumor weighed ninety-two pounds, and the patient, once it was removed, only ninety. Matas invited Ochsner to return the next day and watch him excise the grotesque appendage.

"For the life of me, I didn't see how he could get it off technically," Ochsner said. "The following morning when I went back, I was amazed to see that he had a block and tackle put in the ceiling of the operating room, and he had a pair of ice tongs that had been sterilized. The patient was put to sleep and then put in the prone position, the area prepared, the ice tongs put into the tumor, attached to the block and tackle, and the tumor was lifted up, with the patient lying on the table." The tumor was excised at the pedicle that connected it to the patient's back. "The patient withstood the procedure well. During the operation the patient received intravenous saline. Matas had been the first to use intravenous saline surgically. The patient left the table in good condition; however, she died during the night of hypovolemia because so much blood had been removed in the tumor. I mention this not only because of the ingenuity which Dr. Matas showed in his method of operating on the patient but because, although this was in 1927, blood transfusions were used so infrequently that he did not use them. Had transfusions been used, I think this patient would have survived."[2]

After Alton had been shown around for several days, Bass suggested that he conduct one of Matas' clinics. "Well, I wasn't about to hold one of Dr. Matas' clinics," Ochsner related. "I had heard him speak. Dr. Will Mayo said Matas was the best-educated doctor the world had produced. He had a photographic memory. He would refer to an article and say it was written in 1910. He could tell you the volume number, the page, even the line it was on. He read five languages, and he read incessantly. He had a storehouse of knowledge that no one else had. His clinics were superb, and I wasn't about to hold one." But Bass was insistent, and Ochsner came up with a stratagem that he thought would get him off the hook. "When I arrived in New Orleans in the sunshine, I knew they wouldn't have colds here and I knew they wouldn't have any bronchiectasis," he said. "So I said if you can get me a case of bronchiectasis I'll hold a clinic. I thought I was safe. But I had underestimated Charity Hospital. They trotted out a half-dozen cases."

2. *Ibid.*

Two hundred or more spectators—university officials, medical faculty, students, others—crowded into the amphitheater at Charity Hospital to form their judgments about the crisp-spoken doctor who had completed his training only two years earlier and now was a candidate for one of the important medical jobs in the country. Dr. Matas listened as Ochsner explained how his curiosity had been aroused by the patient in Zurich who could not swallow when the pharynx was anesthetized, and how he had learned about the swallowing mechanism in Wisconsin and devised an easy, quick method of doing a bronchoscopy. He then announced that he would demonstrate the technique. He turned to the patient on the table beside him, swabbed her pharynx with the cocaine solution provided by Charity Hospital, and sent her out for X-rays. He announced that within an hour he would have the pictures of her chest, then launched into a lecture on bronchiectasis and the difficulty of treating the disease.

The film came back. Ochsner held it up and discovered to his amazement and chagrin that it was blank. The demonstration was a complete failure. "This has never happened before," he told the assemblage. "It is the first time that I have been unsuccessful in filling the bronchial tree. I must admit that I do not know what has happened."[3]

The next day he boarded a train for his return to Madison, resigned to the belief that he had forfeited any slim chance that he might have had for the appointment. He settled back into the routine of his duties at Wisconsin. Two weeks later, he received a letter containing the most momentous news of his lifetime. Bass wrote that he had won the job.

Ochsner returned to New Orleans for a week to find out details that he had not discussed on his first visit because he had not thought he would be seriously considered. He learned that he had tilted the balance in his favor because he did not offer excuses for the failure, but frankly expressed his puzzlement. His belief that "there may be a reason for a failure, but there never is an excuse" had served him well. It would be months before he learned why his demonstration was a dud: the cocaine solution was old and had lost its anesthetic effect. For a winner, and Ochsner was one, even a fiasco is not fatal.

The Ochsners' second son, John Lockwood, was born during a Madison blizzard on February 10, between Alton's two trips to New Orleans. Alton completed the school term at Wisconsin, then drove Isabel and the two boys to Chicago to spend the summer with the Lockwoods.

3. *Ibid.*

He set out alone, in the Buick, to take over his duties at Tulane and to find a home for his family. He had observed his thirty-first birthday on May 4.

The drive southward was an eye-opener for Alton: "I wondered what sort of life I had really chosen." In prosperous Wisconsin the barns and dairy buildings were large and immaculate, the homes unpretentious but well kept. As he proceeded through Tennessee and Mississippi, the evidences of poverty mounted. Occasionally he passed a plantation mansion, but mostly he saw unpainted Negro shacks in a region where cotton crops provided a hand-to-mouth existence for a large part of the population. There may not have been a single Negro family in Kimball when he was growing up, and he had no reason to be conscious of the racial distinctions that divided American society. In St. Louis, of course, he had encountered blacks, but only as a student and hospital resident, a situation in which he was insulated from social realities. He did not have the prejudices, rooted over generations, that southern whites had to learn to deal with. Although he instinctively would cast his lot with the segregationist upper class, racial problems in general were of little consequence in Ochsner's thinking at this point. Medical problems were what mattered. Certainly, a great many of the Charity Hospital patients who received his surgical services were blacks, and there is not the slightest suggestion that Alton Ochsner ever did less than his best for any patient, utterly regardless of race.

Probably, as he started for New Orleans, Ochsner never had heard of a rising politician who would be elected governor of Louisiana a few months after his arrival. Huey Pierce Long was a controversial headline maker within the state, but unknown beyond its borders before he won nomination for governor in January, 1928. It was a happenstance that Ochsner was settling into his new job just as Long was beginning to establish his dictatorship over Louisiana affairs. It is possible that if he could have foreseen a clash with Long over the operation of Charity Hospital, Ochsner might have made a U-turn and raced back to the serenity of the Wisconsin campus. Had he done so he would have missed one of his ordeals and one of his triumphs.

He arrived on the last day of June to find the heat and humidity much different from the pleasant weather he had enjoyed during his winter visits. Friends had warned that the enervating summers would sap his resolve and keep him from working. Not Ochsner. The sweat may have dripped from his forehead, but he plunged full-speed into his projects. He registered at the Jung Hotel on Canal Street, a block from the Tulane medical school and two blocks from Charity Hospital. Dean Bass had told him earlier, "Tulane has never given enough care to the patients at Charity, and I want you to do this."

For several months, until he moved his family to New Orleans, Ochsner devoted almost every waking hour to Charity, where he had been appointed chief visiting surgeon by the board of administrators. "I never worked so hard," he recalled. It was time well spent, because the mystique that eventually made him a larger-than-life surgeon in the public mind first developed out of his activities at the big, state-operated hospital on Tulane Avenue. Few, if any, other hospitals in the United States have a record of service longer and of more importance to a community than Charity. It began in 1736 with a 10,000-livre bequest by a sailor, Jean Louis, for the establishment of a haven for sick seamen. It became a state institution, the Charity Hospital of Louisiana, in 1786 under the administration of the Spanish governor Don Andres Almonester y Rojas. The oldest building in the complex that made up the hospital in 1927 had been constructed in 1832.

By Ochsner's time, Charity was one of the largest hospitals in the country, offering 1,732 beds for the care of Louisiana citizens who could not pay for its services. No fewer than 31,363 patients were admitted in 1928, and 72,537 were treated as outpatients. In the surgical area, busy around the clock, 15,967 operations were performed in that year. The sirens of arriving ambulances were a familiar sound, 30,285 victims of accidents having been treated.[4]

While Charity's principal function was to take care of the ill and injured, the institution also was important for training thousands of medical students, interns, and residents. As a teaching hospital, Charity had few equals; it served an army of patients, and they came with a wide range of ailments. The Tulane medical faculty introduced students to clinical practice, the actual treatment of patients. In return for free care, a Charity patient became a lesson in the education of doctors. The wealth of clinical material made the hospital a gold mine for research. The patients were human beings, not experimental animals, but their numbers and the variety of their ailments greatly added to the store of medical knowledge.

Upon his arrival, Ochsner had to choose an associate professor of surgery. The most likely candidates for the job were James D. Rives and

4. Charity Hospital, annual report for 1928.

Idys Mims Gage. Rives's qualifications were beyond challenge: he had emerged as one of the most capable surgeons of his era and was an inspiration to succeeding classes of students at the Louisiana State University medical school and to interns and residents at Charity Hospital. But Ochsner had been impressed by Gage in their encounters during his visits to Tulane.

Gage knew that the doctors who opposed the appointment of the new chairman were waiting to pounce on his first sign of weakness, and he tried to pick an easy case for the appointee's debut in a Charity Hospital operating room. For nearly a week after Ochsner reported for duty, Gage managed to cancel difficult procedures. Then fate forced his hand. A patient with a brain tumor required immediate treatment, and there was nobody else available to do the operation. Ochsner had received some training in neurosurgery in Europe but had done no such work since his return. On July 6, 1927, he performed his first surgery in New Orleans. He was faced with a challenge that would have taxed his capabilities at any stage of his career. In stifling heat, under a skylight that focused the sun's rays upon the table below, Ochsner performed a suboccipital craniotomy for the excision of a left-sided neurofibroma of the eighth nerve in the posterior fossa. In layman's language, he opened the skull and removed a growth from the back of the brain. It was an operation never before done in New Orleans.

Garbed in a heavy gown, his breathing impeded by his mask, Ochsner worked for longer than five hours, losing ten pounds as sweat oozed from every pore. Later he had one nurse assigned to mop his brow to prevent perspiration from dropping into the wound. In the summers before air conditioning blessed the lives of New Orleans surgeons, he sometimes could wring cups of liquid out of a sopping wet gown. Some surgeons stripped off pants and shirt and wore only underwear beneath their gowns.

"I remember finishing in a state of complete exhaustion, nauseated, and although the case was successful, I didn't know how I was going to get through the day," Ochsner related. "We started before eight o'clock in the morning and finished at one o'clock. Dr. Gage and I went down to Gluck's Restaurant [on Royal Street in the French Quarter] to have lunch. The only thing either of us wanted was watermelon, upon which we used a great deal of salt. This was in the days before we knew anything about salt deprivation, and I recall that immediately after eating the watermelon with salt I felt better."[5] He and others learned to take salt tablets before starting a summertime operation. Ochsner also developed a yen for tomato juice, which he gulped by the glassful on operating days.

The brain operation was no comfort for the detractors of the new chairman. "He did a masterful operation which demonstrated to all his versatility," Gage said.[6] It should have become apparent to his adversaries that the new professor of surgery knew his business, and also had the toughness of a formidable competitor. Gage had limited the number of spectators by passing out word that the patient had a cold and the operation would be postponed.

Born at Greenwood, South Carolina, on September 6, 1893, Gage was graduated from the Tulane medical school in 1917 as a protégé of Matas', to whom his devotion was deep and lasting. He became a medical officer in the First World War, and was scheduled for duty in Siberia after the Armistice. But through Matas' intercession, he was released in time to join the Tulane faculty as an instructor in surgery in the spring of 1919. Although still young by medical-school standards in 1927, Gage was one of the eligible prospects as successor to Matas. But as qualified as he was, Gage had no ambition to be a department chairman; he was content to play second fiddle to Matas and then to Ochsner. Michael E. DeBakey would be flabbergasted later when Gage turned down an opportunity to head one of the surgical wards at Charity Hospital, preferring to remain as second man in Ochsner's ward. His lack of aspiration to administrative office takes nothing away from Gage's ability as a surgeon. His almost uncanny flair for diagnosis remained a legend in the Ochsner Clinic long after his death.

In time, Gage would feel toward Ochsner as a brother. During World War II, Ochsner's mother needed a gall bladder operation. The two surgeons succeeded in obtaining a leave for Gage in order that he could do the job in New Orleans. Ochsner looked on while Gage did the procedure. Afterward, Mrs. Ochsner needed blood. Gage's was compatible, and he climbed on a table to provide the needed type for a transfusion. He turned down an offer of coffee and orange juice at Touro Infirmary, where he had operated, and walked to St. Charles Avenue to board a streetcar enroute to the Louisiana Club for lunch. As he left the car at Carondelet

5. AO Recollection, Career.
6. Mims Gage, at testimonial banquet for Alton Ochsner, May 19, 1956.

and Gravier streets, he suddenly felt faint from the loss of blood. He sat on the curb and put his head between his knees to restore the circulation of blood to the brain. Afterward, he could smile when he contemplated what passersby must have thought at the sight of a man in an army colonel's uniform slumped over the gutter.

Ochsner once confided to Mrs. Gage that he knew he had a bad appendix and wanted to have it taken out before he had an acute attack. "Oh, Al," Mrs. Gage responded. "Please don't tell Mims ahead of time, because he'd just die a thousand deaths if he knew he was going to operate on you. You'll just have to make it an emergency. Just don't tell him ahead of time. He won't be in any condition." A few nights after the Ochsners and the Gages returned from a meeting of the Southern Surgical Association, the telephone rang and Gage answered. "Oh, oh," he said, "I'll be right up." He turned to Mrs. Gage. "Al thinks he has appendicitis. Isn't that awful? I'm going right up there."

Mrs. Gage pretended to be surprised. "He called back about nine o'clock and said, 'I've got him in the hospital. It's an unusual case. He has a lot of pain when I palpate but his white blood count isn't high.' I thought, well, of course it isn't high. Mims said Al had decided this was the time to have the appendix out. He said, 'He thinks I ought to go ahead and do it. This is just awful and you don't know how awful I feel, but he doesn't want anybody else to do it.'"

Gage got home at about six o'clock in the morning. "Well, his appendix wasn't too bad," he told Mrs. Gage. "It did need to come out, but it wasn't ruptured." After her husband had slept, Mrs. Gage disclosed the plot.[7]

When the Ochsners' third son was born, on June 24, 1928, he was named Mims Gage Ochsner, and Gage was the godfather. In the course of time, Gage performed appendectomies upon Isabel and young Mims Ochsner. Ochsner said to him, "Mims, you took out my appendix, Isabel's, and Mims's. Now which one was easiest?"

Gage replied, "Well, yours, of course."

"I don't know how you can say that," Ochsner protested. "It seems to me Isabel's was the simplest, and Mims was just a child and that was nothing."

"I'll tell you why yours was the easiest," explained Gage. "It's because

7. Mrs. Mims Gage, interview, June 20, 1977.

I didn't have you looking over my shoulder as I did when they had their operations."[8]

Gage was a raconteur, with a supply of jokes that kept listeners laughing. He specialized in Cajun stories, about the Acadian population of Louisiana. Ochsner, too, could tell Cajun jokes with good effect, although he could not match Gage's delivery. He looked to Gage for a fresh story or two whenever he had a speech scheduled. Gage had a trigger wit, and probably not one of his colleagues could have carried off one of his most noted exploits. As he walked through the hospital one day, wearing a business suit, a nurse stopped him and reported that an elderly woman about to undergo surgery was overwrought. No chaplain was available. She asked if Gage would look in on the patient.

"How are we today?" he asked the taut figure on the bed.

"Oh," she said, "I want to talk to a minister. I need a Methodist minister."

"Why, what a coincidence," Gage said. "I am a retired Methodist bishop. Let us pray." He knelt beside the bed, took the woman's hands between his own, and made an appeal to the Almighty of exactly the kind the patient wanted to hear. The grateful woman thanked him, and he left her relaxed and ready for her ordeal. While she was recovering, Gage walked down her corridor, wearing his doctor's gown. She recognized him and was appalled, upbraiding him for the sacrilegious imposture.

"But, dear lady," he begged, "I am sworn to help the suffering, and my prayer was as sincere as any bishop's." She laughed. "You're right," she said, "and I thank you . . . bishop."[9]

The second faculty member hired by Ochsner was his old friend from Chicago, Earl Garside, who came in as instructor in surgery. Born in Indian territory that became part of the state of Oklahoma, Garside received his doctor of medicine degree from the University of Oklahoma in 1921. He served his internship and residency under Nelson Percy, A. J. Ochsner's associate, at Augustana Hospital. A bachelor, he developed a severe case of hepatitis in New Orleans and was put to bed in the interns' ward at Charity Hospital. After a week—"I was yellow as gold and sick with an infectious disease"—Isabel intervened and took him into the Ochsner home on Green Street, setting up a cot for him in the dining

8. Ibid.
9. Ibid.

room because it was the only available space. With the help of her nursing, he recovered. In 1931 he resigned from the faculty to begin work on a master of surgery degree from the Tulane graduate medical school. Then he returned to Chicago to be associated with Edward Ochsner, A. J.'s brother, who was retiring from the operating room.[10] Edward Ochsner always remained in the shadow of A. J.

10. Garside, interview, April 19, 1977.

6 The Chairman Takes Charge

Alton Ochsner had reason to feel that he was making a big stride in his career when he became chairman of surgery at the Tulane University School of Medicine on July 1, 1927. The school was nearing its centennial—the first classes had convened on January 5, 1835—and it had built a reputation as the most prestigious medical college in the Deep South and as an institution of high national ranking. The medical historian John Duffy has pointed out the school's rare heritage: Louisiana was the first state to be influenced in the nineteenth century by the medical advances in France, then the world standard. French-speaking Louisiana youths studied in Paris and brought back new concepts of healing. Some served on the faculty of the New Orleans school.[1]

The institution was founded as the Medical College of Louisiana, a proprietary venture by a group of young physicians. Then it became the medical department of the University of Louisiana, and finally, in 1884, a school of Tulane University of Louisiana, for which philanthropist Paul Tulane had provided an endowment. Tulane fared well in 1910 in the Abraham Flexner report, a merciless probe that resulted in the closing of about one-half of American medical schools. As chairman of surgery, Ochsner took his place in a distinguished line, beginning with Charles A. Luzenberg, 1835–1837, and continuing with Warren Stone, 1837–1871; Tobias G. Richardson, 1871–1888; Samuel Logan, 1889–1892; Albert B. Miles, 1893–1894; and Rudolph Matas, 1894–1927.

From the beginning, the school and Charity Hospital were interdependent. Charity needed the services of the physicians and surgeons on the Tulane faculty to oversee the treatment of the many thousands of needy patients who relied on the free care furnished by the state of Louisiana. The school, on the other hand, could not have turned out class after

1. John Duffy, *The Tulane University Medical Center* (Baton Rouge, 1984), 3–6.

class of practitioners without access to the material for clinical teaching provided by the patients at Charity.

Although they hardly could get along without each other, the hospital and school had a sometimes stormy relationship. Charity was a public institution, governed by a superintendent and board of administrators subject to the vagaries of politics. Tulane was a private school, not beholden to officeholders. There was reason to hope for smooth sailing, however, at the time that Ochsner came onto the scene. Two years earlier a Tulane Service at Charity Hospital had been formally established, with the Charity board assigning five hundred beds for teaching purposes. The plan was expected to lessen the likelihood of conflict between Tulane teachers and Charity's house staff. But these prospects for amity did not reflect a new presence on the Louisiana political horizon in 1927. Within a few months, the new Tulane surgery chairman would find himself a center of controversy, the unwitting target of Huey Pierce Long.[2]

Gertrude Forshag peered out of a window of the Richardson Memorial Building on Canal Street and got her first look at the man whose secretary she would be for fifty-two years. The new chairman of surgery stood on the sidewalk, waiting for an automobile to pick him up. Miss Forshag, then a clerical worker in the medical department, was on vacation when Ochsner arrived. Upon her return to work one of the stenographers had news: "Oh, you should see the handsome professor of surgery. Oh, he's so good-looking, and he's so cute and so nice." Later, Miss Forshag was in a front office, overlooking Canal Street, when a fellow worker summoned: "Come on, come on. Hurry. Here he is."

"I looked out the window, and there he was at the gate, waiting," Miss Forshag related. "He had on a seersucker suit and a straw katy. Everybody came along, he tipped his hat." Within two weeks outlander Alton Ochsner had become a New Orleanian, on the surface at least. He had bought one of the rather shapeless, gray, washable, quick-to-wrinkle lightweight suits that were the summer uniform of half the adult male population, and had acquired a straw katy (or kelly), the flat-brimmed, saucerlike hat that was apt to go rolling down the street if the wind suddenly gusted. He may have learned in Kimball to lift his headgear in salute. At any rate, the tip was obligatory in New Orleans at the time, and

2. *Ibid.*, 23 and *passim*.

Ochsner caught on quick.[3] A smudge of a moustache was his attempt to look more mature, but did not confuse the impressionable secretaries who knew that, by the standards of his profession, the trim, fresh-faced, vibrant doctor was not much past boyhood. Any of them who might have hoped to be asked to a tryst were disappointed. He was pleasant, accessible, and sympathetic with the women (and men) who worked for him, but always drew a line. Never in their fifty-two years together did he call Miss Forshag by her first name. At office parties, he made the required appearance and left at the proper time. As for any amorous leanings, in his lengthy heyday Ochsner must have had many opportunities, but in years of research into his life and activities, there turned up no hint of an affair, not even in the period when he was a lonely widower.

His youthful appearance could have been a handicap: Ochsner was barely older than some of the students who faced him in classes when the new term began in September. It did not take him long, however, to establish his authority. He was always well prepared for his lectures, spoke with a delivery that commanded attention, and tolerated no interference with the business at hand. If a student nodded off, Ochsner threw a piece of chalk or an eraser at him. Invariably prompt himself, he had no patience with tardiness, and he had a sarcastic greeting for a student who tried to sneak in unobtrusively once a class started. The red-faced culprit was invited to come down to a front row seat and asked whether he usually kept bankers' hours.

Ochsner's introduction at Tulane was recalled by Rufus C. Harris, who himself joined the faculty in 1927 as dean of the law school and who went on to become president of the university. The two discovered that they were fraternity brothers, and they enjoyed a friendship that endured for many years, with only one temporary misunderstanding, which arose much later, during a critical period in Ochsner's life. "I was impressed with him the first time I ever saw him," Harris said, "because there was an air of confidence about Alton Ochsner. There was a friendly air about him, too. I recognized that he was coming there in a more exciting capacity than I because he was the successor to the great surgeon Rudolph Matas, and it was something to be known as the young man who succeeded a doctor like Matas. But it never impressed itself upon him particularly. He was himself all the time. He was gregarious, he was friendly.

3. Gertrude Forshag, interview, November 17, 1976.

He met people on their terms, not his. I don't know of anybody who won people to himself more readily than Dr. Ochsner did. He was very open."[4] Ochsner became the Harrises' family physician.

The so-called downtown quarters of the medical school occupied the Josephine Hutchinson Memorial Building. A solid, sedate structure of three stories and above-ground basement, it had been the last word in medical architecture when it was opened in 1893. The rear windows overlooked a corner of Storyville, the notorious red-light district that had been closed in 1919. The two higher classes of Tulane medical students listened to lectures and did their work in the laboratories of the Hutchinson Building, whereas the two lower classes were assigned to the Uptown campus, on St. Charles Avenue across from Audubon Park.

Ochsner's office was on the Hutchinson Building's third floor, where the cadavers were kept and where the dissecting rooms were located. The third floor also featured a large amphitheater and some laboratories. For nearly three and a half years the chairman spent most of his working hours here, except when he was performing surgery at Charity Hospital. He had given up a promising clinical practice in Chicago because he wanted to teach and do research, and now his opportunity had come. The lights burned late, sometimes throughout the night, as Ochsner and other members of his department plunged into ambitious studies that yielded a series of reports in medical journals. Mims Gage, Earl Garside, George Herrmann, and Reginald A. Cutting enthusiastically joined Ochsner in after-hours efforts, and no fewer than thirty articles were prepared for publication by the time the school moved to a new building in December, 1930. Even Ochsner could not produce a paper a month, but in this period he was averaging better than one every two months.

Research was a factor in the development of Ochsner's reputation outside New Orleans, but it also brought a mishap that might have put a crimp in his skill as a surgeon. He was threatened for a while with the loss of the middle finger of his left hand, and was lucky to come out of the episode with his dexterity unimpaired. In Wisconsin he had become interested in the problem of adhesions, the internal scarring that often follows surgery. George Herrmann suggested that they devote some of their efforts at Tulane toward the control of pericardial adhesions that sometimes can affect heart function. They set out to learn whether papain—a ferment made from the tropical fruit papaya—would hasten the disap-

4. Rufus C. Harris, interview, February, 1978.

pearance of adhesions after an operation through the process of autolysis, or absorption by the body. They were using dogs in the study. Late one evening, after a hard day, Ochsner carelessly began to insert a tracheal tube before his dog was fully anesthetized, and the animal bit him on the left hand.

"I got a perfectly horrible infection with a suppurative arthritis of the distal interphalangeal joint," he related. "Since this was in the days before we had antibiotics, the infection was extremely difficult to control." For a time it appeared that he would have to have the finger amputated. The joint was destroyed, and the finger would have become stiff had not Ochsner kept flexing it during convalescence. "It was a case of haste making waste," he said.[5]

Once the fall term opened in 1927, it quickly became apparent that Tulane had acquired a teacher who not only could make clear the subject matter of his lessons, but also could inspire students to work. Even the faculty members who did not warm up to him conceded his pedagogic skills. One of his innovations was to subordinate textbooks in favor of up-to-date professional journals.

"I felt that learning medicine from textbooks was obsolete," he explained. "By the time a textbook had been written, it was old, and I felt that the students should get their information from current periodicals. The surgical staff developed a suggested reading list for various subjects, and the students were supposed to read some of these lists. Then they were quizzed on the subjects. This meant a great deal of work for the staff in preparing the list and also in quizzing, but I think the students were encouraged to use current literature and to know how they would go about getting current literature when they graduated."

Of course, the approach meant that Ochsner himself could not use the same lectures year after year, the cushion of a lazy professor with tenure. He would work the night before at home, assembling his information and dictating into recording equipment. The next morning he would take the cylinders to Miss Forshag for his words to be transcribed before class.

The new chairman took full advantage of the opportunity for clinical teaching in Charity Hospital. He assigned the junior class to the wards where students saw the more advanced cases. The seniors, meanwhile, worked in the outpatient service with the early stages of disease, and thus

5. AO Recollection, Appendicitis, etc.

could learn more about making diagnoses. Ochsner's "bull pen" was conducted in the A. B. Miles amphitheater in Charity.

In his own words, Ochsner "enjoyed every moment" of his early months at Tulane and at Charity. It was the calm before the storm, but for a while the only ripple in a placid sea was made by a few jealous doctors who held part-time positions on the Tulane surgical faculty. For the time being the atmosphere also was calm at Charity Hospital, where before long there would be turbulence.

Ochsner was not yet seen as a formidable rival by practitioners in the New Orleans medical community. Such anti-Ochsner feeling as there was at Tulane involved surgeons who had strong emotional ties to Matas and who found it difficult to accept any successor to their idol. Frank L. Loria long afterward complained that Ochsner "felt that anybody who started under Matas didn't know what he was doing."[6] But Matas himself seems to have been impressed by the newcomer, and their relationships always were cordial. In 1929 Matas endorsed Ochsner's application for fellowship in the American Surgical Association, writing: "Dr. Ochsner's activity as a contributor to surgical progress and literature is attested by his numerous contributions. . . . Personally he is modest, unassuming, temperate, judicious, honorable and thoroughly dependable in all the social relations of professional life. Though quite young in years, he is ripe in training, accomplishment and experience. He has splendid opportunities for further development in New Orleans, and I am confident that the future will prove that he has not failed to profit by them."[7]

The only recorded clash between Matas and Ochsner involved Isidore Cohn, a member of the clinical faculty, who might have hoped to step in as chairman when Matas retired. Somebody, and Ochsner said he thought it was Cohn, told Matas that Ochsner had blocked Cohn's bid for membership in the American Surgical Association. "Dr. Matas called me down one day," Ochsner related, "and for two hours just castigated me. I couldn't get a word in. I'd say 'but . . . well . . . but . . . well,' but he wouldn't stop. He was a Latin and had a Latin temper, and no one has had such a tongue-lashing as I did for two solid hours. Finally, after two hours, I managed to say, 'Dr. Matas, I had absolutely nothing to do with this.' He just sort of backed out, but he didn't apologize. But somebody had accused me, and I assume it was Isidore Cohn himself. I don't know

6. Loria, interview, May 17, 1978.
7. Rudolph Matas to Lincoln Davis, April 25, 1929.

who kept him out. I'm inclined to believe it was Urban Maes. I was so young then nobody would pay any attention to me in the American Surgical."[8]

In his first two and a half years at Tulane, Ochsner was making an impression in the world of academic medicine. His research was attracting attention, and his talents as a teacher were being recognized. Among the doctors who worked in Charity Hospital's operating rooms, it was evident that an unusually gifted surgeon also was serving an impoverished segment of the Louisiana population. Yet the horizons of his realm did not stretch as far as one might imagine. There were restrictions that limited his future. He went to Tulane as a full-time professor, denied the right to treat private, paying patients as Matas and his other predecessors had done. Under the circumstances, he might go on to make a name for himself in professional circles, but unless he could score some laboratory breakthrough—as, for example, Jonas Salk and Albert Sabin did much later with poliomyelitis vaccines—he never could enjoy widespread public acclaim.

He was in the right specialty: it is the surgeon who excites the layman's imagination with feats of lifesaving legerdemain. The headlines or telecasts, however, belong to the operator who takes out a lung and halts the spread of cancer in a motion-picture star, athlete, or politician, not the one who, in a public hospital, extracts a bullet from the heart of a slum shooting victim.

8. AO, interview, June 14, 1978.

7 Surviving Huey Long's Wrath

Tulane's new chairman of surgery was about as apolitical as any youthful American ever is likely to be. He had moved about too frequently to become involved in local governmental issues anywhere. He was too busy with his surgery, teaching, and research to have more than a headline-scanning interest in national elections. Now he became an innocent target of the master demagogue of the era, the Louisiana Kingfish, Huey P. Long.

Taking office as governor in 1928, Long established himself as a czar who tolerated no enemies or anyone whom he regarded as unfriendly to his regime. He seized control of the Charity Hospital board of administrators, of which he was an ex officio member, and made the huge facility a part of his fiefdom. He ousted the superintendent and gave the job to Arthur Vidrine, son of one of his henchmen. Vidrine, not yet thirty years of age, was a graduate of the Tulane medical school who had spent two years abroad as a Rhodes Scholar. He had served a brief internship at Charity. At the time Long chose him for the superintendency, he was practicing in Ville Platte, a small town in Louisiana's Cajun country.

Although the Charity board in 1925 had designated five hundred beds for Tulane's purposes, the school had no formal training program at the hospital. The Tulane faculty had access to the wards because the teachers were given appointments as house officers by the Charity board. Upon his arrival in New Orleans, Ochsner had been named chief visiting surgeon by the board, and it was in this capacity, and not as chairman of surgery at Tulane, that he performed operations and taught students the clinical phases of medicine in the hospital setting.

Relations between Vidrine and Tulane dean C. C. Bass were strained. Bass had assumed that the setting up of the Tulane Service at Charity gave him the prerogative to select the faculty members who would be involved there. But he found that some of his nominees were not given the required house staff appointments. When the chairmanship of Tulane's department of otolaryngology became vacant, Vidrine asked Bass to give him the post. Bass pointed out that Vidrine had not specialized in ear, nose, and throat. Vidrine suggested that he could "read up on it."[1]

Meanwhile, Ochsner was getting his own introduction to politics, Louisiana style. He was disenchanted because the hospital was run by doctors who were given political appointments to the house staff. Later he noted that Long had announced Vidrine would reduce the mortality rate at Charity. "And he did, on paper," Ochsner said. "They would go out in the parishes and bring in whole busloads of children to have their tonsils out; bring them in in the morning, take their tonsils out, and send them back. Of course, these were admissions and operations and they did thousands of them that way, and of course the mortality rate went right down with the admissions, and none of them died, and this is the way he decreased the mortality rate."

Ochsner apparently offended Vidrine when he refused the superintendent's request to recommend him for appointment as a professor of surgery at Tulane. "I told him, 'Well now, Arthur, if I recommended you for an appointment on the staff as a professor, since you are a political appointee, both you and I would be criticized. Why don't you wait until you are through with this present [Charity superintendent] job, and then we can talk it over?'" Ochsner added, "I didn't dare tell him then what I thought about him."[2] John Duffy wrote that Vidrine yearned for the professional prestige that a Tulane professorship would have given him.

In the spring of 1930 Ochsner received an inquiry asking if he would like to be considered for chief of surgery at the University of Virginia. His frustration caused him to wonder whether a move might be advantageous. Knowing little about the Virginia school, he dictated to Miss Forshag a letter addressed to his friend Allen Whipple at Columbia University:

> You may be somewhat surprised that I should even consider moving from Tulane, and my reason for writing to you is to get your frank opinion concerning the advisability of it. I consider it only because I feel that the outlook at Tulane as far as building up a Department is concerned is absolutely hopeless. The University is dependent upon Charity Hospital, which is a state institution and which is in the control of politics. The University is merely tolerated

1. Duffy, *Tulane Medical Center,* 147–48.
2. AO Recollection, Huey Long and Charity Hospital.

in the hospital, and there is no cooperation at all. The house staff is appointed by the Hospital, and the University has no control whatever over it. As far as the University itself is concerned, it is perfectly free from politics, and my relations there have been very pleasant. I have an excellently equipped surgical experimental laboratory where any type or kind of experimental research may be done. However, under the present system (and apparently there is no better outlook) it is impossible to train men as surgeons.[3]

Ochsner told Miss Forshag to give him a carbon copy of the letter because he wanted to show it to Isabel. He folded the copy and put it into an inner pocket of his jacket. That afternoon, at Charity Hospital, he hung his jacket on a peg in the heart station and donned a white coat to make rounds. At home that evening he thought about the letter and went to get the copy. It was not in his pocket. The next day Miss Forshag confirmed that he had taken the carbon with him when he left the office.

Some six months later, on September 13, 1930, the copy reappeared— in Huey Long's rooms at the Roosevelt Hotel, where the Charity board was holding a meeting. Long used it to get a vote to cancel Ochsner's appointment as chief visiting surgeon and to bar him from Charity. "I should have absolute loyalty," Long replied to a demurring board member who said the action would "annihilate" Ochsner. Vidrine was not present at the meeting. The New Orleans *Times-Picayune* said a source at Charity disclosed that the letter had come into the possession of Vidrine, who sent it to Long.[4]

Ochsner went to his grave without knowing who took the letter from his pocket and how it got into Vidrine's hands, but he once said that Vidrine "was laying for me and apparently took the letter out of my pocket and used it." He cannot have believed the superintendent himself went snooping into the heart station and filched the copy. But somebody else did—unless the paper fell from the jacket pocket and was picked up by a hospital employee who passed it on to Vidrine. Ochsner was advised of the board's action, which occurred on his seventh wedding anniversary, in a note dated September 30. Earl Garside was dismissed from the visiting staff at the same time.

Long's vindictiveness toward Ochsner is puzzling unless it is inter-

3. John P. Dyer, *Tulane: The Biography of a University, 1834–1965* (New York, 1966), footnote 216.
4. *Times-Picayune*, September 18, 1930, Sec. 1, p. 9.

preted as part of a vendetta against Tulane. Ochsner never encountered Long face to face, and of course was no political threat. A few weeks after the dismissal, Long announced plans to open a medical school, based in New Orleans, at Louisiana State University. The first classes were held in the fall of 1931, and Vidrine was named dean, a post that he held while continuing as superintendent at Charity. Vidrine raided the Tulane medical faculty to fill some of the LSU professorships. Mims Gage, who knew Vidrine from their days together as medical students at Tulane, took over Ochsner's activities at Charity for a year. On a motion by Urban Maes, seconded by Isidore Cohn, the Tulane surgical faculty gave a vote of confidence in Ochsner and expressed regret over his dismissal.

Ochsner's reaction to the ouster was one of dismay. "I was so hurt because when I came down here Dean Bass said Tulane had never given to Charity the service that it should, and he wanted me to just give everything to the hospital," Ochsner recalled. "My family didn't come down for months, and I spent all of my time at the hospital. Then and afterward I gave everything I had to it, and then to be kicked out because the man who was head of the institution didn't like me—and for that reason only—I just felt I was cut up. I didn't even want to stay here." At about that time, Ochsner recalled, he had an offer to go to the University of Illinois. "I was going to accept it," he said, but he decided first to talk with C. Jeff Miller, gynecologist-surgeon, an influential figure both at Tulane and in the New Orleans medical community.

"Dr. Jeff, to get a slap in the face like this after having put in so much time and doing so much, I just feel I can't stay here," he told Miller, a father figure for the younger surgeon ("I actually loved the man," Ochsner said). Miller's reaction was not what Ochsner expected. "You cannot go under fire," he insisted. Perhaps nobody else could have changed Ochsner's mind at this time. The loss of access to the teaching hospital had diminished his usefulness to Tulane, and the denial of operating-room privileges might have been a lethal blow to the career of a surgeon whose outside practice was severely limited by the policy of full-time service that he had accepted when he took the chairmanship: a surgeon who cannot operate soon begins to lose his skills. But Miller's logic prevailed.

Indeed, with friends like Miller and the sympathy of Tulane's administrators, Ochsner soon found his position far from hopeless. In December, 1930, the medical school moved to the new Hutchinson Memorial Building at 1415 LaSalle Street, adjacent to the Charity Hospital. The

Hutchinson Memorial Clinic was established there to provide free care for needy patients as part of the instruction of students. The Tulane board subsidized ten beds at Touro Infirmary for clinic patients who needed surgery, and Ochsner once again had the opportunity of operating and of demonstrating techniques to students.

Undoubtedly the prospect of the loss of such a chairman as Ochsner was one of the factors in a gradual relaxing of the prohibition against private practice by full-time professors. The pressure already was building, some of it coming from sick people who had heard of Ochsner's skills in treating Charity Hospital surgical cases and wondered why they were denied services for which they could pay. Not until 1934 would the administrators in effect let the bars down, but already Ochsner and other chairmen were seeing some private patients. For one period they were asked to turn over fees to the school, but they no longer were shut out of the kind of practice in which a gifted doctor can thrive.[5]

Tulane and Bass solicited the aid of the American Medical Association's Council on Medical Education in their resistance to harassment by Long and Vidrine. Approval of the Council was necessary for the LSU school to receive vital Class A accreditation. In 1932, with third-year students nearing senior status, the approval still had not been forthcoming. LSU was notified that there would be no accreditation until its school had been inspected by a special committee. Meanwhile, in an effort to bolster the LSU standing, Long and Vidrine had recruited Urban Maes as chairman of surgery. Maes accepted the job only on the condition that relations between Tulane and Charity be smoothed out, and that some of Tulane's grievances receive action. In September, 1932, two years after his dismissal, Ochsner was notified that he had been reinstated. The AMA Council accredited LSU in February, 1933.[6]

In effect, Ochsner had been pushed out of a third-story window only to land in the executive suite on the fifth floor. He said the smartest decision he ever made was to turn down the Illinois job and stay at Tulane. "It did two things, his kicking me out," he commented. "It identified me with the worthwhile people in this state, the people who hated Huey Long, and here I was being persecuted. It made me become known in a way that I wouldn't have otherwise. It also gave me a chance for two years to do

5. AO, interview, December 8–9, 1977.
6. Duffy, *Tulane Medical Center*, 146.

research that I couldn't have done otherwise. It was a fortuitous thing, although it seemed a horrible blow at the time."

Huey Long had five more years to live from the time of his vengeful move against Ochsner until an assassin shot him in the halls of the state capitol in Baton Rouge. The irony is well known. Urban Maes, summoned from New Orleans to attempt lifesaving surgery, was delayed by an automobile mishap. As Long's condition deteriorated from loss of blood, Vidrine had to make the decision to operate himself in an effort to sew up the internal wounds. Long acquiesced. Fifty years afterward there still is controversy over the question of whether Vidrine bungled the job, whether he failed to find and close a hole in the kidney. The truth may never be known because Long was buried without an autopsy.[7]

In reminiscing, Ochsner liked to tell about an incident that occurred some three decades after Long's death. He had become friendly with Huey's son, Russell B. Long, who as a United States senator occupied the seat once held by his father. "I was astounded to hear him say the other day to me," Ochsner related, " 'You know, if my father had had you to take care of him, he would be alive today.' I didn't know Russell realized this."

7. Alton Ochsner, address to Ochsner Foundation fellows, August 14, 1971.

8 Boss of the Bull Pen

S oon after Ochsner took over the chair at Tulane, he inaugurated the diagnostic clinic that came to be known as the bull pen, and it was here that he engraved his image in the memories of Tulane medical students. Forty, even fifty years later, distinguished practitioners could recite the details of their turns as soon-to-be-graduated seniors in Ochsner's "why clinic." Legends persist to this day about some of the encounters in the surgical amphitheater of first the old and then the new Charity Hospital. The bull pen was not an idea originated by Ochsner, but he made it a teaching tool of rare effectiveness, with the professor pictured as a fire-snorting, razor-horned tormentor bent on goring a clumsy student toreador.

Ochsner borrowed from his experience at Washington University, recalling George Dock's exercise of having a student look at, but not talk with, a patient and then submit to a quiz about what he saw. Ochsner also copied from neurosurgeon Ernest Sachs's technique of allowing a student to make an examination and then explain his diagnosis. The procedure at Tulane was to give a member of the senior class twenty or thirty minutes to examine a patient at Charity Hospital. Then, in the amphitheater, the student had to present his case and defend his diagnosis against Ochsner's relentless questioning. "Why do you say that? Why? Why?" the professor demanded, while two hundred members of the senior and junior classes, along with Charity house staff doctors drawn to the spectacle, watched the student squirm.

Ochsner called the experience a "psychic ordeal," justified because it taught aspiring doctors to think under stress. "The practice of medicine is stressful," he said. He described diagnosis as largely a matter of common sense.

If you know the fundamentals and if you know what makes an organ work and you know the interplay of the various organs, you can figure out the symptoms pretty well. I emphasized that they had to have a reason. Whenever they made a diagnosis, they had to have a reason. I've often said that if your reasoning is correct, if you get the right information and your reasoning is correct, you'll almost invariably come out with the right diagnosis. You may not, but I'd rather have the person reason correctly and come up with the wrong diagnosis—but you usually do not. If a person can think along in a logical sequence, things will pretty well unfold.[1]

Ochsner dominated the scene with his knowledge and his personality, and there never was a question of who was boss. He sometimes played to the gallery—that was part of the concept of the pedagogic exercise, to teach a student to keep his composure under frustrating circumstances, to think under fire. He could be sarcastic and impatient with hazy reasoning, quick to point out obvious gaps in a student's workup of a case. But Ochsner was not sadistic. He did not leave lasting scars on the psyches of the hundreds of Tulane seniors who faced him in his arena and came out better doctors. More than Ochsner, students feared Mims Gage in the bull pen. Gage took it as a personal responsibility to wring any conceit out of medical students. Until they received their degrees, they were fair game for his considerable and sometimes malevolent wit. After that, those who had felt themselves abused found they had a friend.

"Dr. Ochsner liked no tricky cases," explained L. Sidney Charbonnet, Jr., who as an assistant had the job of selecting the patient for the bull pen. " 'Now don't get something that's going to be too obscure,' he would say. 'Get a case that these boys will normally come upon when they go into practice.' " Charbonnet described the routine. "The student would come in to make his presentation. The chief tried his best to make this student coordinate all of his findings and come to a diagnosis. He would feel sometimes that a student was very close to the proper diagnosis, and he would throw in that 'why' that you've heard of. Why take this test? Why not this? He drove in the pegs of why you felt as you did. He would then make the student think deeply. Sometimes the student surprised himself with how well he did."[2]

One bull pen session that lives on in Tulane lore featured the appearance of Maurice Sullivan. Both Ochsner and Gage were in the amphithea-

1. AO, interview, August 14, 1979.
2. L. Sidney Charbonnet, Jr., to Harkey, January 22, 1977.

ter, Ochsner doing the cross-examination as Sullivan presented his case. Not satisfied with the proceedings, Ochsner became aggressive, pursuing Sullivan as he backed around the floor.

"What did you say?" Ochsner asked as Sullivan outlined the symptoms. "Why?" he interposed. "Why? Why?" Gage saw Sullivan grow pale. "Why did you say that? Why?" Sullivan fainted, and Gage caught him as he slumped.

Gage lowered Sullivan into a chair and asked, "Who's the next victim?"

"I don't know who was more scared, he or I," Ochsner recalled. The incident illustrates the intensity of the bull pen and the fear it struck in the hearts of students who knew their time was coming. Sullivan went on to become a successful dermatologist at Johns Hopkins.[3]

There was standing room only in the amphitheater when the word spread around Tulane and Charity Hospital that Ochsner's son, Akky, was to appear in the bull pen. "They knew how rough my dad had been on everybody else and they wanted to see how he would handle me," Akky related. He had a patient with symptoms that made a diagnosis of ulcer indisputable.

> I presented the history. The first mistake I made—and I'll always respect Dad for this characteristic of his, with which I agree 100 percent, that he was a stickler for correct English. He didn't like bastard words, he didn't like Greek and Latin combinations. Most medical professors talk about venograms. He said that is wrong, it's phlebograms, Greek and Greek and not Latin and Greek.
>
> Anyway I said this man *hemorrhaged*. "He what?" Dad asked. Then I knew what I had said, and I explained he *had* a hemorrhage. We got through the symptoms, then I was asked how I would treat him. He agreed with what I said. Then he says, "Suppose this had been a gastric ulcer"—that's one in the stomach proper whereas most are in the duodenum—"How would you handle it?" Well, at the time there was a raging controversy about how you handle gastric ulcers. Most of the internists favored treating them medically. My daddy was in favor of operating because some of them are cancers, and he was afraid if you watched an ulcer it would be too

---

3. AO Recollection, Bull Pen.

late. "If this were a gastric ulcer how would you handle it?" he asked again.

I knew about the controversy, and I knew how he stood and how the others felt. I just had a feeling I had done well and I decided to toy a bit. I said, "Well, do you want to know how *you* would handle it?"

I've never been so scared in all my life. He grabbed me—he wouldn't have done this to another student—by the collar and lifted me up and started shaking my head like this. I could hear everybody howling in the background. He said, "I want to know how *you* would treat it, and Goddamn it, you're not going to treat it any different than I would treat it." That brought down the amphitheater.[4]

Thomas E. Weiss, a Tulane graduate who became one of Ochsner's colleagues in the Clinic, recalled the period when a class spent its first two years on the ivied Uptown campus, concentrating on the basic sciences, then moved to the medical complex in the area of Charity Hospital for the final two years, during which students were introduced to medical practice. "It was a test of your emotions and your stamina in the demanding basic science courses," Weiss explained. "When you got into the clinical years it was supposed to be clear sailing. But from the day you became a junior you would start sweating, thinking of the time when you would be in the bull pen. When it was your turn you would always say a little prayer that Dr. Gage would be out of town because he could take you apart. It wasn't really done maliciously and to belittle anyone. Dr. Ochsner overwhelmed you with his firmness and his knowledge."[5]

There was an element of luck in the bull pen, and John C. Weed's was good. When his number came up, he had only about five minutes to prepare for his confrontation with Ochsner. Then he discovered that his patient, an elderly Cajun from southwest Louisiana, spoke no English. Weed knew only a smattering of the language of French derivation used along the bayous. By the luckiest chance, he spotted in the hospital a medical student from the Acadian country. With the help of his interpreter, he obtained the answers to a few questions about the patient's symptoms, then found himself the center of attention in the amphithea-

4. Alton Ochsner, Jr., interview, June 15, 1977.
5. Thomas E. Weiss, interview, March, 1979.

ter. He recited the history: stomach pain, bleeding, vomiting. The Cajun either had a gastric ulcer or carcinoma of the stomach. "We'll have to operate," said Ochsner, and launched into a lecture on stomach cancer. And what if the student from southwest Louisiana had not been nearby, if Weed could not have communicated with his patient? "I believe Dr. Ochsner would not have accepted an excuse," Weed said.[6]

Ochsner used his rounds of hospital wards, as well as his bull pen, to emphasize his medical lessons in one-on-one contact with students, interns, and residents. One morning in 1944, as an entourage was following him through Charity Hospital, he paused at the bed of a patient who had been admitted during the night. A student presented the history, physical findings, and results of laboratory tests.

"And what did you find on rectal examination?" Ochsner asked.

"Dr. Ochsner, I admitted three patients last night with histories and laboratory work. I just had to get some sleep and went home for a couple of hours. I didn't do a rectal examination."

Ochsner caught him by the lapels and drew him close. "My God, man, how *could* you sleep when you hadn't done a rectal?"

6. John C. Weed, interview, March, 1979.

9   Broken Belt: Father Comes Home

"O f course I'm a Southerner," Ochsner used to joke. "I'm from *South* Dakota, you know." And over the years he came to adopt the attitudes and beliefs of the uptown New Orleans in which he lived, an overall philosophy not unlike that of antebellum Dixie planters. He worked as assiduously to win acceptance in a closed, class-conscious social hierarchy as he did to achieve professional eminence, and with equal success. He rubbed shoulders with debutantes and millionaires, yet he would sit all night at the bedside of a penniless patient, black or white, if he thought he could do any good. In few of the years from early middle age on did he fail to travel abroad as a member of the international scientific circle, yet to the end he remained politically, and in some ways socially, naïve, a dupe for those who wanted to trade on his name. He accepted appointments to directorships of big corporations, yet never knew how much money he had in the bank. Always contradictions.

The overwound spring that actuated the perpetual-motion machine named Ochsner had to snap sometimes. Hours of tension in an operating room, hospital rounds, lectures to students, sessions in the laboratory, writing papers, and doing research for teaching—these were the demands of his working schedule. Ochsner brought additional pressures on himself by joining the busy New Orleans social scene. He believed that the affluent New Orleanians in the Uptown area would look to him for their medical services if they became acquainted with him. Besides, he liked parties and was fascinated by the round of entertainment enjoyed by the old-line families. He was not the only outsider ever to want in, but he was given his visa much more quickly than most. By 1935 he was a member of the Boston Club, the citadel of the establishment that ruled Carnival and the debutante season. He and Isabel accepted invitations and then reciprocated. It further overcrowded his agenda, taxing his energies to the limit and sometimes beyond. When this happened, it was his family that suffered.

Isabel, Akky, and baby John joined Alton in the fall of 1927, settling in a raised cottage at 8221 Green Street, in the tree-shaded Carrollton residential area. It was the first of three rented houses the Ochsners would occupy before Alton bought in 1939 the commodious three-story residence at 1347 Exposition Boulevard that would be his home until he died. The second abode was at 2233 Joseph Street, near Freret Street. From there the family moved to 428 Lowerline Street.

It was not long before the Ochsner circle reached full size. Mims was born on June 24, 1928, completing the triumvirate of boys, and Isabel, known as Sis, came along on November 27, 1929.

Alton's good fortune in marrying Isabel was never more evident than in the period when the four closely spaced children—only five years separated Akky and Sis—were growing up. The career demands were nearly intolerable, stretching his nerves and stamina to the breaking point. And then he came home to a household always on the verge of the turmoil that could be expected in the presence of four high-spirited youngsters. His patience was already at the snapping point when he sat down at the dinner table—sometimes as late as nine o'clock, because he insisted that the family wait for him and have the one meal together. If one of the boys spilled his milk, the tablecloth was hardly dampened before "the fastest belt in New Orleans" went into action.

John and Mims had the most welts to show for their rambunctiousness, although Akky had a share. Alton once broke his belt in administering a whipping to John, who claimed the thong as a trophy and liked to wear it at parties as an exhibit of his Spartan insensitivity to pain, of his father's muscle, or of both. Mims remarked that, in a more permissive age, Alton might have been accused of child abuse, and he was only half-joking. In their preteen years the boys lived in fear of their father, and with cause. Alton did not deny that he was quick to chastise. "My father used to beat the hell out of me," he said, almost certainly overstating the case. He added, "But no one loved him as much as I. I'm a great believer in discipline, and I think the trouble with youth today is that they haven't had discipline. A person who is undisciplined is an unhappy person."

Sometimes, he seemed to realize that he had been hasty. He would rub his whiskers affectionately against the culprit's face and call him "schnickel-fritz." His paternal feelings were aroused when one of his children had the slightest physical problem. Seymour Ochsner, grandson of A. J., told about the occasion when Alton's family was visiting in Chicago and Akky got a splinter in his finger. "My mother made the comment," Seymour related, " 'Isn't it interesting that the famous young surgeon who does all these major operations could be so concerned about a child with a splinter in his finger?' "[1]

Two versions remain in family lore of the time when the stern father got his comeuppance. There is no dispute about the sequence of events. John and Mims were more obstreperous than usual one Sunday afternoon. "I told them that if they didn't behave themselves, I would punish them," Alton recalled. "I no sooner got the words out of my mouth than they did something, and so I took my belt off. They ran out of the house and I chased them." The two boys nimbly avoided a mud hole in the yard over which a plank had been placed. But their pursuer stepped on the loose board and went tumbling into deep mire. In the later retelling, he had on a white linen suit.

The mud-covered surgeon went into the house to complain to Isabel about allowing the boys to dig holes in the yard. She replied she didn't know there were holes. "I didn't learn until twenty years later that they had dug the hole, filled it with water, covered it over, and baited me so that I would fall into it. It is a wonder I didn't break my neck, because it was a deep hole." Sis said her father became angry despite the lapse of time when he finally was told of the plot. And John confirmed that he and Mims had conspired.[2] Mims's memory differed. He said that he and John wanted to dig a swimming hole and found that the pit filled with mud instead of water. Alton's fall was not premeditated, he averred.[3]

As tots, John recalled, the children "thought he was God. He operated on dogs and people." (The dog reference was to his research.) But he was a vengeful deity, and his homecoming was to be dreaded by any offspring whose transgressions were of a magnitude that Isabel had to report. "I'd never have it thought that we didn't love Daddy," John explained. The realization came with time. The memories are bittersweet.

Alton liked to take one or more of the children with him when he made his Sunday morning hospital rounds. They would wait in the corridor while he saw his patients. If a patient were a friend of his, Alton might introduce Sis, John, or whichever child was with him. These encounters brought an early realization that their father was much admired by those he treated, but the full knowledge of his fame did not come until they were in school and were aware of the reaction that the name evoked. Some-

1. Seymour Ochsner, interview, April, 1978.
2. John L. Ochsner, interview, July 14, 1977.
3. Mims Gage Ochsner, interview, April 20, 1977.

times Alton took his children to the Tulane laboratory and showed them the animals in the experimental colony. Much loved was a dog taken home as a pet, known as PU49 (Mims's recollection) because he had been used for peptic ulcer experiments and so listed on laboratory records.

Alton tried to reserve some Sunday hours for a get-together with his children. Sunday breakfast was a special meal, featuring pancakes and bacon. From the time they began having friends, Akky and the others were encouraged to bring them to meals, and the Sunday breakfast was a popular occasion. Afterwards, Alton left for the hospital. Later, the big midday dinner often was followed by an automobile ride over a familiar route, such as two or three laps through Audubon Park, upon which the Exposition Boulevard home faced. In his middle years, Alton was an impatient driver with a heavy foot on the accelerator. (Reportedly, police had informal orders from on high not to halt a certain car with a physician's emblem beside the license plate when it was seen speeding on a New Orleans boulevard.) He did manage to hold to a more leisurely pace on Sunday when the children were along. In the early evening he revived a custom from his childhood of having popcorn and milk for everyone. Then Mike DeBakey or one of the other Tulane colleagues would arrive, and he and Alton would retire to the study for a long session of writing.[4]

When occasionally Ochsner treated the family to a movie, he chose a slapstick comedy, perhaps Laurel and Hardy. His laughter was so loud that others in the audience would turn their heads to see who was making the noise. Somewhat embarrassed, the teenage children would squirm a little and pretend they were not with him.

The central figure in family life was Isabel, whose devotion to Alton was as important in the fulfillment of his career as his own industry, aptitude, and luck. Not only did she do most of the rearing of three sons who became medical doctors and a daughter who had her own talents as an interior decorator, Isabel also was Alton's capable partner in the social activities that go with professional success, and his source of inspiration or solace in life's darker moments. She paid the bills, made the investments, laid out his clothes, and briefed him on what he had to do when he set out on a trip alone. Her personality helped cement the relationships that Alton found helpful professionally.

Her sense of humor helped smooth over the inevitable minor crises. If she and Alton ever engaged in a shouting match, the children didn't hear

4. Alton Ochsner, Jr., interview, June 15, 1977.

it, and obviously the couple had an exceedingly amicable relationship. When there were differences of opinion, Alton took refuge in a stony "I don't argue, Isabel. I state facts." She had a wittier, more subtle approach. Once they drove past a house being constructed in the neighborhood. The exterior walls were gray. Alton commented that the builders were using a veneer of gray asphalt paper made to resemble brick, but Isabel argued that the wall was being constructed of real brick. Neither would concede. Isabel went out in the middle of the night, claimed one of the bricks, and put it on Alton's plate at the breakfast table. Even then he would not admit that he was wrong.[5]

It was a relaxed household when Alton was not home. Isabel played the piano, and she and the children sang. Akky copied his father's example and learned to play the trumpet. Isabel liked people and encouraged her children to make friends. She herself was close to the wives among four couples with whom the Ochsners shared outings, visits, and out-of-town trips. Among their earliest New Orleans friends were Mr. and Mrs. Samuel M. Smallpage. Mrs. Smallpage, the former Margaret Benton, knew Alton when he was attending the University of South Dakota. A resident of Sioux City, she was a girlhood chum of Alton's niece, Pearl Orcutt, and accompanied her to football games and other events at the university.[6]

John's rambunctiousness led to one of Isabel's enduring friendships. Soon after the Ochsners moved to Lowerline Street, he broke a toy piano belonging to the children of neighbors Gary and Lottie Gillis. Mrs. Gillis called on Isabel to discuss the incident, and the two found they had much in common. Alton became fond of Gillis, an insurance executive who later because the first chairman of the board of governors of the Ochsner Foundation Hospital. Mrs. Gillis was amused by what she called the "Yankee qualities" of Isabel, whom she described as being efficient, doing things for practical reasons, and speaking her mind, in contrast to the euphemistic, roundabout approach dictated by generations of southern gentility. Isabel was aware of the differences. "Southern gentlemen do beat their wives," she once told Mrs. Gillis, "but they do it with their coats and ties on."[7]

The Ochsners did not lack support in high New Orleans society when

5. *Ibid.*
6. Mrs. Samuel M. Smallpage, interview, May 17, 1977.
7. Mrs. Gary Gillis, interview, June 21, 1977.

the founding of the clinic that bears Alton's name created controversy in the medical community in the early 1940s. One night at a dinner, the man who was seated next to Mrs. Russell Clark began castigating Alton. She told him she would get up and walk out if he did not hush. "I wish I had a friend like you," he remarked. "Well, he [Alton] has many like me," Mrs. Clark replied. She and her financier husband had been friendly with Alton and Isabel for several years.[8]

Of the four surgeons who joined Ochsner in forming the clinic, the one who was closest to Alton socially was the otolaryngologist, Francis E. LeJeune. He and Mrs. LeJeune were frequent companions at parties and on fishing trips. Their association began when LeJeune performed emergency mastoid surgery on both Akky and John while Alton was away at a medical meeting. Mrs. LeJeune admired Isabel. "She was very wise. Everybody respected her opinion," she explained. "There'd be a lot of yakety yak, and you wouldn't hear anything from Isabel. Then, when everything subsided, somebody would ask, 'Well, what do you think, Isabel?' And you'd find out that she knew more about the matter than any of them."[9]

Isabel had a flair for entertaining. She was adept at planning a menu for a dinner party, and kept records so as to avoid serving a guest the same dish twice. In her later years, when she traveled extensively, she bought presents that pleased her friends when they were distributed at subsequent parties. She joined in the activities that were expected of the wives of prominent New Orleanians. She served as president of the Orleans Club, the most exclusive of the city's women's organizations.

The first empty seat at the dinner table was caused by Akky's departure at the age of nine years to attend the Southern Arizona School for Boys near Tucson. His recurring asthma attacks, recalling Alton's early illness, indicated a change of climate. Tucson was chosen because Alton's college friend Roy Rudolph was practicing medicine there. Alton dropped Akky off in Arizona en route to San Francisco for a meeting of the American College of Surgeons.

Akky grew up to tower over his father and brothers. In his absence John and Mims became close companions. Upon his return Akky often found himself aligned with Sis. Perhaps it is no surprise that when, in later years, a rift developed in the family, it involved Akky.

8. Mrs. Russell Clark, interview, May 5, 1977.
9. Mrs. Francis E. LeJeune, interview, May 5, 1977.

There is no way of knowing whether all three of Ochsner's sons went into medicine mostly because of his campaign to lead them there, or whether their decisions were results of their genes and environment. He liked to tell outsiders that he tried to discourage them, but that was only a cover for his actual tactics. One ploy, whenever the subject came up, was to fling a challenge, in effect, "Oh, don't even think of it. You know to be a doctor you've got to have willpower and dedication. And you have to work." The indirect persuasion started early, before the boys were in high school. Conversation at the dinner table would bring out the fact that summer vacation was starting. "Who's going to come down and watch me operate?" he would ask.

"We'd look at each other and figure out whose turn it was," Akky recalled. "I was usually the one that got stuck with it." John, who was about twelve years old, fainted when he saw his first surgery. When one of the boys accompanied him on rounds, Ochsner would ask, "Did you see how the people respond and appreciate what you do? That's the excitement of medicine."

"If it hadn't been for that, I'm not sure we all would have been doctors," Akky said. "Medicine can give you something that nothing else—not even the ministry—can give you. People are grateful if you are able to relieve their suffering." Mims's recollection was: "I always wanted to be a doctor." As for John: "Nobody told me I had to be a doctor. I just fell into it because that's what Dad was."

All three sons obtained their medical degrees from Tulane. There was a potential for awkward situations, of course, in classes conducted by their professor father, but there were no embarrassments. When Akky, as a freshman, was taking part in an oral quiz, one question went around the class. "By the time it got around to me, my first answer had already been given and was wrong, so I gave him an answer," Akky said. "He hesitated a little bit and said, 'No, no, not quite right,' and he went on to everybody else. The class said, 'Well, what is the answer?' and he gave an answer that was almost the same as I had given. Everybody in the class was wondering, and somebody asked me, 'Wasn't that what you said?' I went to him that night and I said, 'Dad, why didn't you give me credit for that answer?' You know what he said? 'I couldn't have my son the only one in the class to know the answer.' It made me so mad."

As the final examination in the course neared, Akky felt that he was prepared except that he was a little confused about the Ochsner-Mahorner tourniquet test for varicose veins.

"Look, Dad, explain to me one more time how that tourniquet test works," I said. God, he got mad and said, "You figure it out. Just think of physiology. You figure it out yourself." He wouldn't give me the answer. I was sleepy and said "to hell with it" and went back to bed. You know, I got to school and they had four questions, and that was one of them. I spent half the period trying to figure it out, and I don't know to this day. I came home that night and said, "Dad, I asked you that question. Why didn't you tell me?" He said, "Because you had got hold of one of those exams." Of course I hadn't, but he wasn't going to give me any satisfaction, and that was part of his character.[10]

John had an experience with a happier ending. In Alton's study at home he picked up a monograph on shock by John Lockwood, and since that was his given name, he read it. As luck would have it there was a question on shock in the examination. John had a high grade in the surgery course. He experienced no resentment among his classmates because of his relationship with the professor. John finished in the top third of his class, but his father's first greeting upon his graduation was, "Why didn't you make AOA?" Alpha Omega Alpha is an honorary medical scholarship fraternity. Only later did John learn that Alton had not been inducted into the fraternity as a student, but had become an honorary member during his career, as John eventually did.[11] Mims claimed to have gone through the Tulane medical school without experiencing any repercussions resulting from his father's place on the faculty.[12]

Sis was, without doubt, Alton's favorite child. Not only was she the only girl and the youngest, she also was lively, outgoing, witty, and sensitive to her father's moods. She shared Alton's earthy sense of humor, and by the time she was in high school traded off-color jokes with him. Despite her somewhat privileged status, she got along well with her brothers, who sometimes were able to shift the blame for some of their misdeeds to her and who found ways to beat her out of her allowance when they ran short of spending money. Alton did not spare the rod on Sis, although he never laid it on with the same force that he applied when the boys were being punished.

10. Alton Ochsner, Jr., interview, June 15, 1977.
11. John L. Ochsner, interview, July 14, 1977.
12. Mims Gage Ochsner, interview, April 20, 1977.

Sis was a junior in high school when the family was having dinner one night on the porch that overlooks Audubon Park.

Daddy asked me what I was doing that night, and I said I was going out with so-and-so to a Beta party. He said, "I want you home by twelve o'clock." I said, "Daddy, I can't. It doesn't start until ten. We won't get there until eleven." He replied, "That's fine, I still want you home at twelve o'clock." I said he was being unreasonable; we didn't do those kinds of things. Finally he told me, "You will be in this house at twelve o'clock." I got up and said, "I will not go to the damn party," and turned on my heels and went upstairs.

Up I went. Right behind me came Daddy, the belt coming off on the way, and he flew into the room and we really had it out. I said, "Go on, hit me if that makes you happy. I'm too old to be spanked, but if that gets you, go on. I don't care." He looked at me like, "What in the world? What are you saying?" I said, "Look, Daddy, let's face it. You don't care about us. All you do is go to work all the time. You're never home. We never knew you when we were young. We're terrified of you."

The man closed the door and sat down. Between the two of us we must have cried for two hours. He said, "All of my life I have worked to not only do something for mankind, which was the heritage I received when I was a child, but to see that my children had a wonderful education and maybe something material that I didn't have when I was growing up. I know I sacrificed a great part of my life, that I've missed not being a father, not being with my sons and not seeing my daughter at different times in her life that were important to her. But I've done it for you."

I want to tell you, it makes me cry now when I tell you about it. From that day on we were like this [fingers entwined]. My oldest brother came running up and came to the door. Then he went running down, yelling, "Come quick. Sarah Bernhardt has never been this good. She's got him. She's got him."

Sis said the incident was a turning point in her life.[13]

In the years to come, it became apparent that Ochsner was dependent

13. Mrs. Isabel (Sis) Ochsner Mann, interview, May, 1977.

on the support of a feminine confidante with whom he could share his hopes and fears. It did not have to be a romantic attachment; his need was for a woman's unquestioned interest in his well-being. His world fell apart upon the death of his beloved Isabel. That is when he turned to Sis, who played the role at a high cost to her own domestic happiness, until a surprise development lighted up his last days.

10 Launch Pad to Success

The comparison is perhaps too obvious, but nonetheless appropriate: Alton Ochsner in the early 1930s was like a space rocket, fully fueled and poised on the launch pad for lift-off. Considering his attributes, it is unlikely that he ever could have remained a local phenomenon for the duration of his career, but he nevertheless had help in his development into a figure of first regional, then national, and finally international reputation. An early, important boost came from his friend C. Jeff Miller, who had persuaded him not to leave New Orleans when Long took away his Charity Hospital appointment.

Miller enjoyed influence far beyond the borders of New Orleans. He served as president of the American Gynecological Society in 1928 and of the American College of Surgeons in 1931. Miller developed high regard for the ability of the young professor of surgery, and also came to have a fondness for him. Curtis H. Tyrone, Miller's protégé and partner in the practice of obstetrics and gynecology, explained that Miller was glad to refer to Ochsner patients who needed surgical procedures that Miller did not perform, both because of his faith in Ochsner's competence and because he knew that Ochsner would not steal away those with obstetrical or gynecological complaints.

Although Ochsner's election to the first of many professional society offices came in 1933, when he became secretary of the surgery section of the Southern Medical Association, his real breakthrough was engineered by Miller in 1935. Tyrone gave this account:

> I went to the meeting of the Southern Surgical Association as the guest of Dr. Miller. It was brought out that the secretary was being moved up to president. I should mention the Southern Surgical. If you were a member of it from the South, you had to be the number one surgeon in your locality. They didn't want any outsiders or immigrants.

Jeff Miller went to the board meeting to elect new officers, and he came to our hotel room about to freeze to death at Sea Island, Georgia. I'll never forget what he said. "Goddamn it, I've put it over." I asked what, and he had made Al Ochsner secretary of the organization. And that was greater than president because the secretary could serve for a number of years. Now Al Ochsner, except for Jeff Miller, never would have been secretary of that organization. He wasn't from the South, and he had been a member for only a short time. The man who he beat out was from Atlanta. His father was one of the founders of the association. I don't know how Jeff Miller managed. He said, "There was a tie vote, and I rolled them for it and I beat them."[1]

Ochsner remained secretary until he became president in 1944. The job was an ideal power base for an ambitious doctor, offering an opportunity for personal contact with the South's pre-eminent surgeons. With his ingratiating ways, Ochsner made the most of it.

Miller also thrust Ochsner to the forefront through his leadership in the American College of Surgeons. The college sponsored sectional meetings, and Ochsner, always eloquent about surgery, found himself a speaker at such sessions. His presentations impressed Eleanor Grimm, the ACS staff member who arranged the programs for the sectional gatherings.

The appearances resulted in numerous invitations to speak at local meetings of doctors, especially in the South. Ochsner relished the chance to address practitioners, and he quickly accepted every engagement that did not conflict with his schedule. "How much is your fee?" he would be asked by a program chairman. "Just reimburse me for my expenses," he would reply, although he would accept an honorarium from a society that could afford it. Of course, the talks at local meetings helped keep him in the spotlight. They also were the source of referrals of patients from practitioners who had the chance to size up the energetic surgeon from New Orleans.[2]

Jeff Miller died of a coronary thrombosis at his home on March 21, 1936. "Al was there, and of course I was there, standing next to Al when [Jeff] breathed his last," Tyrone recalled. "Al took my hand and said to

1. Curtis H. Tyrone, interview, March 24, 1977.
2. Forshag, interview, 1986.

me, 'You and I have lost the greatest friend we ever had,' and God knows it is true."

The instincts that would have made Ochsner a successful politician had he chosen a career in government—and a rich man had he wanted to be a salesman—emerged in this period of his life. As persuasive as he was on a podium, he could be even more magnetic in one-on-one contact. Handsome, completely engrossed in the subject at hand, he could make a lasting friend in a five-minute conversation. Like a politician, he remembered names and faces, and like any professional officeholder, he knew how to follow up an encounter with a personal note. The filing cabinets that were removed from his office after his death contained the carbon copies of thousands of communications to doctors, patients, and the people he knew from his social or civic activities. Even before the custom of addressing casual acquaintances by their first names became common after World War II, Ochsner used them in his greetings. With him it was a friendly gesture, without a trace of undue familiarity, flattery, or fawning. By the time he turned forty years of age, he had impressed hundreds of practitioners who would be glad to refer patients to him for surgery, or to vote for him in medical society elections.

While he was winning admirers with his medical society activities and his busy schedule of personal appearances, Ochsner in the early 1930s also was making himself known with a stream of publications in professional journals and even chapters in textbooks. His papers were printed in a wide list of journals, enabling him to catch the eyes of American practitioners. Between 1932 and 1936, for instance, his contributions were accepted by such publications as the *Southern Medical Journal, Gynecology and Obstetrics, New Orleans Medical and Surgical Journal, Proceedings of the Society for Experimental Biology and Medicine, Annals of Surgery, Archives of Surgery, Radiology, American Journal of Digestive Diseases and Nutrition, American Journal of Surgery, Southern Surgeon, Modern Hospital,* and *Surgery.* In most of these, he had several papers. He reported on the results of research that he and his associates were doing at Tulane and on his own surgical experiences. His subjects included bronchiectasis, peritoneal adhesions, ileus, varicose veins, sclerosing agents, subphrenic infections, leeches, appendiceal peritonitis, amebiasis, and peptic ulceration.[3]

3. Publications of Dr. Alton Ochsner, listing compiled by Dr. Ochsner's staff.

His surgical exploits propelled Ochsner into the headlines, a circumstance that irked some of those who took the position that a practitioner may be seen but should not be heard or read about. Ochsner never denied that he enjoyed the spotlight, although he was circumspect about courting exposure. Mims Gage used to say there were only two groups more jealous of each other than surgeons: opera singers and whores. Ochsner's detractors in large part were New Orleans doctors who were competitors for patients or for medical school appointment. He came out mostly unscathed because of the reputation he had established in the profession as a whole.

11 Surgeon: "All Day, Every Day"

Alton Ochsner frequently said he wanted to be remembered as a teacher, yet he was happiest when, masked and gowned, he stood over a patient and used his knowledge and skills to overcome disease or injury. As busy as he was—and his own guess that he performed twenty thousand operations probably was conservative—he wanted to do more. "Oh, my God," he remarked when his colleague Guy Caldwell showed him the five rooms equipped for surgery at the Alton Ochsner Medical Foundation's first hospital. "Now I can operate all day, every day."[1] Urologist Willoughby Kittredge remembered more than one busy day at the Foundation hospital when Ochsner would pick up a mop and swab the floor to help the clean-up crew hasten preparation of an operating room for his next patient.[2] Ochsner once told chest specialist Julius Lane Wilson, "I had the best day of my life yesterday. I performed fourteen major operations."[3] But in a serious moment of introspection, he observed: "I've known people who loved to operate. That hasn't been my fascination. My love for it is getting people well, and this is a good way to do it. My love is because I am accomplishing something. It is a means to an end."[4]

In forty-five years of activity, he operated in cities around the world—Tokyo, Frankfurt, Zurich, Paris, Rio de Janeiro, Panama City, Buenos Aires—as well as in Chicago, Madison, New Orleans, and other American localities.

The British master Berkeley Lord Moynihan listed the requisites for the perfect surgeon: "the heart of a lion, the eye of an eagle, the hands of a lady." Terence Millin, vice-president of the Royal College of Surgeons in

1. Guy A. Caldwell, interview, 1979.
2. Willoughby E. Kittredge, interview, 1985.
3. Julius Lane Wilson to Harkey, February 26, 1977.
4. AO, interview, April 13, 1977.

Ireland, once said Ochsner "near fulfills" the standards.[5] He had other assets as well: for one, the nerve of a burglar; for another, what a colleague, Edward T. Krementz, called "an angel on his shoulder," a mystical presence to guide him through desperate circumstances.[6] There were times when he ventured into situations where even his angel must have feared to follow.

Out of the surgical suites emerged the public conception of a lifesaver, of a man who somehow could prevail against the odds in advanced cases, who could provide precious time for the stricken, who could breathe hope into a seemingly lost cause. From far and near, as his reputation spread, came the patients. His fame as a surgeon was the cornerstone for the establishment of what became the South's largest independent medical center. There was the element of luck, of course, in the development of Ochsner's reputation. The layman has no measure for judging the competence of a doctor. A name is made mostly by word of mouth, on the spread of stories about patients who went to hospitals in ambulances, underwent surgery, and walked out unaided. A follow-the-leader psychology is part of the mystique. Even though Ochsner practiced in a setting of high visibility, he might well have gone largely unrecognized but for his luck and his penchant for attracting attention.

In Ochsner's career, where there was smoke, there was fire. The legends that emanated from the operating rooms were based on reality. The professionals who worked with him, or who watched him in action, learned that he was an exceptional surgeon. Accounts of some of his exploits will make it clear that he could rise to an occasion, that he responded at peak efficiency when things went wrong and a patient's life hung in the balance. At the risk of being dubbed "knife happy" by his critics, he was willing to operate if he believed there was any chance of helping the patients. He bridled at the suggestion that he was eager to use the knife, saying that the true test of a good surgeon is knowing when *not* to operate. He explored new surgical territories, and his principal trailblazing efforts were in the removal of whole lungs or parts of the lungs in the treatment of cancer.

Ochsner finished medical school at a time when the surgeon who fiddled around had a dead patient. "They had very poor anesthesia, they didn't understand about intravenous fluids, they didn't understand about

5. Terence Millin, in talk at Dublin, September 6, 1961.
6. Edward T. Krementz, interview, 1980.

shock," explained Paul T. DeCamp. "The big push then was to get in and get out. If a great surgeon could do a procedure in thirty minutes, a greater one could do it in twenty minutes, and a supersurgeon could do it in fifteen minutes."[7] By the time Ochsner completed his postgraduate training, surgery was in an evolutionary stage in the United States, largely because of the influence of the great Johns Hopkins professor William S. Halsted (1852–1922). Halsted's disciples had begun preaching his theories that some speed could be sacrificed to meticulous handling of tissues. Advances were being made in anesthesia, including the tracheal-tube gas-inhalation method that opened up new horizons for thoracic surgery. Still to come, rather late in Ochsner's career, would be the heart-lung oxygenator that made possible open-heart surgery, heart transplants, and other modern accomplishments.

Ochsner earned his place in the medical pantheon with energy and determination more than with inspiration. He never had the sort of genius that brings a Nobel Prize to investigative scientists. No new surgical procedure was named for him, nor was any widely used operating-room instrument. Yet he had the vision to recognize the possibilities of an idea and the dedication to experiment with it until it became a contribution to the art and science of healing.

He was a product of his environment and his education. Younger surgeons who worked with him are near unanimous in the conclusion that he was not a master technician. Yet almost never did his anastamoses leak or his ligatures give way. He knew his anatomy and rarely made a mistake in identifying anatomical features. An associate never forgot an incident when Ochsner thought he was clamping off the artery to one lung and it turned out to be the blood supply for both lungs, with the result that the patient died. It was an error Ochsner surely never repeated. In the operating room he was a commanding but not intimidating presence. He knew what he was doing, reacted with unflappable assurance when things went wrong. His basic approach was learned from A. J. Ochsner, who emphasized: "Never make an unnecessary move. Do the shortest, most direct thing. There are many ways to do an operation. Learn one and stick to that." Of A. J., Alton noted, "If you watched him you'd think he was operating very slowly, but actually he was going very fast. No movement was unnecessary."[8]

7. Paul T. DeCamp, interview, April 26, 1978.
8. AO, interview, December 8–9, 1977.

It was ego-building to carry the good news, to stride out of an operating room and tell a frantic family that a procedure had gone well, that a cancer had not spread and the patient could look forward to a long life ahead. On the other hand, he may have flinched inwardly, but Ochsner never ducked the responsibility when a wife and children had to be given the shocking word of an unexpected operative death. Ochsner used to say that a surgeon might hope for a zero mortality rate if he chose only patients who did not have much wrong with them. "It's the difference between the boys and the men," he said. "The individual who is willing to tackle the tough job and get them well, although he is going to have complications and lose a few because the risk is so much greater." Nobody accused Ochsner of being a boy among surgeons. His operations included hopeless cases, and it was inevitable that he lose his share.

Ochsner's first patient to die on the table succumbed to the anesthesia, ether. "It was an out-and-out anesthesia death," he recalled. "But I was the surgeon, so it was my fault. The surgeon is responsible for the case, no matter what happens. I had to go out and tell the family. I said the patient stopped breathing and we just couldn't revive him. I didn't say it was the fault of the anesthetic and I didn't say it was my fault." Ochsner broke the news to the patient's wife and son. "The wife broke down. They knew it was a very bad risk, but they didn't expect the death. It was a horrible thing to go out and tell them."

Although there were surgeons who might tie a neater knot, none could react to a potential disaster with more aplomb and competence than Ochsner. Some of the legends concern his handling of emergencies, his brushes with disaster. He was a source of strength to the doctors who worked with him, knowing as they had learned that he always could respond when the unexpected occurred. One of the beneficiaries of his coolness was his student Michael E. DeBakey, with whom he worked in close collaboration during the younger man's early career. Long afterward, when DeBakey had made himself a towering figure in the medical world, he still would relate the details of an incident that occurred while he was a resident.

A patient with an infected patent ductus arteriosus was being operated on in the Charity Hospital amphitheater, which was filled with visiting surgeons attending a surgical congress in New Orleans. I was assisting Dr. Ochsner, and during the procedure and following his instructions, I was attempting to dissect and free up the aorta with my index finger on my side of the vessel in coordination with his efforts on his side when I suddenly realized, with a gripping terror, that I had entered the aorta. The infection had made the wall of the vessel very friable. In a whisper that must have expressed my trepidation, I informed Dr. Ochsner of my concern. His equanimity and self-control were reflected in his calm response and his instruction to me to leave my finger there. He then deftly placed occluding sutures around the opening, and as he tied the last suture, he asked me to remove my finger carefully. I am sure you can understand my sigh of relief in observing that there was no hemorrhage. He had met this challenge so skillfully that no one realized that a near-fatal accident had occurred. Moreover, his understanding of my own dismay at this near-fatal accident reflects his benevolent and magnanimous character, for after completion of the operation, he gave me his reassurances and commented kindly on my assistance.[9]

DeBakey said the incident might have hurt his surgical career by shaking his self-confidence had Ochsner reproached him. Ochsner's reaction to this thought, also expressed years later, was that "there wasn't anything to say. It wasn't his fault. Oh, I suppose a lot of people would have tried to blame someone else for it. That's one thing I've tried never to do. Of course, he did it, but he wasn't at fault. I told him to do it. Now when someone does something that he's not supposed to do, then I'll give him hell."

Robert J. Schramel never has forgotten a sudden cloud of smoke that formed in a hotel meeting room. An assembly of surgeons was watching on a television screen the first closed-circuit showing in New Orleans of an operative procedure, one in progress at Charity Hospital. Through the speaker came the voice of the surgeon explaining each move he was making in preparing to remove the lung of a man with cancer. Then it happened. Almost in unison the smokers in the room lighted cigarettes and nervously puffed away. What had started out as a demonstration of surgical techniques had turned into a crisis. The camera overhead pictured a massive hemorrhage. The voice of the surgeon faded away . . .[10]

When the International Society of Surgery met in New Orleans in

9. Michael E. DeBakey, at Ochsner memorial service, New Orleans, October 3, 1981.
10. Robert J. Schramel, interview, 1980.

October, 1949, Alton Ochsner was asked to perform an operation that would be shown on closed-circuit television to the delegates at the Roosevelt Hotel and also at the Tulane School of Medicine. He chose a seventy-four-year-old male patient with advanced carcinoma of the lung.

"It was a bad case and I shouldn't have done it, but it was the only case we had," he explained. "When I got in there, it was a lot worse than I had thought. The tumor was extremely large and had invaded the pulmonary artery. In dissecting the tumor away from the artery I got into the artery. There was an immediate gush of blood." The watching surgeons knew how desperate the emergency was that confronted Ochsner.

"At this moment, of course, I ceased talking and every bit of my effort was directed at controlling the hemorrhage. By then I had forgotten I was on television. Everything except the immediate emergency was blocked out." He squeezed the artery to stem the flow of blood, and held it with one hand while sutures were placed to close the damaged wall. Ochsner got the lung out and the patient survived the procedure, although the cancer had reached a stage that gave him only a day or so longer to live.

Ochsner always cited the incident as one of the memorable crises of his career. "The more experience one gets, the more he becomes able to cope with these situations," he observed. "They do occur, although many of them can be handled by knowing just what to do."[11] Interestingly, although the dilemma caused by the hemorrhage was obvious to the viewing surgeons, it was overlooked by the *Times-Picayune*'s reporter, who was covering the story because of its significance as the first televised surgery. The newspaper's account told only of the excision of the lung, noting in passing that "the pulmonary artery held up."[12]

From his first days in New Orleans until retirement ended his career as a surgeon, Ochsner was pre-eminent in an operating room. There were no tantrums, no cursing, no loud talk, and no doubt as to who was in charge. "The little Prussian," his early students called him before the years changed his black hair and moustache and he became "the Great White Father." Some students tried to walk and talk like him, or take on his mannerisms. Harold V. Cummins, Jr., remembered when students, interns, and residents competed for his eye, a period at Charity Hospital when patients were being figuratively "drowned" because interns were ordering fluids in order to get their names on the charts and senior

11. AO Recollection, Career.
12. *Times-Picayune*, October 12, 1949, Sec. 1, p. 1.

residents were countermanding with their own orders, all trying to come to Ochsner's notice.[13]

His cases always were the sickest; nevertheless, nurses liked to scrub with him because to assist him in an operation was a challenge. Julie M. Carnahan, his personal nurse for almost all of his active years at the Ochsner Clinic, first worked with him in 1937, when she was a student at Touro Infirmary. "He always was a gentleman," she related. "He never failed to thank the nurses who helped him." He specified the instrument he needed, never asking for a thingamajig or a whatchamacallit as some more excitable surgeons are wont to do. "If things went wrong with some other doctors' patients, they were rough on the nurses; but not Dr. Ochsner."

Whenever he was operating, at Charity Hospital, Touro Infirmary, or someplace else, Ochsner usually drew a crowd of observers. Nurse Carnahan recalled that he always had at least three assistants. In her early experience the nurses were kept busy preparing sutures and bits of thread of various lengths, which they handed to the assistants. She learned that the velvet-smooth Ochsner exterior covered a core of iron when she happened to see him take an errant intern to task. The young man was on duty one night when a nurse discovered that one of Ochsner's thyroid patients was bleeding. She called the intern and asked him to come to the patient's bed. He said he was not coming. "But there's blood seeping on the bandage," she insisted. The intern took his time, but eventually appeared. The next morning as Ochsner made the rounds he stood the intern against a wall. "Don't you ever let this happen again to one of my patients. When they call you, you come immediately."

Nurse Carnahan said Ochsner did not raise his voice, but the inflection conveyed an unmistakable message: there had better not be a second time. Usually supportive of those who trained under him, Ochsner was quick to lose interest in a student, intern, or resident who neglected his assignments, was careless, or gave the impression that he did not share the surgeon's solicitude for patients. Ochsner might not dismiss one who raised his doubts, but the suspect afterwards had to make his own way as far as the surgeon was concerned.[14]

For years, Paul DeCamp had the opportunity to watch Ochsner's approach:

13. Harold V. Cummins, Jr., interview, February 2, 1978.
14. Julie M. Carnahan, interview, April 7, 1977.

He saw a lot of patients in a very short time. It would have been very easy for the patients to feel that they were getting slighted. Sometimes it was thirty seconds, forty-five seconds, or a minute and a half, but he had an enormous ability and I think it was genuine, I didn't believe it was a fake, to be totally immersed in a patient for the period of time that they were together. I think the patient recognized that, therefore, the impact was more meaningful than if he had spent five minutes, with less concentration and attention.

He always found something to be optimistic about with a patient. I got the impression that he didn't consider a visit satisfactory unless the patient definitely felt better when he walked out of the room than he did when he walked in. It was very interesting. We might have a patient dying of cancer, and he'd come in one day and find the person had diarrhea. Well, Dr. Ochsner was so happy that the patient wasn't constipated. He'd come back the next day and find the patient constipated, and be so happy that the diarrhea had ended.[15]

Ochsner had no idea that he was about to perform a surgical first when, in 1944, he opened the chest of a forty-four-year-old patient believed to have a mediastinal tumor. What he found instead was a saccular aneurysm in the arch of the aorta. A weak spot had developed in the wall of the body's main artery near the point where it arches over the heart. It was, figuratively, a blowout. The wall had given way, and the aneurysm ballooned out of the aorta. The diagnosis was missed because the aneurysm did not pulsate. Ochsner's dismay upon discovering the patient's real problem was heightened when he found the lung adhered to the aneurysm. As he carefully dissected—peeled—the aneurysm away from the lung, it began to bleed, "wildly," he related. He feared that the aorta would explode in his face, showering him with blood while the patient expired.

"I was afraid to do nothing at all," the surgeon recalled. He improvised. He placed Ochsner clamps—named for A. J.—across the base of the aneurysm and proceeded to excise the bulge. Then, in a maneuver that might be likened to wrapping tape around a hole in a garden hose, he closed the gap in the aorta wall with cotton sutures. "I was frightened of what was going to happen when I removed the clamps," he said, "but, fortunately, there was very little bleeding and that stopped almost imme-

15. DeCamp, interview, April 26, 1978.

diately." Thus he accomplished the first recorded successful resection of a saccular aneurysm of the arch of the aorta. A French surgeon had employed the procedure earlier, but his patient bled to death.

Ochsner could not enjoy his triumph for weeks because of a doubt planted by Thomas Findley, head of the Ochsner Clinic internists. At the time, doctors believed that most aneurysms were a result of syphilis. "What are you going to do when the spirochetes start gnawing away at those cotton sutures?" Findley asked. "Of course, I was scared and didn't sleep for weeks, but the man got well and lived for a number of years before he died of a heart attack," Ochsner said.[16]

Seldom did it happen, but even Ochsner lost his calm in one stressful surgical situation. Patrick H. Hanley, a chief resident, happened to wander into an operating room when Ochsner was having bleeding difficulties with a five- or six-year-old girl. Inflammatory changes inside a blood vessel caused the sutures to pull out when Ochsner attempted to close an opening in the vessel. "I could see he was in very serious trouble," Hanley explained. "He looked up and said, 'Pat, I want you to exsanguinate the patient [draw out blood]. Place a cannula on the radial artery.' The idea was that the patient would go into temporary shock, the blood pressure would go down and give him an opportunity to sew the vessel without blood flowing over the entire field." Hanley had trouble finding the tiny artery, about one-third adult size, in the child's wrist. The tense Ochsner exploded. "Goddamn it, Pat, you don't know where the radial artery is? You're a senior resident? Hell, I don't see how the hell you're a senior resident. I don't know how the hell you ever got into surgical training."

"He just kept insulting me, talking about my knowledge, my ability," Hanley went on.

I never raised my head, never said a word. I thought of saying, "Now, chief, I know what the hell I am doing; just don't bother me." But I just kept my head down and kept working. Finally I got this little bit of artery. It looked like a number eight thread almost, it was so spastic. I had to make a hole in it, not cutting it completely, and put a hot ethylene tube in it.

As I was holding it up he said, "Pat, Goddamn it, you know that's not the radial artery. That thing's too small. You don't even know a damned thing about anatomy. I don't know how the hell

16. AO, interview, April 13, 1977.

you got in here." The room was full of people, residents, visitors, nurses. You could hear a pin drop.

I didn't pay any attention to him. I finally got the little tube in there and the blood started coming out. I exsanguinated the patient. It didn't take too much, but I removed a couple of units of blood from the child. Then he went on and sewed the thing up, and put some gelufoam on, and everything else. Later he told me to transfuse the patient with the blood I had removed. I gave the blood back and everything was fine.

I never said one word. After I got through doing what I had to do I walked out of the room and went to the dressing room. I was taking my operating room clothes off when he came in. He came to my aisle and said, "Pat, I want to apologize. What I did in the operating room is the most unbecoming thing for a surgeon. I have insulted you. I thank you." I said, "Don't thank me, chief. Hell, I knew you were in a big hole and anything I said would have made matters worse."[17]

Hanley went on to be one of Ochsner's associates in the Clinic, and a devoted friend. He said the incident was the only time he ever knew Ochsner to get ugly. "I think the only thing that did it was this was a child and he was in real trouble and he was maybe a bit afraid."

The original Foundation Hospital, alongside the Huey P. Long Bridge, was a former army facility known to personnel as Splinter Village. Operating there one day, Ochsner had made the incision preparatory to removing a cancerous lung from an elderly man. Gas anesthesia was being used. Without warning, the gas machine exploded and burst into flames, apparently set off by a static spark. The patient was knocked from the table, receiving a fractured skull in the fall. Attendants extinguished the fire, and Ochsner·sewed up the chest. Two weeks later, after the fracture had begun to heal, the lung operation was carried out successfully. The patient lived for years. Prodded by his family, he sued for damages and received an award. But at the trial, when he first entered the courtroom and saw Ochsner, he went directly to the surgeon and hugged him.

Getting ready for a pneumonectomy in a Tokyo hospital, Ochsner began to worry about the problem of communicating with the Japanese scrub nurses, how to tell them what instruments he wanted. Then he saw one of the nurses pick up an instrument, and heard her refer to it by the

17. Patrick H. Hanley, interview, November 24, 1978.

German name. "Do you speak German?" he asked in the language he learned in Zurich and Frankfurt. "Ja," she replied, and explained that she had trained in Germany, as had other nurses on the team. Ochsner's Presbyterian luck was at work again.[18]

Ochsner used to note that he was a member of the first generation of surgeons to be trained in physiology as well as in anatomy and pathology. Physiology is the science that deals with the normal functions of the body; pathology with the structural and functional changes that result from disease processes; and anatomy with the structure of the body. The added knowledge was valuable to Ochsner, not only in his clinical practice but also in his investigative efforts.

Early in his career his understanding of physiology led to a contribution toward the treatment of intestinal obstructions. Such obstructions were a frequent aftermath of abdominal surgery. Ochsner realized that when normal passage through the intestines failed, the bile, pancreatic juice, and gastric secretions stagnated in the stomach. These fluids needed to be removed, but he concluded that purgatives and enemas only aggravated the situation. His solution was to put a tube down the throat to get rid of the accumulated secretions, meanwhile holding off drugs and allowing peristalsis to resume when the body was ready.

In connection with his generation's being "the first to introduce physiological methods in the treatment of patients," Ochsner added: "We were able to think for ourselves. Otherwise, we would have done exactly what our predecessors did. All they knew was what was handed down by rote." In New Orleans, he developed a method of positioning patients for X-rays in diagnosing obstructions. The ileus, or blockage, occurs when there is an accumulation of fluid or gas in the loops of the intestine. A picture made from the proper angle reveals the contrast between gas and fluid.[19]

The memory of those night-long ordeals in Frankfurt when a delay meant death impelled Ochsner, working with Michael DeBakey in New Orleans, to devote efforts toward control of blood clots, potential pulmonary embolisms. Not only did the two score a marked advance in treatment, but their research also attracted attention and led to perhaps the most publicized of all of Ochsner's surgical exploits.

18. Merrill O. Hines, interview, 1985.

19. Alton Ochsner, "Acute Intestinal Obstruction," *Southern Medical Journal*, XXIV (1931), 93–97.

Analyzing the material at Charity Hospital, Ochsner and DeBakey succeeded in differentiating between two types of blood clots in the veins, one life-threatening and the other likely to be crippling although not fatal. In so-called phlebothrombosis, a "red" thrombus (clot) does not adhere to the wall of the vein and may break loose and be swept to the heart or lungs, with instant death the likely outcome. In thrombophlebitis, a "white" clot stays in place, blocking the flow of blood in an extremity. The patient's life is not in danger, but he is subject to pain, fever, and perhaps an incapacitating swelling of a leg.[20]

Ochsner determined that thrombophlebitis should be treated conservatively with therapy to increase the circulation of blood in the leg. But in the case of phlebothrombosis he went back to his idea, dating from the Frankfurt experience, of ligating, or tying off, a vein to keep the clot from reaching vital areas. For one period, Ochsner and DeBakey advocated ligating the superficial femoral vein in the upper part of each thigh as a means of blocking the clot. Coincidentally, during this time Ochsner had a midnight telephone call from Dr. Joseph M. Perret, Sr., of New Orleans. In thumbing through the current *Journal of the American Medical Association* as he was going to bed, Perret had come across an article by Ochsner discussing the presence of tachycardia (rapid heart beat) as an unexplained symptom of phlebothrombosis. The article alarmed Perret because he was treating the aging and overweight archbishop of the Roman Catholic archdiocese of New Orleans, Joseph Francis Rummel, who had been immobilized by a broken hip and who had the symptoms of which Ochsner wrote.

Ochsner routed his colleague Paul DeCamp out of bed, and in the Hotel Dieu hospital at 2 A.M. on a Sunday, the two surgeons ligated the superficial femoral veins, a procedure that Ochsner believed saved the prelate from a fatal pulmonary embolism. The operation was done under local anesthesia, and DeCamp was annoyed when he discovered that nuns were sneaking whisky toddies to Rummel while the surgeons were at work.[21] The grateful churchman arranged for Alton and Isabel Ochsner to have an audience with Pope John XXIII when they visited Rome several years later.

The femoral vein operation worked for Rummel, but subsequently patients were lost to embolisms because thrombi had bypassed the tied-

---

20. Alton Ochsner and Michael DeBakey, "Thrombophlebitis and Phlebothrombosis," *Southern Surgeon*, VIII (1939), 269–90.

21. DeCamp, interview, April 26, 1978.

off vessel and reached the lung through the collateral circulation. Then Ochsner and DeBakey settled upon ligation of the inferior vena cava—the body's principal vein—as the effective procedure. This was the method that Ochsner employed in 1949 when he was summoned to El Paso, Texas, on an errand that made nationwide headlines.

The reigning professional golf champion, Ben Hogan, had survived serious injuries received in an automobile-bus collision, but within a week his life was being threatened by vein clots that had caused the collapse of one lung and were continuing to form. Hogan's physicians knew about Ochsner's work on clots and made an emergency call to him. Ochsner flew from New Orleans to El Paso in an Air Force B-25 bomber. In a lifetime of globe-trotting and domestic travel, Ochsner logged almost as many hours aloft as an airline pilot, but he never had another ride quite like this one. The only space available was in the bombardier's seat in the nose. As the plane circled the El Paso airfield, the surgeon noted furious activity below. Fire equipment and ambulances were speeding toward the runway, and other emergency equipment rolled into place. After an uneventful landing, Ochsner learned that warning lights in the cockpit had signaled trouble in the landing gear. Precautions were taken, but the signal turned out to be a false alarm.

At the hospital, Ochsner found Hogan's condition precarious. In an effort to halt formation of the clots, physicians had given anticoagulants. His blood was thinned to the point that he was, Ochsner said, "bleeding from every body orifice." Hogan's wife, Valerie, was reluctant to authorize ligation of the vena cava because she understood that his legs would be affected and he might not be able to play golf. "I promise you that he will play," Ochsner told her. He gave medicine to thicken Hogan's blood to the point that he would not bleed to death during the operation, then he did the ligation. Hogan's recovery began almost at once. From a deathbed, he not only went back on the professional tour, but in fact won many of his titles in subsequent years. Hogan served as honorary chairman of a campaign for public donations to finance the Ochsner Foundation Hospital and remained Ochsner's devoted friend.[22] Hogan's later successes excited the golfing world and led Ochsner to add a joke to one of his papers. "A number of my friends have threatened to have their cavae ligated prophylactically, in order to improve their golf game," he wrote.

The Ochsner-DeBakey approach remains valid today, although the

22. AO Recollection, Stars.

blood thinner heparin and the availability of bypass blood-vessel grafts give practitioners alternative means of treating patients.

William H. Meade, a graduate student working at Tulane toward a master's degree in surgery, spent a couple of hours in Ochsner's office one day making arrangements for an experiment, using dogs, in which he would test the reaction of tissue to the surgical sutures in use in the 1930s—silk, catgut (actually sheep intestine), and wire. As Meade was leaving, Ochsner said, half-facetiously, "Bill, we're a southern state. You ought to try cotton." Ochsner had no idea that Meade would take him seriously. He forgot about his remark until two or three weeks later, when he went into the laboratory to see some preliminary results and was astonished to learn that Meade was trying out cotton along with the other sutures. The test results in dogs were good, and Ochsner arranged for one group of surgeons at Charity Hospital to use cotton sutures in their operations, while a second group employed silk. A third group evaluated the results, which demonstrated that cotton sewing thread is a good material, easily sterilized, flexible, strong, and productive of little tissue reaction. Regular cotton thread of the kind sold in stores on spools is used. Ochsner had the cost of sutures in Charity cases computed on a per case average, and learned that the outlay for catgut at the time was $1.30, for surgical silk 92 cents, and for cotton a fraction more than 1 cent. Serendipity again.[23] Ochsner Clinic surgeons continue to prefer cotton, as do some outsiders.

Ochsner and DeBakey, then a young resident, were annoyed when a patient with milk leg—a crippling swelling of a limb in which the blood circulation is impaired—was transferred by obstetricians to a surgical ward at Charity Hospital. No form of surgical relief was known, and such a patient often stayed for six weeks in a bed that otherwise would be occupied by somebody who could be helped by an operative procedure. In the course of grand rounds one day, Ochsner and DeBakey noted a paradox. The patient had a fever of 103 degrees, and the surface temperature of her body was hot, except that the affected leg was cold. Teacher and student had become interested in the role of the sympathetic nervous system in arterial disease, and one suggested that they try a sympathetic block and see what the result was. They injected novocain into the sympathetic nerve leading to the leg. "Immediately," Ochsner recalled, "her

23. William H. Meade and Alton Ochsner, "Spool Cotton as a Suture Material," *Journal of the American Medical Association*, CXIII (1939), 2230–31.

extremity, which had been white, turned red. It became warm and her pain was relieved."

It was a breakthrough that was followed up to advantage by Ochsner, DeBakey, and Mims Gage. They led the way in the development of sympathetic nerve blockage as an important diagnostic and therapeutic procedure. It still was being used half a century later, although most surgeons now turn to the installation of bypass grafts when they want to restore circulation. Some practitioners divide the sympathetic nerve as well as provide a bypass. The sympathetic, or involuntary, nervous system controls the degree of vasospasm that affects the blood flow in the presence of a clot or arterial disease in an arm or leg. As early as 1943 Ochsner was able to report that anesthetization brought permanent relief of pain to 90 percent of his patients, the disappearance of fever in almost all, and an almost invariable decrease in swelling.[24]

Along with Oscar Creech and J. P. Woodhall, Ochsner succeeded in lowering the death rate from tetanus in Charity Hospital, where patients still appeared at a rate of about three each month long years after immunization became available. The three men found that most victims could be saved by the early provision of tracheotomies, surgical openings in the throat to maintain airways when the breathing difficulties that accompanied the disease developed.[25]

None of his other pioneering surgical accomplishments provided more satisfaction for Ochsner than did his separation of Siamese twins in the Foundation Hospital on September 17, 1953. Catherine and Carolyn, the daughters of Mayor and Mrs. Ashton J. Mouton of Lafayette, Louisiana, had been born at Lafayette nearly two months earlier, weighing a combined eleven pounds, eight ounces. They were pygopagus Siamese twins, connected at the sacrum, the bottom of the spine. The literature revealed no instance of twins of that type having previously been parted by the surgeon's knife to begin normal lives.

Ochsner prepared the babies for the separation procedure with preliminary surgery to provide temporary colostomies (intestinal outlets). Then, once it was determined that each of the girls was born with her vital

24. Alton Ochsner and Michael DeBakey, "The Role of Vasospasm in Thrombophlebitis and Its Treatment by Novocain Block of the Sympathetics," *Tri-State Medical Journal*, XIII (1941), 2654–56.
25. Oscar Creech, J. P. Woodhall, and Alton Ochsner, "The Necessity for Tracheotomy in the Treatment of Tetanus to Prevent Lethal Respiratory Complications," *Surgery*, XXVII (1950), 62–73.

organs, the way was clear for the delicate parting. The surgeon found that the fusion extended for the full length of the sacrum, and that the spinal canals also were joined. A bungled job would mean paralysis, but Ochsner was in what may have been his finest period, when his rich experience reinforced his judgment and when he showed no sign of losing any of his youthful dexterity. The separation, accomplished with bone-cutting forceps and scissors, was clean. Ochsner took care of closing the surgical wounds for Catherine, while Rawley M. Penick did the sewing for Carolyn. For the remaining three decades of his life, Ochsner watched with affection the growth and development of these beneficiaries of his skill.[26]

In 1949 Ochsner and W. B. Ayers had removed an epignathus from the mouth of a girl, born in a south Mississippi town, who weighed eight and a half pounds when she was brought to the Foundation hospital four and a half hours after birth. From her mouth protruded a growth almost as large as her head, an epignathus, also known as a monster, the un-developed beginning of a twin. Ayers opened the tiny throat and provided an air tube to the windpipe because the baby could not breathe through the mouth. On the next day he installed a gastrostomy through which food could be introduced directly into the stomach. On the fourth day Ochsner excised the growth, which extended far down into the pharynx. He managed to salvage two-thirds of the hypertrophied tongue, and the first recorded excision of an epignathus with the survival of the host had a happy ending. With the help of plastic surgeons and other Ochsner Clinic doctors, the girl grew up without handicaps to remind her of the ordeal and triumph that marked her first days on earth.[27]

Even earlier, Ochsner and Neal Owens, a plastic surgeon, had per-severed for seven years in a project to provide a new passageway through the throat for a tiny girl whose esophagus was closed by a stricture caused by drinking lye. The four-year-old tot, who weighed only twenty pounds because of her difficulty in swallowing food, was one of numerous chil-dren taken to Charity Hospital during the 1920s and 1930s for treatment of injuries resulting from the ingestion of household cleaning solutions that contained lye. Usually a careless parent had left a container where the little one could reach it. In a protracted series of operations, Ochsner

26. AO Recollection, Stars.
27. Alton Ochsner and W. B. Ayers, "Case of Epignathus," *Surgery*, XXXI (1951), 560–64.

and Owens fashioned a substitute esophagus from a length of the child's jejunum and a skin tube.[28]

The painstaking care of Ochsner and DeBakey's research efforts is illustrated in a paper they prepared in 1941 for the *Journal of Thoracic Surgery*. No fewer than 295 published articles were cited in their exhaustive review of the experience of American and European surgeons in dealing with cancer of the esophagus. Ochsner and DeBakey also described four operations in which they excised cancerous sections of the esophagus. They recommended restoration of the connection of the esophagus to the stomach by raising the stomach into the chest cavity. Three of their patients died postoperatively, but the other was alive a year and a half after surgery.

DeBakey's interest in heart surgery, an area in which he would go on to win renown for his work in Houston, began in the 1930s while he and Ochsner were teaming up in their tireless and wide-ranging quest for new ideas. It is intriguing to speculate about what the two bold operators might have accomplished together if the heart-lung apparatus had been developed earlier, while they were collaborating. The device that enables a surgeon to invade the heart itself in order to make repairs came along in the waning period of Ochsner's surgical career, and he never became a cardiac surgeon. Nevertheless, he and DeBakey delved into the possibilities then offered by surgical treatment of coronary disease. In 1937 they published one of their studies of the techniques then in use: alterations of the sympathetic nervous system, thyroid operations, and attempts to develop collateral blood supply to the heart by grafting tissues to the heart muscles.[29]

As Ochsner was starting practice in Chicago, a general surgeon was expected to be versatile. "We did everything from pulling teeth to working on ingrown toenails," Earl Garside said. One of the employees at the stable where A. J. Ochsner kept his horses had a toothache. "I'll pull it," Alton said. He applied a local anesthetic, planted forceps around the base of the tooth, and yanked. The tooth broke off at the root. "You'll have to get a dentist to drill it out," Ochsner told the stablehand.[30] "That was the

28. Alton Ochsner and Neal Owens, "Anterothoracic Oesophagoplasty for Impermeable Stricture of the Oesophagus," *Annals of Surgery,* C (1934), 1055–91.

29. Alton Ochsner and Michael DeBakey, "The Surgical Treatment of Coronary Disease," *Surgery,* II (1937), 428–56.

30. Garside, interview, 1977.

beginning and end of my career as a dentist," he commented when, years later, Garside told the story.

His career as a veterinary surgeon was just as short. Not long after he moved to New Orleans, he offered to bob the tail of Sport, a blooded bulldog that its owner, Grace Lewis, planned to show. Ochsner bungled the job and made it impossible for the dog to compete. Miss Lewis forgave but did not forget.[31] According to one of his sons, Ochsner belonged in the ranks of celebrated surgeons who always made a mess of carving the family Thanksgiving turkey.

Although Ochsner eventually directed much of his attention to the treatment of lung cancer, in his earlier days in New Orleans he was busy dealing with bronchiectasis, tuberculosis, and empyema. He was one of the pioneers in using surgical methods to combat these conditions before the discovery of antibiotics made them less of a problem. He became proficient in performing thorascopy in patients with pulmonary tuberculosis. The technique is to excise a sufficient number of ribs to cause a tubercular lung to collapse. A collapsed lung has an opportunity to rest, allowing healing to begin. For bronchiectasis, the approach was to remove the affected lung lobe. When Ochsner first began doing the procedure, the nationwide experience was that more than half of the patients were operative casualties. The mortality was greatly reduced by the time antibiotics came along to make the disease rare. In empyema, Ochsner and his associates reported good results from either surgery to provide drainage or from aspiration and air injection into the lung.[32]

The jazz musician Muggsy Spanier, who was a patient, wrote a song: "Oh, Dr. Ochsner, Oh." Juan Perón, the Argentine dictator, sent an expensive alligator handbag as a gift to Mrs. Ochsner. United States Senator Theodore C. Bilbo of Mississippi underwent surgery for cancer of the jaw. General Clair Chennault, wartime leader of the Flying Tigers, entered the Ochsner hospital when it was too late to do anything about his lung cancer. Not surprisingly, as Ochsner's reputation spread, his services were sought by the headline makers as well as thousands who had no claim to fame.

Chennault's final days, spent in Splinter Village, provided what

31. Woodard D. Beacham, interview, 1980.

32. Alton Ochsner, "The Surgical Treatment of Pulmonary Tuberculosis," *New Orleans Medical and Surgical Journal,* LVIII (1929), 876–88; "The Treatment of Acute Empyema," *International Surgical Digest,* XI (1931), 67–74; "Surgical Treatment of Pulmonary Tuberculosis," *International Surgical Digest,* XII (1931), 321–28.

Ochsner said was the "most touching meeting I have seen in my life." Madame Chiang Kai-shek paid a farewell visit to the air warrior who had helped her husband battle the Japanese even before the United States entered the fighting. "I went into the room with her," Ochsner related. "To see the affection between those two! She turned to me and said, 'Doctor, you have in this room one of the greatest men in the world.'" They talked about the days when the generalissimo's wife joined Chennault at four o'clock in the morning to act as his interpreter in his instructions to Chinese pilots before they started out on forays against the enemy; in the afternoon she returned to assist in the debriefing. Chennault, who had had a lung removed in Washington, was dying of hemorrhage when he entered the New Orleans hospital. He was somewhat paranoid in his last days and insisted that Ochsner himself handle a blood transfusion because he feared that some of the residents may have come under Communist influence.[33] Ochsner was a friend of Chennault's Chinese journalist wife, Anna, who was active in conservative causes.

Bilbo also died in Splinter Village. Almost to the end he tried mightily to conceal from Ochsner the fact that he continued to smoke cigars after his surgery.

In 1941 Ochsner spent two of the busiest weeks of his life in Panama. He performed forty operations, gave twenty-eight illustrated lectures, and saw some 150 patients in consultation. The Santo Tomás Hospital, a government institution, paid him a thousand-dollar fee and must have turned a tidy profit because the hospital billed all of those who were served. But Ochsner had developed at Tulane an affinity with Latin Americans and seldom turned down an opportunity to make an appearance in South or Central America. Thinking back in his late years, he estimated that he had made no fewer than one hundred trips to the area. The two weeks would have been memorable enough because of the work volume, but turned out to have been only a prelude to one of the tense, nail-biting adventures of his lifetime.

One of the patients about whom he was consulted was Tomás Gabriel Duqué, a newspaper publisher and former president of the Republic of Panama. Ochsner concluded that Duqué's cardiac problem was the result of a thyroid heart, but Panamanian doctors would not agree since they could find no evidence of unusual thyroid activity. In January, 1943, Ochsner received a telephone call from Cordell Hull, the United States

33. AO Recollection, Chennault and Chiang.

secretary of state. Duqué, Hull disclosed, was seriously ill. The Panamanian *médicos* now agreed that Duqué had to undergo thyroid surgery, but the patient insisted upon the procedure's being done by Ochsner. Hull explained that the United States government owed a favor to Duqué because he had helped engineer a ruse that ousted a pro-Nazi president of Panama. Hull said all of the wartime priorities that Ochsner would need to travel would be arranged. At the time patients with hyperthyroidism were prepared for surgery with doses of iodine. Ochsner arranged by telephone for physicians in Panama City to give the medicine; after two weeks he felt that Duqué was ready. The surgeon was concerned about the expertise of the Panamanian anesthesiologists, so he arranged to take Ansel Caine, a leading New Orleans anesthesiologist, with him. Ochsner knew two young surgeons in Panama City who would help him with the thyroidectomy.

Edgar Burns, the urologist partner in the Ochsner Clinic, warned that Duqué was not likely to survive and advised Ochsner not to operate. "You know those Latins and the temper they have. If he doesn't get well, they are likely to liquidate you." Burns was serious. Ochsner already had misgivings about walking into a ticklish situation. He and Caine flew to Miami to make connections with a flight to Panama City. At Miami, curious airline officials asked what connections the two doctors had with the White House. They were impressed because Ochsner and Caine had the absolute top travel priorities. "We arrived in Panama the night before Mardi Gras," Ochsner recalled.

> I went out to the Santo Tomás Hospital to see Duqué, and he was so sick that I didn't think he was going to live through the night. I canceled the operation for the next day and sat at his bedside, thinking that each breath would be his last. Finally I realized that I had to do something, because I knew that he was not going to get better if we didn't operate upon him, so we rescheduled him for the next day. After the operation he developed a terrific thyroid crisis, and I stayed right with him in his room for five days, nursing him as no one else had ever been nursed, and he gradually got well. I couldn't forget the admonition Edgar had given me about not letting him die.

Duqué lived on for some twenty years and was ever grateful to the surgeon. Ochsner once related that the single largest fee he ever received was a $10,000 check from Duqué.

Another of Ochsner's Latin patients was Eduardo Weiss, the Argentine air attaché in Washington. After undergoing a sympathectomy in treatment of a vascular disorder, Weiss made a checkup visit to Ochsner each January. Shortly after seeing Weiss in 1955, Ochsner went to Lima, Peru, for the inter-American meeting of the American College of Surgeons. There he encountered old friends, Professor and Mrs. Ditto de Sola. The professor was chairman of surgery at the University of El Salvador.

Upon returning to New Orleans, Ochsner went to the Clinic on Monday morning and was surprised to find Weiss waiting for him. "Eduardo! What's wrong?" he asked. "I must see you alone," the attaché replied. Ochsner asked the nurse to leave.

Weiss described a fifty-year-old patient whose health had been perfect until two weeks earlier, when he developed a severe pain in his left leg while playing tennis. The leg was cool and there was no pulse below the femoral. The attaché wanted to know if anything could be done for the man. When Ochsner said the patient could be helped, Weiss swore him to secrecy and revealed that the man was Juan Domingo Perón, the president of Argentina. Weiss asked Ochsner to fly with him to Buenos Aires to treat Perón. The trip was made in secrecy. It was the first occasion on which Ochsner ever left the Clinic without telling associates where he was going. It also was a time when Pope Pius XII was seriously ill in Rome. The rumor spread that Ochsner had been called to Rome for consultation, and when the Pope's condition improved, some people thought Ochsner should be given credit.

Ochsner and Weiss flew to Miami and boarded a flight to Buenos Aires, arriving on Monday afternoon. "The plane was stopped at the end of the runway," Ochsner continued. "A staff car met us and we were taken off. We went to the leading hotel, the Plaza. When we were going up the steps of the Plaza, whom should I run into but the de Solas, whom I had just seen in Lima." The couple asked what he was doing in Argentina. "Of course, I didn't dare tell them. I told them they knew of my interest in the relationship between tobacco and cancer of the lung, and since I realized that the only animal that used tobacco was the penguin, who smoked Kools, I was down there to see if there was a high incidence of cancer of the lung among penguins. The de Solas didn't press me further."

Ochsner saw Perón in the presidential summer palace, about thirty miles from Buenos Aires. "I examined the president and found that he had an obstructive vascular lesion in his left lower extremity," he related. "I told him that he first should have an arteriogram and then, depending upon what was found, should have either an endarterectomy [a reaming out of a vein], a bypass [the installation of a substitute vein], or a sympathectomy [obliteration of a nerve]." Perón asked if these procedures could be done in Argentina. "I told him that the arteriography and sympathectomy could be done in Argentina, but I wasn't willing to do the others, because he was such a prominent person I thought that he should be given every advantage of being operated on where the surgeon had his team. He agreed to come to New Orleans after the [Argentine] congress had met six weeks later."

On January 25, 1955, in the presidential palace, Ochsner performed a novocain sympathetic ganglion block to provide temporary relief. "He never got to New Orleans because six weeks later, when the congress met, they had a revolution and he was kicked out," Ochsner concluded. "I did admonish him to stop smoking because he had been a very heavy smoker, and he, incidentally, suggested that everyone stop smoking in Argentina, and particularly the youth. I have subsequently seen him in Madrid, where he was in exile, and he has never been operated upon, has been perfectly well, and has had no more trouble since he stopped smoking."

Another famous person who turned to Ochsner for surgical treatment was Gary Cooper, the motion-picture star. He was scheduled to begin his work in the classic Western *High Noon,* but was bothered by the reappearance of a right inguinal hernia, which two operations had failed to correct. At the suggestion of Ben Hogan, Cooper made an appointment with Ochsner, explaining that he had to have quick action or hold up the filming of the movie. On March 14, 1952, in an operating room at Splinter Village, Ochsner provided a repair that not only allowed Cooper to meet his *High Noon* engagement, but also solved the problem in the right inguinal area. A year and a half later, however, Ochsner was summoned to Paris because Cooper had developed a hernia on the left side. The actor could not return to the United States at the time because he would lose tax advantages if he did so. Accompanied by Mrs. Ochsner, the surgeon flew to Paris and did a successful hernioplasty in the American Hospital. The Ochsners also enjoyed a week of sightseeing with the Coopers and Gary Cooper's friend Clark Gable.[34]

Twenty-eight years after he moved to Tulane, Ochsner performed what Mims Gage said was "the greatest piece of surgery I have ever seen." On the evening of October 27, 1955, chest physician Joseph K. Bradford was

34. *Ibid.*

called out of a meeting of the Clinic staff in the Ochsner Hospital auditorium. Upstairs a patient with a cancer of the trachea was gasping for air.

"When I got to him he couldn't get air into his lungs," Bradford related, "and there was no way we could get it there because the trachea was closing off. I went downstairs and called Dr. Ochsner out of the auditorium. My first question to him was, 'What do you know about cancer of the trachea?' He replied, 'I've never seen one.' "

Bradford said the patient would die unless some kind of airway could be provided. A tracheotomy could not be used because the cancer was in the way. "We'll try to do something," Ochsner responded.

"He started about ten at night and finished about two in the morning," Bradford recalled. "Without ever having done it before, he removed about two and one-half inches of the trachea and replaced it with a tantalum mesh and some fascia from the thigh. Dr. Gage watched the operation and told me the next day it was the greatest piece of surgery he ever had seen because Dr. Ochsner was working behind the great vessels, the innominate artery and the right innominate vein. The patient lived for nearly five years and died of a heart attack."

Bradford, one of the few clinic staff members who didn't try to conceal a cigarette when Ochsner approached and who freely argued over the evidence linking smoking and cancer, may have questioned the conclusions Ochsner reached from his research. But he never doubted Ochsner's surgical skill.[35]

Merrill O. Hines, medical director of the Ochsner Clinic, knew he was going to meet resistance when he went to Ochsner's office on a Sunday morning in 1967 to deliver a reminder. Hines owed allegiance to the chief, as he called him. Ochsner had selected him as a recipient of a Commonwealth Fund scholarship to the Tulane medical school, had hired him on the Clinic staff, had arranged for him to establish a department of colon and rectal surgery, and had supported his rise through the Clinic hierarchy. Now it fell Hines's lot to tell the active surgeon that on April 30 he was through, that he no longer could do operations as a member of the Clinic and in the Foundation's hospital. Regulations adopted years before—with Ochsner's support—declared a Clinic partner ineligible to do surgery as of the end of the Clinic fiscal year in which the doctor's seventieth birthday fell. The Clinic's fiscal year ended on April 30, and

35. Joseph K. Bradford, interview, November, 1976.

Ochsner's Presbyterian luck already had given him one reprieve: because his birthday was on May 4, he had remained eligible until he was only four days short of being seventy-one years of age.

As Hines expected, Ochsner's reaction to his message was brief and definite. "I won't quit," he said. Hines waited a couple of weeks, then made another Sunday morning call. With him he had a copy of the regulations. "We have this rule that was passed with your approval. If you won't abide by it then there is no alternative but to tear it up and we'll rewrite it." And Hines ripped the page in two. "Goddamn it," Ochsner blurted. "You get out of here. I'll quit."[36]

On his last day, April 28, 1967, he made a silent point to the Clinic administration. He performed seven operations, showing that he could have gone on and on. Doctors and nurses staged a cake and punch party for him as he left the operating room.

36. Hines, interview, 1985.

12   Scientist at Work

"Early to bed, early to rise, / Work hard, and publicize." The couplet recited by irreverent Tulane doctors-to-be captures the essence of the Alton Ochsner of the 1930s and 1940s, although the "early to bed" part was well off the mark. "Late to bed, early to rise" would have been more accurate. Sleep was a luxury Ochsner was willing to do without, and often he worked until midnight or later. It is true that he sometimes would lie down immediately after dinner, but only to bounce back up at 2 A.M., when the household was quiet, to dictate pages of a paper that he was preparing for publication. The "work hard" allusion needs little comment: Ochsner's industry could be exceeded only if the limitation of a twenty-four-hour day was somehow lifted. As for "publicize," it was professional exposure that Ochsner most sought, and the most effective medium was the medical journal, through which he could report on his research projects and describe his experiences in the practice of surgery.

Research was necessarily a sort of moonlighting activity since teaching and surgery had prior claims on his efforts. In this circumstance, it is one of the remarkable accomplishments of his life that he published work of a volume that would have taxed the productive capacity of a scientist who spent an entire career in the laboratory. Of course, he had help. Associates such as Michael DeBakey, Paul DeCamp, and John B. Blalock took up part of the load, and for years Ochsner trained a succession of residents who could be assigned to search through the literature for the references he needed.

Critics claimed that much of his work consisted of repetitious papers dealing with topics previously covered and adding a minimum of new data or conclusions. He would report on fifty cases, then a hundred, two hundred, and so on. Conversely, a single subject might be reported in two or more journals. There also were recurring themes. He wrote on blood clots, for instance, beginning in 1939 and continuing until 1977. Finally, his output included numerous tributes to departed surgeons, editorials, reminiscences, philosophical discussions, and the like. But he obviously had something to say; otherwise, editors would have rejected his contributions.

Ochsner himself set rigid standards for reporting on his work: "A physician who has been placed upon a pedestal by his grateful, admiring patients is obviously pleased and flattered. Unless he is analytical, he is likely to become imbued with his therapeutic successes and to acquire an exaggerated concept of himself, and this is regrettable. Not only does it warp his subsequent judgment in the practice of medicine, but it may exert a detrimental effect on his medical writing."[1]

As an example of the dangers, Ochsner noted that some investigators excluded hospital deaths in determining survival rates among cancer patients. This practice, he said, skewed statistics to make results of a therapeutic procedure appear to be more successful than they actually were.

Ochsner's first published paper, the one on blood transfusions, appeared in a Viennese clinical journal's September, 1923, issue.[2] His last saw print in November 1981, two months after his death. Not one of the intervening fifty-eight years passed without contributions. The documented record shows 584 published articles, written alone or in collaboration. The tally includes books, chapters in books, scientific studies in professional journals, historical and philosophical articles in medical and lay publications, and reprints of lectures and speeches. As a young exchange fellow, he enjoyed the peer recognition that came from publishing, and he never forgot it. He thought of himself as a teacher, and the journals gave him a podium.

He was every bit as thorough in his writing as he was in his surgery. His papers had voluminous bibliographies because he expected his coauthors to dig painstakingly through the literature. It was not wasted effort. The references were a guide to readers who wanted to pursue a subject. Clarity was another hallmark of the work. The scientist in Ochsner demanded precise language, and the literary Ochsner responded. A layman who keeps a medical dictionary open has little difficulty understanding the discussion.

In January, 1937, the first issue of the journal *Surgery*, produced by the Mosby Publishing Company of St. Louis, made its appearance. Coeditors were Ochsner and Owen H. Wangensteen, chairman of surgery at the

1. Alton Ochsner, "Judgment, Accuracy and Honesty in Medical Reporting," *Mississippi Valley Medical Journal*, LXXXI (1959), 45–47.
2. Alton Ochsner, "Die Bluttransfusion nach Percy," *Klin. Wchnscher*, XXXVI (1923) 697–712.

University of Minnesota. Will Mayo wrote the foreword for the initial issue. Ochsner and Wangensteen solicited papers from their friends, and the journal soon had a wide readership. *Surgery* later became the official organ of the Society for Vascular Surgery and Society of University Surgeons. Ochsner and Wangensteen remained active editors until 1971, when they took on emeritus status. Ochsner also found time to serve as coeditor of the *International Surgical Digest.*

An enterprising medical student, John A. Zieman of Mobile, Alabama, profited from Ochsner's lectures. He took longhand notes, combined them with the notes of fraternity brothers, and produced three volumes of printed material that he sold, he recalled nearly fifty years afterward, for twelve dollars to fellow students. He reckoned that he cleared about two thousand dollars before he graduated in 1940. Ochsner frowned on the project because he could not review the notes before they were printed, but students found them helpful, especially as the professor did not work from textbooks.[3] George D. Lilly used recordings of Ochsner's lectures and made typewritten transcripts, which he had bound into a volume of 389 pages plus index. Lilly was one of Ochsner's early Tulane students.

In view of the lengthy period over which Ochsner wrote, perhaps it is not surprising that no fewer than 135 coauthors joined him in publications. The number, however, is an impressive reminder of the army of doctors whose careers he influenced, one way or another. Next to DeBakey, his most frequent collaborator was DeCamp, who put his signature on thirty joint papers. His friend Mims Gage collaborated on nineteen works, and Blalock, a longtime stalwart on the clinic surgery staff, on eighteen. Alton's cousin Seymour Ochsner provided a double-Ochsner byline on eight papers.

The fact that in less than one year in Europe Alton honed his college German well enough to write scientific papers in that language is testimony to his linguistic acumen. His works also appeared occasionally in Latin American journals, but in these instances translators converted his English into Spanish.

A highlight of Ochsner's long involvement in research was his association with DeBakey. The two also were linked as practicing surgeons and teachers, but the lasting legacy from a fruitful partnership was their investigative work. Together, they published no fewer than seventy-one papers,

3. John A. Zieman, interview, 1986.

covering subjects ranging from surgical treatment of coronary disease to hair balls in the alimentary canal, from bone cartilage disease to gall bladder operations, from skin disease to cancer of the esophagus, from blood clots to intestinal obstructions, from hepatitis to diseases of the mouth.

DeBakey, twelve years younger than Ochsner, was a sophomore in the Tulane medical school when he first came to Ochsner's attention. Ochsner was immediately impressed with the shy student "who seemed to have a great deal of intelligence and who was a very hard worker." The more he saw of DeBakey the more he realized that the young man had great potential; Ochsner resolved that he himself was going to train this talent.

Upon graduation, DeBakey served a year as an intern at Charity Hospital. "I remember very well," Ochsner said, "one day after I had done a thyroidectomy at Charity, he called me and told me I ought to come over because the patient wasn't doing very well, and I went over and found that he wasn't. The neck was distended, and I immediately opened up the wound because the patient was having a great deal of respiratory distress and evacuated a large clot. The ligature on the superior thyroid artery had slipped, and this was the cause of the bleeding. Had it not been for the fact that Dr. DeBakey was such an alert intern, the patient might have succumbed." Ochsner added, "I realized then what a valuable man Mike was going to be."

DeBakey joined the Tulane surgical staff as an assistant. "He loved to write and loved to do research," Ochsner recalled. "He didn't have much desire to operate except just to become proficient in doing an operation. After he had become proficient in doing an operation, he didn't have much desire in operating any more. But he was particularly desirous of doing research and writing."[4]

Later, DeBakey concentrated his attention on surgery, making contributions in the use of grafts to replace damaged blood vessels and in cardiac surgery, including the development of an artificial heart. Those who worked with him in New Orleans believe that if he had not been diverted from the laboratory, he eventually might have won a Nobel Prize for his research. One of his accomplishments in New Orleans was the invention of a device that facilitated blood transfusions.

Ochsner and DeBakey developed a close personal association. The

4. AO Recollection, Mike DeBakey.

younger man sometimes served as a supervising baby-sitter for the four Ochsner children when Alton and Isabel went out of town. In his earlier years DeBakey had a convoluted writing style. Once while baby-sitting, he sent a telegram to Alton and Isabel that alarmed them. Their quick telephone call cleared up his message: he had been trying to tell them that all was well at home.

Ochsner said he and DeBakey "did a tremendous amount of work together on many subjects, spent many long hours together writing complete resumés of subjects that still today are classics. It was a lot of fun working with Mike because he was so stimulating. He worked from early morning until late at night and never seemed to get tired."[5]

They were separated for the first time in 1942. By then DeBakey was an assistant professor of surgery at Tulane, as well as a member of the staff of the newly opened Ochsner Clinic. Mims Gage left to become commanding officer of the Tulane hospital unit that served in Europe in World War II. Ochsner expected that DeBakey would stay with him and the two would run the Tulane department of surgery. "I knew that as hard a worker as Dr. DeBakey was, we would have no difficulty," he explained. "After a while, however, when [the war] began to get pretty hot, he came to me and said that his family had come to America as immigrants and that he felt he was not doing his duty by not getting into the service. I told him I didn't know what I could do, because we had planned he would stay here, but I admired him for wanting to go into service, and of course I let him go." Colonel DeBakey served for the duration in the personnel department of the surgeon general's office.

After the war he returned to his New Orleans jobs. But he did not stay long, leaving in 1946 to become professor and chairman of surgery at the Baylor University medical school in Houston. Some insight into his departure is provided by Hyman S. Mayerson, the admired and respected chairman of physiology at Tulane:

> We were at a meeting in Atlantic City. I had a note in my mailbox at the hotel saying Mike would like to see me. I got in touch with him and told him to come on up to the room. Mike never drank, but he started pacing up and down; I took a tumbler and filled it half full of whiskey and said, "Mike, here. Take this before you go through the ceiling. What the hell's wrong?" I'd never seen him like

5. *Ibid.*

this. He never got upset. "I've got an offer from Texas," he said. He didn't know what to do.

We talked for a couple of hours and he almost got drunk. I told him, "Look, Mike, you can go along with Ochsner, but you'll be his little boy Friday the rest of your life. You're not going to take that easily. You'll take it now because you're getting something out of the training, but pretty soon you're going to want to be God, too, and it won't work with Ochsner. My recommendation to you would be to accept the job. They want you out there. Go. You deserve it. You're not going to be happy in Dr. Ochsner's shadow. You've got much pent up in you that's coming out. And when it does, it won't work."

About eleven o'clock he thanked me and left. The next morning he says, "I wired them I'm going." I asked him if he had talked with Ochsner and he said yes.[6]

When DeBakey asked Ochsner about his reaction to the offer, Ochsner said, "We'll miss you, but I think you should go, and with my blessing."

If DeBakey's growing fame stirred any envy in Ochsner, he kept it to himself. His only recorded public remark about the younger man was, "That boy works too hard." Ochsner arranged for two of his sons, Akky and John, to train under DeBakey at Houston. Because of the proximity to New Orleans, there obviously was some rivalry between the fast-emerging Houston medical institutions and the already-established Ochsner Clinic. Houston practitioners knew that Sid Richardson, Clint Murchison, and other wealthy Texans passed up medical centers in their own state and sought treatment at the Ochsner Clinic and hospital. Akky, who did not have a close personal relationship with DeBakey, quoted him as telling visiting doctors—possible sources of referrals—that Houston surgeons were doing procedures that were beyond the capability of those at Ochsner. However that may be, DeBakey and Ochsner maintained a warm friendship obviously based on mutual respect and affection. De-Bakey went out of his way to give public credit to Ochsner for training and inspiring him. And Ochsner left no doubt that he regarded DeBakey as his prize pupil and collaborator.

One of Ochsner's most cherished honors was his election in 1947 as the first president of the Society for Vascular Surgery, and a preponderance of his operations in the later years of his career were in the chest, but

6. Hyman S. Mayerson, interview, June 14, 1978.

his research activities reflected the true breadth of his medical interests. Although he became essentially a thoracic surgeon, he had trained in internal medicine and had started practice as a general surgeon. He was literally a head-to-toe doctor: he treated craniocerebral wounds at Charity Hospital, sledders' foot injuries at Zurich, and all kinds of ailments in the in-between areas of the body.

One of his early projects at Tulane not only resulted in a procedure that sharply reduced the death rate from amebic hepatic abscess, but also helped bring about grants of more than three million dollars to the university. Oddly enough, surgeon Ochsner's advice *against* an operation was a key factor.

Until he began his duties at Charity Hospital, Ochsner had never seen a case of amebiasis and the associated liver abscess, caused by a parasite that enters the body in contaminated food. The abscess presses against the diaphragm that separates liver and lung, and an exploratory needle reveals that the lesion is filled with chocolate-colored pus. The patient is weak, but an abscess is not immediately life-threatening. Before Ochsner came upon the scene, the practice was to make an incision through the pleural or peritoneal cavity and provide open drainage. The problem was that one-third of the patients who underwent this operation died of infection.

Going over the records, Ochsner observed a similarity between the fates of those who submitted to the hepatic abscess operation and those who had open drainage for tuberculosis abscess, which also caused infection. Checking the literature, Ochsner learned that Sir Leonard Rogers, an Englishman practicing in India, had reported in 1905 that aspiration of hepatic abscess pus through a needle and the administration of amebicides resulted in a relatively low mortality. Ochsner and DeBakey began using the needle technique at Charity, accompanied by doses of emetine, and the death rate dropped to one-tenth of what it had been with open drainage. Years afterward Ochsner, who seldom raised questions about the practices of Rudolph Matas, commented, "Smart as he was, this was one thing that Dr. Matas had not worked out. It is hard for me to understand why."

Ochsner earlier had been called into consultation by Sarah Henderson, a wealthy New Orleanian, when her young grandnephew suffered a head injury. Another surgeon had recommended an operation, but Ochsner ruled it was unnecessary. The child got well, and Miss Henderson was grateful because he had been spared surgery. While Ochsner and

DeBakey were working on the liver abscess problem, Miss Henderson inherited Coca Cola bottling company stock in Chicago worth half a million dollars. She told Ochsner she wanted to give the half million to the Tulane medical school, assuming that it would be matched by a donation from the General Education Fund. She intended for the money to go to the tropical medicine department, but Ochsner learned that the General Education Fund would match gifts only to the surgery or internal medicine departments.

Miss Henderson felt that too many operations were being done, and she did not want to help the surgery department. She almost had decided to give the money to the University of the South at Sewanee when Ochsner suddenly thought, "My God, this is exactly what she is talking about. Amebiasis is supposed to be a tropical disease, and here we have been able with a nonoperative method to reduce the mortality from 33 percent to 3 percent." Miss Henderson was won over, and the million-dollar windfall was used to establish the William Henderson Chair of Surgery, of which Ochsner was the first occupant. Miss Henderson later gave $2,250,000 to the department of tropical medicine. Amebic hepatic abscess now is controlled with antibiotics.[7]

Research and experience impelled Ochsner to advocate vastly different approaches to the treatment of gastric (stomach) ulcers and peptic (duodenal) ulcers. In a study of gastric cancer cases at the Ochsner Clinic in a period of thirteen years, he and Blalock found that the five-year survival rate was only 7.2 percent. They attributed the dismal record to the long delay—averaging 8.4 months—between the appearance of the first symptoms and the beginning of treatment. By the time the diagnosis was made, the cancer almost always had spread. The surgeons wrote that gastric ulcers are precancerous lesions and even benign ulcers can undergo malignant change. Therefore, the practitioner "is obligated to subject all patients with chronic ulcers and gastric polypi to gastric resection." They advocated radical subtotal gastrectomy—removal of almost all of the stomach and the sites to which cancer had spread. The recommendation would have been for removal of the entire stomach, except that the retention of a gastric pouch no larger than a man's thumb minimizes the disturbances that follow total gastrectomy.[8]

7. AO Recollection, Benefactors.
8. Alton Ochsner and John Blalock, "Carcinoma of the Stomach: Need for Earlier Diagnosis and More Adequate Therapy," *Journal of the Florida Medical Association,* XLII (1955), 99–107.

In the case of peptic ulcers, Ochsner believed in conservative, non-surgical measures. With Mims Gage and Kiyoshi Hosoi, one of his fellows, he did investigative work with dogs, concluding that peptic ulcers result from inherent, predisposing factors, such as tissue susceptibility and constitutional predisposition, and from precipitating factors, chiefly the overproduction of acid in the stomach. He noted that nothing can be done about inherent factors, but the secretion of acid can be controlled. He told patients that most ulcers would be healed if they refrained from smoking, from drinking alcohol, from drinking coffee and other beverages containing caffeine, from eating highly seasoned foods, and from fretting and stewing over life's stresses.[9]

He practiced what he preached. For example, for years the Ochsner Clinic remained in Uptown New Orleans, while the Ochsner Medical Foundation operated hospitals in Jefferson Parish, first alongside the Huey P. Long Bridge on the site of the wartime Camp Plauché, and later at 1516 Jefferson Highway. Ochsner and other doctors making the drive between hospital and Clinic often were delayed at railroad crossings. "I used to allow plenty of time, but every once in a while I'd get held up by a train," Ochsner related. "I used to sit there and stew. Later I realized there wasn't anything I could do, so I began turning off the engine and turning on the radio. Now that didn't get me there any sooner, but I was in a hell of a lot better shape when I got there." He would seat his ulcer patients and tell them, "Don't get upset when things don't work out. Do the best you can, and if it doesn't work out, realize that there's nothing you can do about it. You'll be surprised how simple it is if you try." If the driven, overworked surgeon could learn to take disappointments in stride, most patients could, too.[10]

Ochsner's work on varicose veins attracted interest in the late 1930s. He and Howard R. Mahorner developed a multiple tourniquet test with which to determine the extent of surgery needed to strip unsightly veins in the legs. Their method added a dimension to the classic Trendelenburg test. By applying tourniquets at various places on a patient's leg, they found that they could pinpoint the faulty valves that stopped the circulation of blood. Their knowledge permitted more effective treatment by stripping or by injecting sclerosing agents such as sodium morrhuate. The

9. Alton Ochsner, Mims Gage, and Kiyoshi Hosoi, "Treatment of Peptic Ulcer Based on Physiological Principles," *Surgery, Gynecology and Obstetrics,* LXII (1936), 257–74.
10. AO, interview, August 14, 1978.

test was widely used for a time, but now has been supplanted by other methods.

Earlier, Ochsner and Mahorner had reached back into the medical past and resurrected the leech—once an important therapeutic tool—in dealing with phlebitis, inflammation of the veins of the legs. In 1933 they reported good results in three of four cases. They attributed improvement to the secretion by the leech of hirudin, a substance that inhibits the coagulation of blood.[11]

The dog bite that threatened the loss of a finger was not Ochsner's only mishap in a laboratory. Soon after the medical school moved to Hutchinson Memorial adjacent to Charity Hospital, he had a scare involving his eyes. He came upon the description of a formula that might duplicate lipiodol, which he used as a contrast medium in bronchography. Since lipiodol, imported from France, was expensive, he decided to try out the formula. He was boiling ingredients when the container exploded, spewing hot oil and glass over him, two women technicians, and a porter. "I'm blind!" he shouted, groping about the laboratory. He instructed Gertrude Forshag to telephone George Hardin, an ophthalmologist whose office was near Touro Infirmary. By the time she had made the call, Ochsner could see, but he and the other three went to Hardin as a precaution. It was determined that there were no serious injuries.[12]

Ochsner's wide-ranging interests even led him into experiences with melanoma, a type of skin cancer that has been viewed with dismay by doctor and patient alike. His never-failing optimism caused him to conclude that the prognosis is not good "but is not hopeless," even though the five-year survival rate among patients on whom he kept note was only about one-third. He learned firsthand that melanoma can lie dormant for a long time. A woman who remained perfectly well for twenty-five years after losing an eye to malignant melanoma died of melanosis. Ochsner advised wide and deep extirpation of cancerous moles and of the regional lymph nodes.[13] When the cancer was on an arm or leg he advocated treatment with a regional perfusion technique developed by his successor as chairman of surgery, Oscar Creech, and other Tulane surgeons. The

11. Howard R. Mahorner and Alton Ochsner, "The Use of Leeches in the Treatment of Phlebitis and the Prevention of Pulmonary Embolism," *Annals of Surgery,* CVIII (1933), 408–21.

12. Forshag, interview, 1985.

13. Alton Ochsner, "Prognosis of Malignant Melanoma as Influenced by Therapy," *Arizona Medicine,* CLV (1962), 539–45.

technique involves use of the heart-lung apparatus to pump massive doses of anticancer drugs into the affected area.

The abundance of knife and gunshot wounds treated at Charity Hospital gave Ochsner ample opportunity to practice vascular surgery. He also gained experience in dealing with aneurysms. One therapy that helped in a few aneurysms was to insert a length of wire into the part of the blood vessel where the wall had weakened and was bulging. The wire was guided into place through a hollow needle. The rationale was that the wire would coil around the periphery, cause clotting, and strengthen the wall. Sometimes an electric current was passed through the wire to further encourage clotting. Ochsner conceded that the technique was crude, but when there was a chance that a procedure would work, he was willing to try it.[14]

Ochsner spent some sleepless nights in his early Tulane years, taking his turn with others in carrying out around-the-clock experiments to determine whether applications of heat or of cold were more beneficial in the treatment of peritonitis. Some doctors applied heat, others cold, to the abdomens of patients, and there was controversy over the relative effectiveness. Ochsner and his co-workers devised a study in which peritonitis was induced in dogs by ligating the appendix. A coil was placed into the abdomen of an animal, which was kept asleep for long periods while ice water or hot water was circulated through the coil. While the study indicated a slight advantage for heat, as Ochsner had predicted, the results were inconclusive.[15]

Ileus, or intestinal blockage, was one subject of Ochsner's early efforts in the Tulane laboratory. Working with dogs, he, Gage, and Reginald Cutting reported by 1930 that drugs are of little value in treatment.

The dog bite that might have cost Ochsner a finger occurred while he was experimenting with the use of the papaya ferment, papain, to prevent the formation of adhesions after abdominal surgery. He demonstrated that the fluid was indeed effective. He and his associates worked out a method of pouring about a liter of papain into the peritoneal cavity as an operative incision was being closed.[16] He prevailed upon the Parke-Davis

14. DeCamp, interview, April 26, 1978.

15. Alton Ochsner, I. M. Gage, R. A. Cutting, and Earl Garside, "Relative Values of Heat and Cold on Experimentally Produced Peritonitis," *Proceedings of the Society for Experimental Biology and Medicine*, XXVII (1929), 220–22.

16. Alton Ochsner and Ambrose Storck, "The Prevention of Peritoneal Adhesions by Papain," *Annals of Surgery*, CIV (1936), 736–47.

Company to produce phials of papain commercially, and for several years a supply was available. But demand fell off and production was discontinued. The need largely had disappeared as meticulous surgery was followed by fewer adhesions and a method was developed for preventing obstructions caused by kinking of the loops of the bowel.

In the 1950s Ochsner became involved in a public dispute with the New Orleans Board of Health and the New Orleans Dental Association over the fluoridation of the city's water supply. As a member of a committee named to study the issue, he voted to oppose the addition of fluoride to the water, even though the preponderance of scientific opinion was against him. He conceded that fluoridation substantially reduced the incidence of caries in children, but he raised fears that in later years it would result in an adult disease that causes sound teeth to fall out. Privately, he said most of those on his side of the question were crackpots, but nevertheless he held his ground in what turned out to be a losing cause. He said he favored fluoridation at first, but changed his mind after talking with his old friend, C. C. Bass, by then retired as dean of the Tulane medical school. The episode was a tempest in a teapot, but Ochsner's stand caused much concern among the dentists and doctors who eventually won the battle.

At the risk of being regarded as a faddist, Ochsner extolled the benefits to be derived from vitamins C and E given to patients postoperatively. His views have remained controversial. Vitamin C, he contended, promotes the healing of wounds and also helps prevent blood clots. He prescribed vitamin E for his surgery patients because he was convinced that the alpha tocopherol factor was the best defense against clotting. He attributed some of the skepticism about the value of vitamin E to claims that it was effective in treating everything from heart disease to falling hair. "Of course it doesn't work [for those things], this is the reason it has gotten into disrepute," he said. His interest in vitamin E dated back to 1948, when Jack H. Kay, a young assistant in Tulane's department of surgery, found that alpha tocopherol would prevent clotting of blood in a test tube. The factor was tried out on patients who were candidates for clots, and Ochsner reported good results.[17] He never won over a majority of surgeons to his views on either vitamin.

Ochsner blamed bureaucratic inefficiency for a delay in research that

17. Alton Ochsner, "On the Role of Vitamins C and E in Medicine," *Executive Health,* X (1974), 1–6.

might have improved treatment of Americans who were wounded in the Japanese attack on Pearl Harbor. In the spring of 1941 he was called to Washington as a member of a National Surgical Council committee set up to study the use of sulfonamides, the only antibiotics known and available in useful quantities at the time. Armed services medical personnel wanted to know whether sulfonamides should be given systemically or simply poured directly onto a wound. Twenty or more institutions, including Charity Hospital, were selected to test various methods. Ochsner said authorization was delayed because the original budget for the project was less than $100,000, too small to be seriously considered by the Bureau of the Budget. As a result, he said, "when Pearl Harbor came December 7, we had no answer." He added that when sulfonamides were poured into wounds most of them became infected. "Had the project got under way when we originally outlined it, I am sure we would have had the proper answer by the time Pearl Harbor was attacked. It simply illustrates how inefficient bureaucracies are."

Although his thousands of hours in laboratories would suggest that Ochsner was preoccupied with the science of medicine, in practice he believed that the art of diagnosis and treatment took precedence. "I've always maintained," he said, "that if you take a very good history and do a good physical examination and then reason, from this you can make a diagnosis. Then one should get the laboratory work as a confirmation. Then if the laboratory results don't confirm the clinical impression, disregard the laboratory work. I've seen this work time and again. Nothing takes the place of the reasoning of the human mind."

He liked to relate the story of a woman from South America who was referred to the Clinic after doctors in Chile concluded that she had a psychiatric problem that did not respond to treatment. "I don't know anything about psychiatry," Ochsner protested when a friend asked him to examine her. But he interviewed her and learned that she had a happy and secure family life. She said she awakened every morning full of vigor, but by midmorning was utterly exhausted.

The interview convinced Ochsner that the trouble did not lie in her mind. Upon examination, he found tenderness in the appendix area and over the kidney. "I think you have amebiasis," he told her. "Oh, no," she said. "They've looked for that in Chile." Ochsner sent her to an internist at the Clinic, who ordered tests and who then insisted that she did not have amebiasis. "Put her on treatment anyway," Ochsner suggested. The internist was reluctant but agreed to do so. "Three days later," Ochsner

reported, "she came into my office and announced: 'I'm well! I'm perfectly well!'" Ochsner explained that the tenderness and loss of energy
were classic symptoms of the disease. The scientific approach to diagnosis
had not worked because the telltale amebae did not happen to be in the
stool at the time samples were taken. "Nobody had listened to her story
before," Ochsner said. "They were looking for laboratory evidence and
did not pay attention to what the patient was saying."[18]

There are compelling reasons why Ochsner's larger-than-life statue
stands beside the fountain in front of one of the country's principal medical complexes. The thousands upon thousands of hours that he spent in a
search for new knowledge were rewarded. Because he lived and worked,
medical science is richer. Although he never took the time to sit down and
articulate his credo, it is written in his every activity: A doctor is blessed
with an opportunity to serve mankind by keeping people well and by
caring for the sick. He is able to do his job as well as he does because of the
lore passed along by preceding generations of practitioners. He owes a
debt that he can repay only with his own contributions to the body of
medical knowledge.

18. AO, interview, April 13, 1977.

13   The Clinic Gets a Name

The lasting Alton Ochsner legacy is the medical center that keeps his name alive. Most of his surgical innovations have been eclipsed by newer discoveries, and his research is half-forgotten in the rapid march of the healing arts. Almost all of the students and trainees who found his teaching inspirational are dead or retired. Gone are most of the patients on whom he performed operations, and of the many thousands of others who received his nonsurgical ministrations. His two surviving sons approach the age when they must give up their practices, and the grandchildren who seek to follow in his footsteps have yet to prove themselves. He could be but a fading memory, as are most of the medical achievers who gained fame in their own times yet come to mind now only in the reading of textbooks or the scanning of the literature. With Ochsner, it is different. The tree that he planted nearly half a century ago continues to bear fruit, and in yields of increasing size.

The founding of the Ochsner Clinic, which opened its doors on January 2, 1942, was an important event in New Orleans. Ochsner and his four partners inaugurated a new system of delivering health care in the Gulf South. They shook the medical establishment, introduced concepts of modern practice, and took the lead in restoring New Orleans to its former status as a regional health center. In the end they prevailed, proving that the public likes group practice conducted by specialists in one setting. Even some of their most outspoken critics, defenders of old-fashioned solo practice, eventually organized groups or clinics of their own. By then, Ochsner and his associates had a head start. They captured an outsized share of local patients and at the same time attracted hosts of others from the Deep South and from Latin American countries. Ochsner's dreams came true.

By the late 1930s, with medicine's golden age well begun, specialists were taking over a majority of patients from the generalists, the family practitioners. As a logical consequence, many specialists were forming group practices, or clinics where sick people could find under one roof whatever types of care they needed. Some of the clinics became identified in the public mind with good results, and patients were streaming to such places as the Mayo Clinic in Minnesota, the Ford Hospital in Detroit, the Crile (later Cleveland) Clinic in Ohio, and the Lahey Clinic in Boston. Solo practitioners resisted as well as they could—for example, by mounting an unsuccessful attempt to have the American Medical Association rule that group practice is unethical. The resistance was especially strong in New Orleans, where the proliferation of clinics had not yet begun and a large majority of the medical community maintained separate practices. The only clinic in town was too small to be a threat.

It was inevitable, however, that in a metropolis where two medical schools and several hospitals were turning out trained doctors, somebody sooner or later would disregard the sentiments of the establishment and initiate a group practice. When one did come, bearing Ochsner's name, it fulfilled the worst fears of the standpatters.[1]

Nobody realized it at the time, but the first step toward the organization of the Ochsner Clinic was taken in 1938, when Ochsner enlisted Guy Alvin Caldwell as professor of orthopedics at Tulane. He had been impressed by Caldwell's work in Shreveport, Louisiana, where the surgeon was in private practice and doing much of the surgery at the Shriners' hospital for crippled children. A native of Alcorn County, Mississippi, Caldwell graduated from the Columbia University College of Physicians and Surgeons. He was an innovator in the development, after World War I, of surgical methods for repairs that permitted crippled children to run and play. He and Ochsner became friends as well as faculty colleagues.

Caldwell's proficiency as a surgeon was unquestioned, and he also had shown, in the army and later, a flair for medical administration. He believed in the concept of group practice and had explored the possibilities of forming a clinic at Shreveport, giving up the idea because he concluded that suitable doctors were not available. In New Orleans he became convinced that the time was ripe for a clinic, and he began talking about it with Dean H. Echols, Tulane's neurosurgeon.

Even before Caldwell moved to New Orleans, Ochsner had discussed the advantages of a clinic with Echols, Mims Gage, and others. "He

1. John Wilds, *Ochsner's: An Informal History of the South's Largest Private Medical Center* (Baton Rouge, 1985), *passim*.

would say sooner or later we've got to do it," Echols recalled, "in order that 'the faculty isn't running all over town with their private patients. We've got to get a group together so that we can refer patients back and forth and know that they will see competent people.'" Echols concluded, "Dr. Ochsner was dreaming about it before Dr. Caldwell came to town. But Dr. Caldwell was the one who put it into words and said, 'Let's do it now.'" When Caldwell asked Echols whether Ochsner would look favorably upon the idea, Echols was able to give assurance that indeed he would.

When Caldwell brought up the subject, Echols related, "Dr. Ochsner, with all his tremendous enthusiasm, said, 'Guy, that's what I've been dreaming about. We've got to do it. Why don't you keep working on it?'"[2]

The originators saw the Clinic as a project involving only members of the Tulane faculty. Although the sequence in which they approached others is not documented, it is probable that the first man enlisted was Francis E. LeJeune, otolaryngologist. Not only did LeJeune have a busy New Orleans practice, he also was making a national reputation and was destined to win nearly all the honors that his specialty has to offer. "Duke" LeJeune was born at Thibodaux, Louisiana, and as a child lived in Mexico and Puerto Rico. He was a graduate of the Tulane medical school.

The next surgeon to be asked into the fold was Edgar Burns, urologist, already on the road toward the presidency of specialty societies and toward winning coveted medals. Born at Maud, Alabama, Burns obtained his doctor of medicine degree at Northwestern University and trained at the University of Tennessee. He qualified in every way for the elite group that was in the making.

Burns told Ochsner and Caldwell that he would join up only if the Clinic included his friend Curtis Hartman Tyrone, gynecologist and obstetrician. Unlike the other four, Tyrone had no aspirations for professional standing outside the New Orleans area in which he practiced, and he took little or no part in the activities of national societies. But having inherited much of Jeff Miller's practice, he was one of the busiest doctors in New Orleans, drawing many of his devoted patients from exclusive Uptown circles. He was an obvious asset. Tyrone was born at Prentiss, Mississippi. He started studying medicine at the University of Mississippi and obtained his M.D. at Tulane.

2. Dean H. Echols, interview, 1977.

The five surgeons were rebuffed when they asked John Herr Musser to come in as principal internist, a post they regarded as important to the functions of a well-rounded clinic. Musser complained of high blood pressure and pleaded that he was not physically up to the demands of the job, although he did agree to serve as a consultant.

From the start the organizers envisioned the Clinic as an affiliate or adjunct of the Tulane medical faculty. But when Ochsner presented such a proposal to Esmond Phelps, president of the board of administrators of the Tulane Educational Fund, and to C. C. Bass, medical school dean, he found them opposed to the idea. "They believed it would create discord and jealousy among the faculty members not included in the group, and probably would be criticized by the school's alumni in the surrounding area," Caldwell explained. Phelps and Bass offered no objections if the five formed a private clinic, and both agreed that the participants could stay on the faculty. "We can have our cake and eat it, too," Phelps commented.

The medical economics in the late years of the Great Depression precluded any likelihood that the five surgeons would be able to launch a clinic with their own resources. They approached several wealthy New Orleanians, only to discover that there was no sentiment at all in favor of supporting a private, fee-for-service group practice on a philanthropic basis. Such gifts would not be tax deductible. Nor was there a positive response from bankers who were asked about loans. From a hardheaded business standpoint, the prospects of a clinic did not justify the risk.

Then the combined power of Ochsner and Caldwell came through. One of Caldwell's orthopedic patients was Mrs. Rudolf S. Hecht, wife of the chairman of the board of Hibernia National Bank. Rudolf Hecht was a driving force in a campaign to promote New Orleans as an international trade center. In a house call on Mrs. Hecht, Caldwell had the opportunity to tell her husband about the plans for a clinic, and to arrange a luncheon meeting between the banker and Ochsner. Ochsner was at his eloquent best:

> "Mr. Hecht," I said, "here we are at the gateway to Latin America. I know the Latins well because, since I have been at Tulane, we have had a lot of Latin American students. I have gone down there myself, and I have learned about them. The Latins are more sensitive than we; their family life is very close, for instance. When a patient comes from Latin America, the whole family comes along.

They are very sensitive. If we could have an institution here such as the one we are talking about, I think we could attract Latins.

Mr. Hecht listened, and then he said, "This is good; this is good for New Orleans, it's good for Louisiana, it's good for the South and good for the United States."

I said, "Yes, Mr. Hecht, but we have no equity."

"Oh," he said, "but you have your reputation."

And Hecht arranged for the Hibernia Bank to lend the partners up to half a million dollars on their signatures alone.

"If it had not been for Mr. Hecht, this clinic never would have been," Ochsner emphasized. "He took a chance. He is entirely responsible for the organization."[3]

Ochsner's predominance in the group never was challenged. "The others were successful surgeons," explained Merrill O. Hines. "Nonetheless, they were glad to hitch their wagons to his star."[4] Ochsner's years of hard work at Tulane were bringing national recognition, and in New Orleans he was enjoying prominence such as only Matas had known before him. When it came to naming the new partnership, Ochsner suggested New Orleans Clinic and Southern Clinic. Crescent City Clinic was another title that was considered. When Ochsner was off attending a meeting in Ogden, Utah, the other four acted. "The baby has a name, the Ochsner Clinic," they told him by telegram. "No matter what we named it, the public was going to refer to it as the Ochsner Clinic," Caldwell said. He noted that other clinics also bore the names of their chief surgeons, Mayo and Lahey, for instance.

When word of the plans came out, the medical community reacted angrily. On the night of Holy Thursday, April 13, 1941, a messenger appeared on the doorstep of each of the founders. He bore a small leather sack containing thirty dimes, with a note: "To help pay for your Clinic. From the Physicians, Surgeons and Dentists of New Orleans." The senders who equated themselves with Jesus Christ probably did not consider the anxiety their stunt would cause among the children of the recipients. The "Judases" themselves shrugged off the incident.[5] Years later, when the Clinic was a major success, they chuckled over the memory. The outburst of hostility was a continuation of anti-Ochsner sentiment that

3. AO Recollection, History of Clinic.
4. Hines, interview, 1985.
5. Wilds, *Ochsner's*, 30.

had been festering in some quarters since the surgeon moved to New Orleans.

Inevitably, he ran afoul of the clique that controlled the Orleans Parish Medical Society. It was a time when the society brandished a big club as a de facto arbiter in local medical affairs and held a tight rein on the activities of its members. An example had occurred in 1933: three doctors were censured, and even threatened with expulsion, because they were members of the Charity Hospital board of administrators that planned to expand the hospital and provide some beds for private, paying patients. There was some opposition to the high-handed action by the society. John Signorelli said it was "absolutely reprehensible" to go on record "as intimidating the membership from expressing an opinion." Erasmus D. Fenner said he was against the society telling members that they "shall keep their mouths shut and forego their privileges as citizens of this state, or be expelled." But Emmett L. Irwin, chairman of the judiciary committee, said the committee believed the three doctors "assumed an attitude antagonistic to the best good of the society and the membership at large." The recommendation for censure was adopted.[6]

L. Sidney Charbonnet, Jr., who had trained under Ochsner at Tulane and Charity Hospital and was devoted to the chief, found out how vehement the anti-Ochsner feeling was when he attended a caucus at Hotel Dieu. On the agenda was a discussion of the next officers of the parish society. "I was relatively young in the profession," Charbonnet related. "They were planning to make me historian. Then a discussion about Dr. Ochsner came up. I got up and said, 'Gentlemen, I can't concur in what is going on. Do you realize that nothing we do is going to impede his progress? I am saying this because of my knowledge of this man. Why not ask him to be on our side?'

"My coat was being pulled down from both sides by friends between whom I had been sitting. 'Rather than oppose him,' I continued, 'I think we'd get much further . . .' I was pulled down and a friend said, 'You are ruined.' I wasn't elected historian at that meeting." Eventually, after many years, Charbonnet became president of the society.

Ochsner was not always on the unpopular side on issues that divided the medical community. There was the occasion when Sister Celestine, administrator of Hotel Dieu, wanted to install a classification system for surgeons on the staff. Surgeons would be graded on the basis of their

6. John Wilds, *Crises, Clashes, and Cures* (New Orleans, 1978), 112–13.

training, ability, and experience, and would be allowed to do only procedures for which they were certified as qualified. There was opposition from some members of the staff who contended that anyone who had earned a doctor of medicine degree should perform any operation that he felt was within his capability. Hot words were exchanged in a debate at a meeting of medical society members. Although Ochsner rarely operated at Hotel Dieu, he learned of the controversy and was present for the discussion. As those present were about to vote on the question, he asked for the floor.

"Our primary motive is the care of the sick," he said. "We doctors are a group who have had various degrees of training. In surgery, in particular, some doctors have an advantage over others in handling operative situations. Here we have the administrator of a hospital trying to protect its surgical patients from falling into the hands of incompetent doctors. How can any organized group of doctors possibly condemn this?" Charbonnet recalled that there was prolonged applause. The majority of those present voted in favor of the plan, which was put into effect by Hotel Dieu.[7]

The reaction to Ochsner not always was so favorable, and Charbonnet attributed some of the jealousy felt by many parish society members to the publicity that Ochsner was receiving. Since he was busy presenting papers at meetings and occasionally performing surgery that resulted in headlines, his name appeared in print and was heard on the radio. He undoubtedly was prominent in the minds of the publicity committeemen when in 1940 they sent a letter to society members decrying "a deluge of articles in the daily papers. Many of these are contrary to the policy of organized medicine." Although not identifying Ochsner by name, the committee said stories about doctors attending out-of-town meetings and reading papers "are a detriment to organized medicine in that they are giving certain members undue publicity, and lead the lay public to regard them as views of organized medicine." Committeemen wanted any publicity to be given to the newspapers through the society's publicity committee.

In 1947 the judiciary committee presented what would have been a virtual news blackout, condemning the American Medical Association for sending out releases on articles appearing in AMA publications, and even proposing to ban the publication of the names of doctors elected to

7. Charbonnet, interview, August 12, 1979.

office in medical societies. The suggestion was summarily rejected by the society. In 1972 the society adopted a publicity code that recognizes the modern reality that medicine need not be practiced under a veil of secrecy.[8]

Ochsner's response to the enmity toward himself and the Clinic was a shrug. He went his way, aware of the feeling but not dismayed by it. He tried not to wave any red flags, but he did not back away from conflicts. He was circumspect about appearing to court publicity, yet remained accessible to news reporters and responsive to their questions. Perhaps he would have been more sensitive to the prevailing sentiments if he and the Clinic had depended upon referrals from local practitioners. As it stood, referrals would not be forthcoming.

No matter how they regarded Ochsner and the Clinic, the powers in the parish medical society could not afford to be too arbitrary or arrogant. Ochsner was not without friends, and in the organization of the Clinic he acquired some allies with power. In the year that the Clinic opened, Edgar Burns was president of the society. In time, doctors in the growing Clinic became a sizable bloc of the society membership. The only elective office Ochsner ever held was that of librarian. But in his late years the society recognized his accomplishments by making him an honorary life member. Ochsner once explained that he never was much interested in holding office in such politicoeconomic medical organizations as the AMA or the state or parish societies.

Once the financing was arranged, the five partners raced ahead with their plans. One of their early decisions was to share and share alike in the matter of salaries and any other monetary returns from the Clinic. They had been informed about groups that fell apart in disputes over income, and were resolved not to dig that trap for themselves. Ochsner's only advantage was that he was allowed to continue to receive his salary as a Tulane professor. The others carried on their duties as teachers on Tulane's clinical, or unpaid, faculty. Ochsner's willingness to accept the even-pay arrangement was lasting proof that he did not practice surgery to get rich. He was forty-five years old at the time and coming into the most productive period of his career, with almost unlimited prospects for earning; yet he was content to toss his fees into a common pot because he believed group practice was good medicine. The highest salary ever given

8. Wilds, *Crises, Clashes, and Cures,* 114–18.

to a founding partner was $42,500 a year, on which the income taxes were paid by the Clinic.

Early in the organizational phase, J. Blanc Monroe was retained as attorney, and the Clinic was fashioned according to his ideas. On May 2, 1941, the Ochsner Clinic Associates was formed as a partnership to conduct a group practice. At the same time, the Ochsner Clinic, Inc., was incorporated as a property-owning business. Ochsner was elected president of the corporation, which was set up as the vehicle for owning office space to be leased to the associates and acquiring the needed medical equipment and furniture, which also would be rented to the associates. On May 3, using funds borrowed from the Hibernia on the signatures of the partners, the corporation bought for a total of $101,000 the five-story Physicians and Surgeons Building at the corner of Prytania and Aline streets. The price included two residences in the same block that would provide extra space. Conversion of the Physicians and Surgeons Building into a fully equipped clinic facility soon began. The building was directly across Prytania Street from what was then the main entrance to Touro Infirmary. As members of the Tulane faculty, Ochsner and the others had staff privileges at Touro and could send their patients there.[9]

In later years it was suggested that selection of a site so close to Touro, then by far the leading hospital in New Orleans, with a staff that included successful and highly regarded doctors, may have been interpreted as a flaunting gesture. It was not intended to be. An effort to acquire facilities on St. Charles Avenue was blocked by a zoning dispute, and the Physicians and Surgeons Building became the most logical choice.

No matter where the Clinic set up shop, it would have met a chilly reception from the medical community. There was reason for the city's physicians and surgeons to be concerned. The traditional system of delivering health care was being challenged, and by a formidable interloper. The most effective way of striking back was to try to steer patients away from the Clinic. As a result, referrals to the participating specialists from local doctors ceased. Caldwell felt the impact more than the others because he had been practicing in New Orleans for less than four years, not enough time to build up a long patient list. Practitioners had been impressed by his competence and had sent increasing numbers of patients with bone problems to him, but once the Clinic was in business, local

9. Wilds, *Ochsner's*, 33.

referrals fell to nothing. The other four began with pools of patients to draw from and were less affected by the local boycott. But they, too, got no more business from New Orleans doctors who previously had recommended them. Fortunately for the partners, word soon got around about a new facility where almost any kind of illness could be treated, and local people began coming in on their own, without referral. Almost from the beginning the volume was swelled by people from other parts of the South and from Latin America who were attracted by the reputations of Ochsner and the others.

Painters and carpenters were in the final stages of refurbishing the interior of the Physicians and Surgeons Building when the Japanese bombed Pearl Harbor. Within months as many as one-quarter of New Orleans practitioners were called into war service. Ochsner and the other four partners were too old to be summoned and were left to help care for the civilian population, which had grown with the influx of workers at shipyards and other war plants.

In a way the Clinic exacerbated the doctor shortage because so many of its patients came from out of town. New Orleans hospitals had nowhere near enough beds to meet the needs, and but for the fact that Touro Infirmary made available a share of its 424 beds for the patients of the Tulane medical faculty, the Clinic's staff would have had no place to turn. Even at Touro, there was evidence of anti-Clinic feelings. On the name tags posted on room doors, the occupants would not be identified as patients of the Ochsner Clinic. Instead they were listed as patients of Tyrone, or LeJeune, or one of the other staff members.

The war years tested Ochsner's stamina. He turned down an army commission and assignment as chief of the subdivision of surgery in the professional service division of the surgeon general's office. The job would have been simple in comparison with the responsibilities that he chose to take on, namely, keeping the surgery department at Tulane in action with a depleted staff and, at the same time, doing most of the general surgery for the Clinic.

Perhaps bothered because he did not join the armed services, Ochsner committed himself to serving on a commission that advised the surgeon general. The assignment meant that he had to fly to Washington about every ten days for day-long meetings. The airlines used the lumbering but dependable DC-3 prop planes. A sort of routine developed. Ochsner would leave New Orleans in the afternoon, arriving at Washington in the evening. The advisors would meet the next day for several hours, then he would take off for New Orleans about 9 P.M., reach home around 3 A.M., sleep a couple of hours, and head for the hospital. Sometimes he would be busy until midnight.[10] For fifteen years after the war, Ochsner was a consultant to the surgeon general of the U.S. Air Force, once making a round-the-world trip to inspect the service's medical installations.

Ochsner was not the only busy partner in the Clinic. The others also had their hands full. Patients converged in numbers well beyond expectations on the up-to-date, well-equipped facility that was strategically situated in a medical crossroads. Curtis Tyrone recalled that, in the entire year of 1943, he did not have time to go beyond the city limits of New Orleans, not even to cross the Mississippi River to Algiers. The first months were lean financially for the founders, who were up to their necks in debt. They had to wait until collections finally began to mount up before they could declare a payday for themselves. Time would prove that they had chosen a promising moment for getting started. The golden age of medicine had to be financed, and the flow of dollars already was beginning.

The early success of the Clinic encouraged the founders to think not only about the direct care of patients, but about moving into the realms of research, education, and charity. A prod came from Dean Echols, the "sixth founder," who was not invited to be a partner at the start but who identified himself with the Clinic from the first day. On his own, without consulting anybody in advance, Echols went off to Rochester to study the organization and activities of the Mayo Clinic, a household name in the United States. He came back convinced that the Ochsner Clinic would not survive and prosper unless it emulated Mayo by setting up programs for training interns and residents and for engaging in scientific projects aimed at adding to medical knowledge. Echols outlined his thoughts to J. Blanc Monroe. The Clinic attorney did not respond immediately, but he eventually drew up the organizational framework for the Alton Ochsner Medical Foundation, which was launched on January 15, 1944.[11]

The Foundation owes its existence to the generosity of the founders. They dissolved the Ochsner Clinic, Inc., and contributed its assets of slightly less than $300,000 to the nonprofit organization. Each also put up $4,300 in cash and collectively donated $128,500 in notes owed to them by the Ochsner Clinic, Inc. The Foundation thus became the landlord for the Clinic, as it remains today. Echols became director of educa-

10. AO, interview, December 9, 1977.
11. Wilds, Ochsner's, 61–62.

tion for the first class of medical school graduates brought in as fellows. A modest start in research was made with the hiring of three scientists, whose projects were the first of a series that has been continued in all the years of the Foundation's existence. Through the Foundation, the partners subsidized ten beds at Touro Infirmary, these to be occupied by nonpaying patients from all over the South who would be treated by the partners and other Clinic staff members as part of a charitable and training program.[12]

Ochsner was elected the first president of the Foundation. LeJeune and Caldwell were vice-presidents, Burns treasurer, and Tyrone secretary. The five served on a seven-member board of trustees. Monroe was the sixth member, and the seventh was Theodore Brent, a shipping company president who donated liberally to the Foundation and upon his death left the institution's first major legacy, more than a million dollars. Brent House, the patient hotel and office building on the present Ochsner campus, bears his name.

The end of the war brought an opportunity to enlarge the medical staff. Mike DeBakey and Mims Gage returned, and a number of promising young doctors were hired from the ranks of those discharged from the service. Yet the Clinic was close to being strangled by a shortage of hospital beds in New Orleans. Repeatedly, patients from out of town who needed operations had to go home without treatment because Ochsner's surgeons could obtain no rooms for them. Antipathy of the medical community closed most hospitals to Clinic patients.

Only Touro could be depended upon to make beds available, and even there the share was limited. The institution was established through the generosity of the Jewish philanthropist Judah Touro and is administered by a board of trustees made up of Jewish members, but the staff always has included more non-Jewish than Jewish doctors. In the Clinic's time of need, Touro's trustees were friendly and allotted as many beds as Ochsner could have expected under the circumstances. Many of the staff, however, remained inimical.

In 1942, with the Clinic already unpopular in the medical community, Tyrone made what he conceded to be an unfortunate remark that increased the tension. When an operating-room nurse at Touro was slow in providing an instrument called for by Tyrone, the impatient surgeon said he would bet that it would have been at hand if one of the Jewish doctors

12. *Ibid.,* 64–65.

wanted it. A petition signed by some of the staff suggested that Tyrone's privileges be canceled. Eldon Lazarus, president of the trustees, lectured Tyrone at length about making the anti-Semitic comment. "I was in a hell of a fix," Tyrone recalled. "The other four men in our organization [the Ochsner Clinic] couldn't help me do anything about it. They were ready to kick me off the Clinic staff." He feared he might be shut out of other New Orleans hospitals as well. Rabbi Emil W. Leipziger of the Touro Synagogue interceded to ask that animosities be forgotten.[13] Two years later Tyrone was elected to the Touro executive medical committee, and when the hospital considered establishing a department of gynecology, Lazarus said there was only one man who could head the department properly, "and that is Curtis Tyrone."

The wounds were healed, to the relief of Ochsner and the other Clinic partners. In subsequent years the Touro board negotiated on several occasions with the Ochsner Clinic over the proposed establishment of a Touro-Ochsner hospital. One of the reasons why the plan fell through was the opposition of the Touro medical staff.

Bigotry had little place in Ochsner's outgoing personality, and whatever biases he did have were lightly worn. For example, somehow or other he developed a notion that although Jews are fine artists, accomplished musicians, and capable diagnostic physicians, they do not make good surgeons because they do not respond well to operating-room crises. Yet he conceded that he had known some first-rate Jewish surgeons, and from the beginning the Clinic staff, which he helped to choose, included Jewish doctors as well as Catholics, Protestants, and adherents of other religions. Similarly, Ochsner's relationships with the Roman Catholic hierarchy in New Orleans were cordial, although son Akky remembered as a boy hearing his father make critical remarks about Catholic practices. Akky said the Ochsner forebears were Catholics when they came to the United States, but dropped out and turned to the Presbyterian faith. Alton had occasion during his long years to welcome both a Catholic and a Jewish daughter-in-law into the family circle. (On the other hand, every one of his children would have known better than to bring home a *Communist* mate.)

The hostility of some practitioners and of some members of the Tulane faculty was partly responsible for the inability of the partners to work out a cooperative arrangement with Tulane, Touro, or both for building new hospital facilities. Finally the Ochsner group reluctantly decided to go it

13. Curtis H. Tyrone, interview, May 24, 1977.

alone, only to run into more opposition. After the war the government, no longer needing two military hospitals in the New Orleans area, made them available for civilian use. Ochsner and his associates bid on the facilities at the LaGarde General Hospital on the New Orleans lake front, but lost out to a group of returning veterans headed by Charles B. Odom, General George S. Patton's staff surgeon.

Next, the partners went after the sprawling post hospital at Camp Plauché, on the bank of the Mississippi River in Jefferson Parish. Once again, Odom's group intervened, topping Ochsner's offer and claiming that the Plauché equipment was needed at their newly named Lakeshore Hospital. However, in the face of public and newspaper support for Ochsner, Odom withdrew his bid, and the Ochsner Foundation Hospital was opened on January 21, 1947.[14] It was there that Ochsner, upon seeing the surgical facilities for the first time, remarked that he could operate all day, every day. And it was there that he sometimes would pick up a mop and help clean an operating room for the next case.

The Camp Plauché hospital, housed in fifty-three one-story frame buildings and known to the Ochsner staff as Splinter Village, was obviously a temporary solution. By the time it was in use, a search already had begun for a permanent hospital site. After five years the roles of the founders had been established. Caldwell, with the best brain for administrative affairs and the smallest patient load, was medical director of the Clinic and chief planner for the Foundation. He and the attorney Monroe were the designers for the structure of the Ochsner institutions. Burns involved himself in business affairs. LeJeune and Tyrone were less concerned with day-by-day executive direction of the Clinic and Foundation.

Ochsner set his own course. "He was the neon light" that attracted patients, explained Merrill Hines. In a way, he also was the pivot around which the group revolved. His relationship with each of the others was based on their respect for him and on his warmth and charm. He was the peacemaker who on occasion mediated among clashing personalities. The rule was that there would be no three-to-two votes. All conflicts had to be settled behind closed doors, and the outside world faced with unanimity. Ochsner was a valuable asset in representing the Clinic or Foundation in public, and cheerfully did his share and more of the glad-handing that is needed for goodwill purposes. Of course, in his active

14. Wilds, *Ochsner's*, 73–75.

years he was a major source of the Clinic's revenue from patient fees.

He took part in making important decisions but never bothered himself with minutiae. Sometimes the others grumbled about his frequent absences while he was attending meetings or presenting papers. And there were occasions when members of the surgery staff interrupted Clinic schedules while they covered his Tulane classes. When objections were raised to using Clinic funds to pay for his frequent trips to Latin America, he said he would dig into his own pocket (but apparently never had to do so). He made commitments without consulting others, sometimes with unfortunate results—such as offering a fellowship to an unqualified Latin with connections in high places. Whenever he wished, he arranged to do operations at times that disrupted the hospital surgery schedule. Yet in all of this he never unfairly pressed the fact that it was his name out front.

Caldwell took the lead in the discussions with Touro and Tulane about building a university hospital or the expansion of the Touro facility, only to have his plans wrecked on the anti-Ochsner shoals. On the occasion when the Touro board approved a proposed joint venture, the arrangement was presented to staff doctors and was rejected by unanimous vote. At the time members of the Touro staff and Tulane faculty doctors who were not connected with Ochsner referred patients to each other, excluding Ochsner men. Opposition of some of the Tulane faculty figured in failed negotiations between Ochsner and the medical school. Talks with the Southern Baptist Hospital and Mercy Hospital also got nowhere.

The trustees of the Alton Ochsner Medical Foundation finally decided to go it alone. Since three-quarters of their patients came from outside the New Orleans area, the Ochsner doctors planned to sell a new hospital as a regional facility where southerners and Latin Americans could go for treatment not available anywhere else except at America's most famous centers. A list of ninety-six wealthy men in the region was drawn up, and the staff doctors were assigned to call on them for donations.

Now a latent talent possessed by Alton Ochsner emerged. One of the prospects assigned to him was Colonel Thomas H. Barton, chairman of the board of the Lion Oil Company. Ochsner went into Barton's office at El Dorado, Arkansas, and began telling him about the project. Barton listened for a time, then interrupted. "Just a minute, doctor," he said, and called to an associate next door. "Tom, come in here. I want you to meet the best Goddamned salesman I ever met." Ochsner responded, "No,

Colonel. I just have the best product to sell." The company donated $15,000 for the new hospital, and followed with a gift of $15,000 every year until Lion was merged with the Monsanto Company.[15]

On another trip into Arkansas, Ochsner drove through the little town of Crossett and thought, "I've never seen a prettier place." He was surprised to learn it was a mill town. He concluded that the dominant company, the Crossett Lumber Company, "ought to be interested in good medicine." Two weeks later he went to Crossett, telephoned company president Peter F. Watzek, and made an appointment at nine o'clock the next morning. Ochsner told Watzek of the Foundation and its plans. "He listened attentively," Ochsner related. "And he said, 'Doctor, we've never made a donation out of Arkansas, but this appeals to me, and I'm going to recommend it to our board.'"

A few weeks later the company made a $20,000 gift, and for several years followed up with an annual donation of the same amount. There were sequels. Mrs. Watzek suffered a broken arm in an automobile accident in New Orleans and was treated at the hospital for which Ochsner was raising money. Later, Peter Watzek, ill with a kidney ailment, hastened to New Orleans. Edgar Burns, a leading authority on the ailment, performed successful surgery. Watzek told Ochsner, "If you hadn't walked into my office, I'd probably be dead today."[16]

Ochsner had sought the advice of Samuel Zemurray, president of the United Fruit Company, in the effort to work out a deal with Touro and Tulane, and when the fund-raising drive was begun he approached another wealthy New Orleanian, Edgar B. Stern, whose wife, Edith Rosenwald, was a daughter of one of the owners of Sears, Roebuck and Company. "I was very fond of Edgar and Edith," Ochsner explained. "I went to him, and he listened and said, 'I'll give $100,000.' I told him I almost had not gone to him because Touro also was in the middle of a fund-raising campaign and I thought there may be a conflict. 'Oh, we're going to give money to Touro,' Stern said, 'and I don't mind telling you it's only $25,000.'" Ochsner was flabbergasted. "Then Edgar said the reason is that Touro is just another hospital. This is a different institution." The Sterns subsequently contributed another $100,000 to Ochsner.[17]

From the oil millionaire William G. Helis, Jr., a personal friend, Ochsner

15. Alton Ochsner, address, Ochsner Foundation Fellows, August 14, 1971.
16. AO Recollection, Benefactors.
17. Ochsner, address, Ochsner Foundation Fellows, August 14, 1971.

obtained a gift of more than $250,000 to finance X-ray facilities at the new hospital.[18] From the Louisiana and Mississippi industrialist L. O. Crosby, Sr., and his family, Ochsner's efforts produced $300,000—the first installment of bequests that over the years amounted to $6.5 million.

Ochsner's successes underscore his knack for dealing with wealthy people. It bears repeating that, clearly, he was not motivated to make a lot of money for himself. But he liked the comfort and the prestige generated by riches, and was quite willing to exert himself to foster his relationships with millionaires. He had a healthy sense of his personal accomplishments, was not easily awed, and once he was established in his career met people on an equal basis. His demeanor was marked by a lack of pretentiousness. He liked jokes and banter, and made everybody feel comfortable in his company. Of course, he played with strong cards in his hand. His reputation as a healer was well established, and the man does not live who, when illness strikes, does not want to turn to an expert who also is a friend.

For several years he enjoyed dealings with a set of Texas nabobs that went beyond the everyday doctor-patient relationships. Clint W. Murchison, Sid Richardson, and Richardson's nephew, Perry R. Bass, came to the Clinic for checkups and treatment. Murchison and Richardson periodically invited Ochsner to join them in outings at their ranches or hunting and fishing preserves.

Ochsner was recommended to the Texans by David Lide, a Dallas businessman who had been a surgery patient.[19] In 1956 Murchison became ill during a stay on his island in the Bahamas, and he stopped off in New Orleans on his way home to Texas. He developed a liking for Ochsner and for A. Seldon ("Sam") Mann, the internist who was assigned to treat him. Afterward Murchison frequently sent his airplane to pick up Ochsner and Mann and take them to his ranch in Texas or the one in Mexico or to the Koon Kreek Klub, a fishing hangout for wealthy Texans. On one excursion Bass asked Ochsner and Mann to go with him to Fort Worth to see Richardson, who was ill. They persuaded Richardson to fly with them to New Orleans for treatment, and another friendship developed. Sometimes Richardson invited Ochsner to go quail hunting on his island in the Gulf of Mexico.[20]

18. AO Recollection, Friends.
19. AO Recollection, Patients.
20. *Ibid.*

At one freewheeling party at Koon Kreek, H. Peter Kriendler, of the Twenty-One Club in New York, was the first to pass out. The revelers decided to shave off his moustache, and since Ochsner was a surgeon he was elected to wield the razor. Kriendler had a shock when he looked into the mirror next morning, but on every trip to New York, Ochsner received the red carpet treatment at Twenty-One. Another time, Ochsner was disappointed when Murchison joined the others in a drink, although he and Mann had instructed him to lay off. "Tell you what I'll do, Clint," Ochsner said. "If you'll go on the wagon, I will, too." Both abstained for several months, then Murchison, feeling better, released Ochsner from his pledge. Ochsner enjoyed a sociable nip. Once while his mother was visiting, he went to a medical school banquet where the seniors plied the faculty with liquor in the hope of seeing a drunken professor embarrass himself. Ochsner made it through the night without incident, but the next morning Isabel had to explain to his mother that his nausea was the result of food poisoning. During a wartime visit to the Tulane hospital unit at Fort Benning, Georgia, he partook of hospitality and became a little mellow, to the amusement of his friends. But he performed well in a speech that night. With all the excitement life offered him, he did not need a boost from alcohol.

Sid Richardson had an ideal, if not exactly sporting, arrangement for hunting on his island. A Jeep was fitted with two seats extending forward alongside the headlights. Armed with shotguns, hunters occupied the seats. The driver would approach a clump of bushes and gun the engine, flushing birds out at point-blank range. Even with this advantage, Ochsner's shooting was not spectacular. When Richardson was in Ochsner hospital, Isabel joined Alton in a visit with him. She told Richardson how much Alton enjoyed the expeditions and asked whether her husband was a good shot. "Oh," replied the patient, "he shoots good, but he doesn't hit good."

After Murchison's first visit to the Clinic, Ochsner drove him to the airport in his aging Buick. Soon thereafter Murchison sent him a new Cadillac, the first of a series provided by the millionaire. During the period when he was frequently undergoing treatment in the Ochsner Foundation Hospital, Murchison was a principal in a mammoth real estate development. He and associates bought 30,000 acres in eastern New Orleans, about one-third of the city's total land area. What was mostly a swamp has been turned into residential, industrial, and commercial neighborhoods. The Richardson estate became the foundation upon which Perry Bass and his sons built one of the largest family fortunes in the United States.

Other wealthy Texans became friends and patients of Ochsner's. An association with Mr. and Mrs. Robert L. Slaughter of Fort Worth and San Antonio began when the surgeon removed a small keratotic (nonmalignant) lesion from Mrs. Slaughter's hand. Slaughter told Ochsner he had been kind, and gave $18,000 to the Foundation, his first of a number of gifts. Once Ochsner flew to Colorado Springs in an ambulance plane and escorted Slaughter to New Orleans for treatment of a severe leg infection, and again he made a flight in an ambulance plane to West Texas and took his wealthy patient to New Orleans after a heart attack. Slaughter also presented Cadillacs to Ochsner.[21]

For once, Ochsner's luck deserted him in the disposal of an inheritance that he had hoped to obtain for the Foundation. He and Isabel were long-time friends and neighbors of Ike T. and Posey Rea, whose encouragement had helped persuade him to take the risk of organizing the Clinic. The childless couple moved to Memphis, where more than once Ochsner was summoned because Rea appeared about to succumb to a kidney ailment. During one of the episodes Mrs. Rea told the surgeon that her husband wanted her to have the use of their money while she was alive, but upon her death their considerable wealth would go to the Foundation. She told Ochsner to have attorney Monroe draw up the legal documents to put the plan into effect. Ike Rea's immediate crisis passed. Ochsner, upon his return to New Orleans, called Monroe and found the latter was away on vacation. "I felt there was no urgency about it and did nothing about it," he related. Shortly afterward, Mrs. Rea died unexpectedly of a cerebral hemorrhage. Rea was in a coma at the time and died two weeks later without knowing of his wife's death. The estate went to Rea's sister.[22]

On another occasion, Ochsner's persistence kept the Foundation from losing a gift that was crucial to the construction of the present Ochsner Hospital. It was the $300,000 promised by the Crosby family, as noted earlier the first segment of the most generous support the Foundation ever has received from a single source. The problem that threatened this source developed from the Clinic's remaining in the building at Prytania and Aline after the first Ochsner hospital moved out alongside the Huey P. Long Bridge, five miles away. Ochsner made an appointment for R.

21. AO Recollection, Colleagues.
22. AO Recollection, Patients.

Howell Crosby, L. O. Crosby's eldest son, to see internist Thomas Findley at the Clinic at two o'clock. Crosby appeared on time, but Findley was delayed at the hospital. In a few minutes Crosby walked out in a huff, vowing never to return. When Ochsner strode into the Clinic an hour later, he was told by the receptionist, Mrs. Enid Cary, what had happened. "I thought, of course, that this would mean we would get nothing of the Crosby pledge," Ochsner recalled. "It was one of my darkest moments." He telephoned Mrs. Russell Clark, a friend of the Crosbys, and asked her what to do. She told him to face Howell Crosby immediately.

Ochsner hastened to the Pontchartrain Hotel, where Mr. and Mrs. Crosby were staying. He sat for an hour and a half with Mrs. Crosby, awaiting Crosby, who had gone to see another doctor. Ochsner spent an hour mollifying Crosby, who finally said, "Oh, I can't get mad at you." The next morning Findley was on the dot for another appointment, and the Crosby family's long association with the Clinic was solidified.[23]

The early influx of patients from the Gulf South reflected the word-of-mouth spread of the Ochsner Clinic's reputation among the lay public. The campaign for funds for a new hospital that began in 1950 showed that the professor and his group had become no more popular among practitioners in Mississippi, Alabama, Florida, Arkansas, and Texas than they were in the medical community at home. Directors of the drive misjudged the prevailing sentiments and at first planned geographical money-raising committees that included physicians and surgeons. They soon encountered antipathy toward "building up the Ochsner crowd," and afterward centered their efforts on former patients and well-to-do citizens with a history of philanthropy. There were pleasant surprises. Public donations in the metropolitan New Orleans area ran to nearly a million dollars. A few donors were unexpectedly generous.[24] Theodore Brent made a $400,000 gift.

Passage of the Hill-Burton legislation to finance new hospitals made federal funds available, and a million-dollar mortgage cleared the way for groundbreaking on a twenty-one-acre tract at 1514–1516 Jefferson Highway. (The weed-choked plot once had held a small horse or pony stable and a riding oval, and so was dubbed the "Riding Academy" site.) On June 12, 1954, the Ochsner Foundation Hospital, a 250-bed facility, was opened. The total outlay of $6,507,651 paid for a five-story hospital, a two-story nurses' home known as the Libby Dufour Building, and a

23. *Ibid.*
24. Wilds, *Ochsner's,* 120–21.

four-story, eighty-one-room hotel for patients and their families. It was only the beginning.

Murchison and Ochsner's other Texas friends came through with key donations that made possible the addition in 1963 of a building for the Clinic, which had remained in the original Prytania Street structure, three miles from the new hospital. Murchison wanted to provide the Foundation with a revenue-producing property that would help support activities for years to come. For this purpose he and his associates bought the Charles Town horse racetrack in West Virginia, not far from Washington. A short while afterward, Ochsner received a telephone call from Murchison's attorney, who said a syndicate had offered half a million dollars for the track. Ochsner asked whether Murchison favored the sale, and was told that he was in Mexico and unavailable for consultation. The attorney said the price was good, and recommended acceptance. The Foundation trustees, who were not thrilled by the idea of owning a track where betting was conducted, agreed to the transaction. Murchison was miffed, and his relations with Ochsner cooled.

In 1981 Ochsner had lived to see the Riding Academy site, almost hidden in the undergrowth, transformed into a campus dominated by an eleven-story building that houses a 550-bed hospital and office facilities for more than two hundred doctors on the Clinic staff and two hundred interns and residents. Other structures in a facility valued in 1985 at $200 million include the six-story Brent House hotel, a six-level parking garage, and a cluster of smaller buildings used for research activities and for special diagnostic and therapeutic purposes. At one time the sign out front said Ochsner Medical Center, but this later was changed to Ochsner Medical Institutions, which is more descriptive of the vast conglomerate that grew out of a clinic started with only thirteen full-time doctors on the staff. Even Alton Ochsner, with his limitless ambition, could not have asked for more.

By the time of Ochsner's death, the institutions that he inspired had revenues exceeding $250 million a year, yet he had no monetary interest of his own in them to bequeath to his survivors. He had joined the four other founders in providing that the Clinic would be perpetuated as a partnership of the doctors who made up its staff. In 1957 the five founders sold half-interest in the Clinic to thirty-two senior staff members. Each of the five men received just over $120,000 in payment. When he left the partnership in 1972 upon reaching the age limit, Ochsner was paid $165,000 for his last remaining stake.

Ochsner converses with Rudolph Matas, his illustrious predecessor at Tulane.
Courtesy Isabel Ochsner Mann

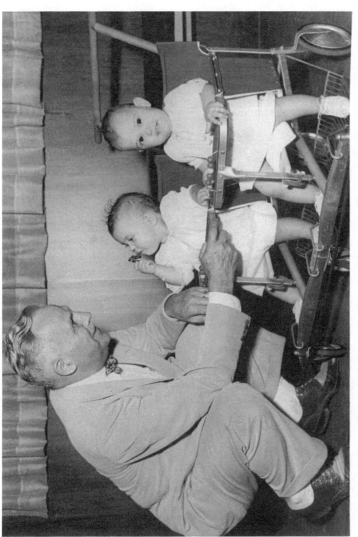

Ohsner admires Carolyn and Catherine, pygopagus Siamese twin infants whom he successfully separated.

Courtesy Ochsner Medical Foundation

Although he was never happier than when doing surgery, Ochsner devoted much time and energy to research.

Courtesy Alton Ochsner

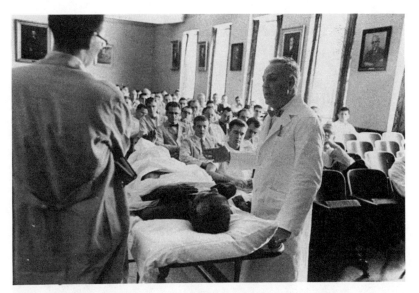

Ochsner frequently said he wanted to be remembered as a teacher.
Courtesy Isabel Ochsner Mann

Ochsner receives the *Times-Picayune* Loving Cup, one of his first major civic awards, from Leonard K. Nicholson in 1946.
Courtesy Times-Picayune

The original trustees of the Alton Ochsner Medical Foundation: *seated,* Guy Caldwell, Ochsner, and Edgar Burns; *standing,* Francis LeJeune, Theodore Brent, Blanc Monroe, and Curtis Tyrone.
Courtesy Ochsner Medical Foundation

In a considerably later photo, the five founders of the Ochsner Clinic: Burns, Caldwell, Ochsner, LeJeune, and Tyrone.
Courtesy Ochsner Medical Foundation

San Francisco, 1957: In his years as an advisor to the Air Force surgeon general's office, Ochsner experienced jet flight long before commercial airlines offered it.

Courtesy Isabel Ochsner Mann

At a meeting of the Alton Ochsner Surgical Society in 1960, Ochsner is reunited with his former prize student and colleague Michael DeBakey, *center*. Oscar Creech, occupying Ochsner's old seat as chairman of the department of surgery at Tulane, is on the right.
Courtesy Isabel Ochsner Mann

Ochsner poses with Michael DeBakey (*left*) and his brother Ernest DeBakey.
Courtesy Isabel Ochsner Mann

At the 1961 congress of the International Society of Surgery, in Dublin, Ochsner was chosen to preside over the 1963 congress—much to his chagrin as chairman of the nominating committee.

Photograph by Studio 'J,' courtesy Isabel Ochsner Mann

Alton and Isabel return home from the Dublin meeting.
Courtesy Alton Ochsner

Left to right: Merrill O. Hines, chairman of the Foundation's board of trustees; Arthur Lord Porritt, who spoke at the Foundation hospital in 1975; Frank A. Riddick, Jr., medical director of the Ochsner Clinic; Ochsner.

Photograph courtesy of C. F. Weber Photography, Inc., and Ochsner Medical Foundation

At the groundbreaking for a major expansion of the Ochsner Medical Institutions campus, Merrill Hines, Ochsner, and Richard W. Freeman examine an instrument rather less subtle than a scalpel.

Photograph courtesy of C. F. Weber Photography, Inc., and Ochsner Medical Foundation

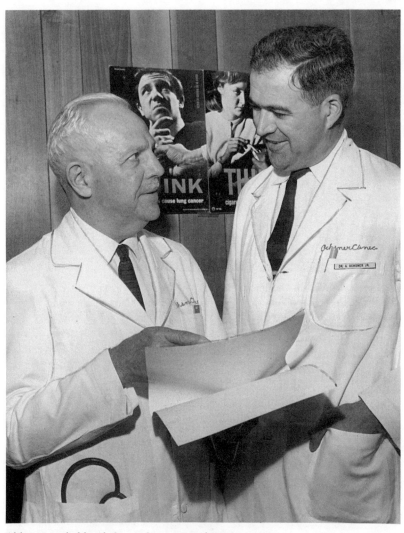

Akky seconded his father in his antismoking campaign.

Photograph by P. H. Guarisco, courtesy Times-Picayune

Ochsner with a celebrity patient, the national Cystic Fibrosis Child, 1976.
Courtesy Ochsner Medical Foundation

A friend and colleague said that Ochsner "looked like a doctor should look."
Photograph by Bauerlein, courtesy Alton Ochsner

By 1980, the year before the principal founder's death, the Foundation's board of trustees was larger than the original staff of the Clinic.
Courtesy Ochsner Medical Foundation

Till the end, Ochsner worked hard and long to cure patients, but one thing he never remedied was the notorious clutter of his office.
Courtesy Isabel Ochsner Mann

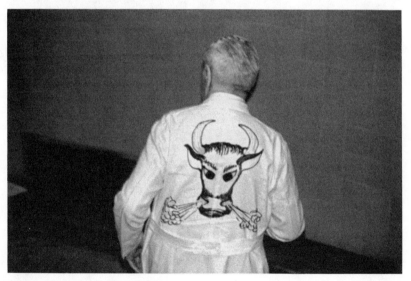

Ochsner as Boss of the Bull Pen.
Photograph by Donald J. Palmisano, courtesy of Ochsner Medical Foundation

Frank Riddick and Foundation president George Porter III, under the gaze of an old friend.

Photograph by Jackson Hill, Southern Lights Studio, courtesy Ochsner Medical Foundation

14 Battling Smoking and Lung Cancer

When Alton Ochsner was a junior in the Washington University medical school, a patient at Barnes Hospital died of carcinoma of the lung. Professor George Dock called in the upper classes to witness the autopsy because, he told them, "You may never see another of these cases in your lifetime."

"Being young and impressionable," Ochsner said, "I was extremely impressed by the rarity of this condition." Seventeen years passed before, in 1936, he observed nine cases in Charity Hospital in a six-month period. "This was an epidemic and there had to be a cause," he reasoned. Upon inquiry he found that all of the patients were men, and all were heavy smokers who had acquired the cigarette habit in World War I. Before the war, relatively few people smoked cigarettes. The epidemiological evidence convinced Ochsner that there is a relationship between smoking and lung cancer. In February, 1939, in a paper published in *Surgery, Gynecology and Obstetrics,* he and Mike DeBakey observed: "In our opinion the increase in smoking with the universal custom of inhaling is probably a responsible factor, as the inhaled smoke, constantly repeated over a long period of time, undoubtedly is a source of chronic irritation to the bronchial mucosa."[1]

By strict scientific standards, they went off half-cocked. The cautious approach would have been to go into the laboratory, do experiments proving beyond reasonable doubt that cancer could be induced in the lung by the presence of tobacco smoke, and then—and only then—report their findings. The only direct evidence available at the time to Ochsner and DeBakey were studies in Germany reporting that the application of tobacco to the tissue of animals would produce malignant tumors. Subsequently, scores of investigations that met scientific requirements backed

1. Alton Ochsner and Michael DeBakey, "Primary Pulmonary Malignancy," *Surgery, Gynecology and Obstetrics,* LXVIII (1939), 433–51.

up the reasoning of Ochsner and his collaborator. Ochsner would live long enough to see cigarette advertising banned from television and radio channels, and every cigarette package bearing a printed warning that smoking can be injurious to health. As it was, however, for much of his career his never-ending campaign against cigarettes remained controversial.

He conducted this campaign on two fronts. On the one hand, he tried to persuade people not to risk lung cancer by smoking. On the other, he persevered—in the face of an appalling number of early fatalities—in developing techniques for lung surgery that would provide palliation and perhaps add years of life for those who were already afflicted. His theory that cigarettes caused cancer was disputed, even ridiculed, by some of his medical peers. Among smokers generally there was a sort of guilty, self-defensive rejection of his thesis, although a decline in cigarette usage did begin. Not surprisingly, he was not hailed as an oracle by the tobacco industry. A request to the Tobacco Institute at Washington for its view of Ochsner for inclusion in this volume brought the reply: "We would have no comment on the old gentleman but appreciate your contacting us."

In New Orleans, the man in the street came to recognize Ochsner as the crusader against smoking more than as the accomplished surgeon. He made smokers feel uncomfortable about their habit, especially before corroborative evidence began to build up. He knew what it was like to have people defiantly light up in his presence. Jokes were staged at his expense. A club raffle was rigged to make him the winner of a store of cigarettes. He went along good-naturedly, but seldom passed an opportunity to get his message across. It was not his nature to be obnoxious, but sometimes he would snatch a cigarette from a companion's lips, or grab a pack and throw it away when he knew he could make such a demonstration without causing resentment.

Some of his colleagues at Tulane or the Clinic avoided smoking in his company and tried to hide their cigarettes when he approached unexpectedly. Hard-bitten Mims Gage would hang out of an open window, even in wintertime, to sneak a smoke, and more than once risked self-destruction to hide a lighted cigarette in his coat pocket when he saw his friend nearby. A dissident on the Clinic staff was Joseph K. Bradford, pulmonary internist, who sometimes argued with Ochsner about his thesis. Bradford continued to puff away if Ochsner came up, but did not light a cigarette in the surgeon's company. One night, at Ochsner's request, Bradford looked in on an elderly woman patient at the Splinter Village hospital.

I was led in and this woman lying in the bed said, "Doctor, have you got a cigarette?" I said, "Yes, ma'am," and she said, "Well, would you give me a cigarette? These damn people in here won't let me smoke. I've been smoking for almost seventy years, and I've smoked almost everything that burns, and I don't want to stop now." I gave her a cigarette. We talked for awhile. I examined her and then looked at her X-ray, and it didn't look tumorous to me. I wrote on the chart: "I do not believe Mrs. Jones has cancer of the lung for the following reasons." At the end I wrote: "If she should have, then tobacco is indeed a slow poison."

That was Saturday night. About five the next morning my telephone rang. "This is Alton Ochsner. I'd like you to come out to the hospital right now." It was still dark. I jumped up, dressed without shaving, didn't have any coffee, and zoomed out there. I located Dr. Ochsner and his entourage and he said, "I want you to make rounds with me." "What did you say?" I asked. "I want you to make rounds with me." He had a lot of patients and to every one, whether they had a gall bladder problem or a gangrenous big toe, he introduced me as, "Dr. Bradford, the great authority on smoking and lung cancer."

He did this all the way down the hospital, and I was getting madder by the minute, and the others were just chuckling away. We got through and he said, "Joe, I appreciate your coming out and making rounds with me this morning." I said, "Well, you know I didn't do this from choice, don't you?" He said, "Yes, but it's good for you." And I said, "Well, if you don't mind I'd like to get some breakfast." As I started off he said, "Try to be a little careful about what you write on people's charts."[2]

Ochsner said he complied with his father's wish that he not smoke until he was twenty-one years old. "On my twenty-first birthday I was emancipated, so I declared my independence by smoking half a pack of cigarettes, and got so sick I promised myself never to smoke again."[3] His sons John and Mims used cigarettes surreptitiously as youths. John used to look forward to the day when he could openly put a package of cigarettes on his desk and have one whenever he wished. By the time he

2. Joseph K. Bradford, interview, November, 1976.
3. AO, interview, December 8–9, 1977.

was grown, he had forgotten about smoking. The story with Sis was different. One night Akky was at a fraternity house. Sis, then a teenager, and her date came in and lighted cigarettes. When Akky got home he went into his parents' bedroom for a chat with Isabel. Alton was snoring. Akky mentioned that he had seen Sis smoking. "Out of a sound sleep Dad sat up and yelled, 'Sis lit a cigarette?' Oh, my God. I thought I had done it. Boy, he had been snoring and he came up in a second." Ochsner handled the situation by putting antismoking literature on Sis's bed so that she could not miss seeing it every night. Eventually, she quit cigarettes.[4]

One doctor who criticized Ochsner's smoking-cancer theory was his long-time friend Evarts Ambrose Graham, professor of surgery at Washington University during Alton's last year there. Warren H. Cole, a classmate of Alton's, told of sitting with Graham and Ochsner at a surgical meeting, apparently in the late 1930s or early 1940s. "Al said, 'Dr. Graham, I believe I have found a possible etiological factor for cancer of the lung,'" Cole related. "Dr. Graham stated, 'That would be quite a discovery, Al. What is it?' Al replied, 'Cigarette smoking.' Dr. Graham flashed back, 'How dumb and how stupid.' Al defended himself by repeating, 'But practically all of the fifty or more cases we just reviewed have that history.' Dr. Graham added, 'But, Al, you forget the importance of coincidence. So has the use of nylon stockings increased.' Since Dr. Graham was his teacher, and considerably older, Al dropped the discussion."

Two facts added significance to this dialogue: Graham in 1933 had performed the first pneumonectomy (the removal of a whole lung) in the United States in treatment of cancer. The patient was still alive at the time of the conversation and, indeed, he outlasted Graham. Also, Graham himself had been a heavy cigarette smoker for some fifty years.

About three years later, Cole said, the three surgeons again were talking together at a meeting.

> Shortly after we sat down, Dr. Graham said, "Al, I'm afraid I owe you an apology." Al said, "What do you mean?" Dr. Graham replied, "You may or may not recall a few years ago that you told me you thought cigarette smoking was the cause of cancer of the lung, and that I pooh-poohed the idea. Well, recently [Ernest L.] Wynder [an associate] and I completed a study of our patients with

4. Alton Ochsner, Jr., interview, June 15, 1977.

cancer of the lung, and, as you said, nearly all of them were heavy cigarette smokers." Al replied, "Thanks, Dr. Graham. Yes, we have continued our studies and the evidence seems more convincing than ever." Dr. Graham seldom apologized to anyone, so I thought it the more significant that he would do so on this occasion.[5]

In late February, 1957, Ochsner received a letter "which simply crushed me." Graham wrote, "Perhaps you have heard that I have recently been a patient in the Barnes Hospital because of a bilateral bronchiogenic carcinoma which sneaked up on me like a thief in the night. I am taking nitrogen mustard and as a result feel like the devil. You know, I think, that I quit smoking more than five years ago but the trouble was that I smoked for fifty years."[6]

Ochsner replied on February 19, "It is a perfectly horrible thing to think that you have bronchiogenic carcinoma, a condition for which you have done so much." He said he was glad Graham was trying nitrogen mustard. "I think we have had more experience with the use of nitrogen mustard than anyone else in the world, at least Merck [the drug house] tells us that we use more of it than anyone else, and we have a tremendous amount of respect for it and we have worked out a technique which works very well."[7] Two weeks later, on March 4, Graham died. Eleven years would pass before lung cancer in another patient would bring the deepest sorrow Ochsner ever experienced.

Three years after Graham showed the way with the first pneumonectomy in this country, Ochsner followed his lead by becoming, on April 15, 1936, the first surgeon to perform the procedure in the Deep South as a means of dealing with a malignant bronchial lesion. The word had spread and the operating area at Touro Infirmary was crowded with curious doctors. By one count it was the tenth pneumonectomy recorded in the world literature. It was an important date in Ochsner's career, because afterward, for as long as he was surgically active, he devoted a considerable part of his operating room efforts to the removal of whole lungs or lobes. If he could not persuade people to eschew cigarettes, at least he could try to salvage something of their lives for them after they paid the price for their indulgence. He never had witnessed a pneumonectomy, and could rely only on his knowledge of anatomy and the published

5. Warren H. Cole to Harkey, November 5, 1976.
6. Evarts Graham to Alton Ochsner, February 5, 1957.
7. Alton Ochsner to Evarts Graham, February 19, 1957.

reports of the few previous operations. Perhaps he telephoned Graham to ask for guidance, although there is no record of such a call. There were questions about the best route for entering the chest, for ligating the hilar structures, and for dealing with the empty space left in the chest.

The first patient was Woodrow Wilson Robertson of Hattiesburg, Mississippi, nineteen years old. Francis LeJeune had determined by bronchoscopy that Robertson had a sarcoma of the bronchus, a subdivision of the trachea that conveys air to and from the lung. The cancer was bleeding, and LeJeune concluded that the only hope lay in pneumonectomy. Ochsner proceeded cautiously until at last he got the lung out and sent it to the pathologist. He was closing the bronchial stump when the report came back from the laboratory: there was no cancer in the specimen. LeJeune, who was one of the spectators, explained that the lesion was situated near the bifurcation, the place where the trachea divides into the bronchi. Ochsner reopened the wound and took out an additional length of the bronchus. This is where the cancer was. The first case was one of the most successful in Ochsner's lengthy series. Robertson lived into old age, and occasionally he communicated with the surgeon. Ochsner said the outcome emboldened him to go on. "I am sure if he had succumbed, I would not have had the heart to have done any more," he confessed.[8]

Even so, he surely had doubts as he continued. Only two of his first seven patients left the hospital alive. It must be remembered that these came to him as desperate cases. Ochsner and DeBakey were not gambling with lives: the patients were doomed anyway unless surgery could save them. A more positive view, the one taken by the eternally optimistic Ochsner, was that two humans had been pulled back from the brink of early graves with a procedure that had promise of greater success once the technique could be perfected.

Ochsner's detractors did not fail to spread the word that the deaths proved he was venturing into territory where he had no business. Thomas E. Weiss was doing autopsies at Touro. He remembers critical surgeons coming to him making such remarks as, "I understand Dr. Ochsner is going to do another lung procedure. Let me know when the patient arrives in your department [the autopsy room] so that I can watch the post [mortem]." One critic said Ochsner "knew damn well that he was going to kill the patient."

8. AO Recollection, Smoking.

"I don't think they saw the total picture," Weiss commented. "He knew these people were up against a fatal disease and were going to die. He felt that with his skill as a surgeon and with the team he had to back him up—Drs. Gage and DeBakey and others—he could get in and do something. He saw this tumor as a monster, and if he could get his knife in between the monster and the patient he could cure him." Weiss said Ochsner was well aware of the criticism but accepted it without recriminations. "He had tremendous feeling for his patients, which I was most impressed by. He had the strength of his conviction that he had to go ahead. He seemed to sense the tremendous responsibility that was his." Weiss added, "No one else had been brave enough to play around in the chest in those days." He noted that some of the surgeons who were the most vocal in condemning Ochsner for operating later did pneumonectomies themselves, using techniques that Ochsner had perfected with his pioneering work.[9]

Ochsner became a widely recognized authority on lung cancer: at one time, he had treated more cases than anybody else in the world. "It was a new disease and there were few people treating it, and many cases were referred to me." During World War II he did as many as four lung operations in a day. He always lamented that lung cancer was an affliction that developed in his own lifetime.

His experience brought dividends. By the time of his retirement from the operating room, he was helping as many as three-fourths of the patients who were deemed candidates for pneumonectomy. For years, however, he stubbornly insisted that the only effective treatment was removal of the entire affected lung and excision of the mediastinal nodes. He condemned the method of R. H. Overholt of Boston, who advocated less radical procedures such as the excision of a lung lobe or even only part of a lobe. "I was very critical of them [Overholt and his associates] because I felt they were denying their patients the best chance of a cure, and I said so openly," Ochsner related.

Michael B. Shimkin of the National Cancer Institute asked if Ochsner would submit the results of his cases for comparison with Overholt's data. "It was very humiliating for me to learn that the five-year survival rate was almost identical in the two series," Ochsner admitted, "ours being no better than the Overholt series. The only difference was that

9. Weiss, interview, August 15, 1979.

theirs had less morbidity because they had more functioning lung left."
Ochsner publicly conceded that he had been wrong, and afterward used
Overholt's approach when it seemed workable.[10]

In the first pneumonectomies, Ochsner collapsed the affected lung (by
injecting air into the chest) before taking it out. "In the beginning, of
course, we didn't know what would happen if you removed a lung," he
explained. "We wanted to see if the patient could tolerate the procedure."
Later, lung function tests were used to determine whether the surviving
lung was competent to do the work of both of the organs, and the collapse
procedure was eliminated.

Ochsner never was in a mood to compromise with smoking. He would
not operate to deal with a problem that he attributed to cigarettes unless
the patient gave a pledge to stop smoking. Later John Ochsner and his
cardiac surgeon associate, Noel L. Mills, also refused to perform open
heart surgery unless their patients promised to give up cigarettes.

Because of his activities with the Women's Field Army, an early organization devoted to the control of cancer, Ochsner was named to the board
of directors when the American Cancer Society took over the field army's
functions. The chief biostatistician for the society was Dr. E. Cuyler
Hammond, who contended that the only way of proving a causal relationship between cigarette smoking and cancer was to determine the
incidence of carcinoma among smokers as opposed to the rate among
nonsmokers. Ochsner agreed that, from a biostatistical standpoint,
Hammond was right. They helped to persuade the directors to sponsor a
prospective study. It was a massive effort, involving 22,000 women volun-
teers who did repeated interviews and follow-ups with 200,000 men
between the ages of fifty and seventy years. After seven years the statistics
revealed a much higher incidence of lung cancer among smokers.

Most of the directors agreed that the results of the study should be
released as a warning to the public. But one, Ian McDonald, objected; he
said the relationship had not been proved. "I couldn't let that statement
go unchallenged," Ochsner related, "and I said that I wasn't going to
discuss the resolution because the other directors knew how I felt. I said I
simply was going to discuss Mr. McDonald's statement that the relationship had not been proved." He told the fable of the Russian nobleman,
Ivan, who was madly in love with his beautiful wife, Olga, despite nag-
ging doubts about her faithfulness. Finally, Ivan decided to test her. He

10. Alton Ochsner, "Lobectomy or Pneumonectomy," *Surgical Clinics of North America,* XLVI (1966), 1255–64.

announced that he was going away for a four-week trip. After four hours he drove past his mansion and saw a carriage in front. Olga emerged from the mansion on the arm of a handsome captain. They got into the carriage. Ivan followed, unnoticed by the two. They drove to a hotel. Ivan peered from outside as they entered an elevator. He saw the light go on in a bedroom. Olga and the captain disrobed, then embraced and got into the bed. The light went out. The distraught Ivan tormented himself. "Oh," he said, "if I only had proof. There is always doubt, doubt."

When the resolution for publicizing the study came to a vote, McDonald was the lone dissenter. Ochsner liked to think that his story was more convincing to the other directors than a debate with McDonald would have been. In 1949 Ochsner was elected president of the American Cancer Society.[11]

While not an out-and-out obsession, smoking and the attendant dangers claimed for years a sizable share of Ochsner's attention. His was not exactly a voice in the wilderness, yet he undoubtedly was the most outspoken foe of cigarettes at the time. He eagerly accepted invitations to speak to small groups, such as garden clubs, and his remarks invariably included a warning that his listeners risked lung cancer and perhaps other horrors if they used tobacco. Sometimes those who heard him hoped the world-famous surgeon would talk about his experiences or discuss symptoms and treatment instead of hammering away at his theme.

An experienced public speaker and academic lecturer, he knew how to use tricks if necessary to win the ears of his audiences. Once, in the 1960s, he addressed the Detroit Surgical Society. After a sumptuous meal, the smokers lighted up and settled down to listen. Ochsner took his place at the lectern, ordered everybody to extinguish cigarettes, and directed the waiters to circulate through the room and take away all of the ashtrays. There was some muttered grumbling, but everybody listened to what the guest had to say.

Perhaps Ochsner never set off the kind of demonstration that a preacher might inspire at a religious revival meeting. The listeners never streamed down the aisle, vowing abstinence and piling their cigarette packages at Ochsner's feet. Yet he did not admit discouragement. The crusader always could find a bright omen, and to the end he continued to forecast that the day would come when nobody smoked. He was the author of four books on the subject. Julian Messner, Inc., of New York published

11. AO Recollection, Smoking.

the first three, *Smoking and Cancer: A Doctor's Report,* 1954; *Smoking and Health,* 1959, and *Smoking and Your Life,* 1964. Simon & Schuster, New York, produced *Smoking: Your Choice Between Life and Death* in 1970.

Ochsner was glad to lend his help to anybody who went to war against smoking. He contributed a foreword in 1964 to a booklet, *Here's How You Can Stop Smoking: Successful Methods That Will Work for You,* produced by New Orleans banker Robert D. Hess in celebration of his own victory over the cigarette habit.

In 1960 Ochsner went on the offensive in his battle. He worked closely with the attorney for the plaintiff in one of the first test suits for damages against a tobacco company growing out of the death of a smoker. Mrs. Frank Lartigue brought the case in federal court at New Orleans against the R. J. Reynolds Tobacco Company and the Liggett and Myers Tobacco Company, charging that their cigarettes had caused the lung cancer that was fatal to her husband. Ochsner helped counsel, H. Alva Brumfield, line up witnesses, and he took the stand himself to testify under oath that he was convinced that Lartigue was a victim of a smoking habit that had lasted longer than fifty years.[12] Similar testimony came from Overholt, who headed the Overholt Thoracic Clinic of Boston, and from George Moore, director of the Roswell Park Memorial Institute of Buffalo, New York. Ochsner said:

> My only interest is that the industry keeps stating that there is no evidence to show that cigarette smoking has anything to do with cancer and because of this a good many people are deluded into smoking. I think it behooves those of us who are concerned about this to speak out. If they would only admit that there is a calculated risk, then we would have no criticism of the industry, and our only obligation then would be to call the attention of the public to the dangers. However, until the industry does admit the risk, I think we must fulfill our obligation to the public and try to force the industry to admit the risk. Apparently nothing short of court action is going to do it.[13]

The jury of six men and six women—seven of the twelve being smokers—returned a verdict in favor of the tobacco companies. The case

12. New Orleans *Times-Picayune,* September 23, 1960, Sec. 2, p. 2.
13. AO, interview, April 18, 1977.

did not end litigation; twenty-five years later suits still were being brought in an attempt to establish liability.

While the elder generation in New Orleans still remembers Ochsner as the vociferous foe of cigarettes, in the rest of the world his efforts largely have been forgotten. Doctors once knew of his role because of his publications and speeches, but in medicine old research becomes obscured. In writing papers, investigators cite the latest publications, and the names of original researchers give way to those of a younger group.

At the very least, in assessing Ochsner's contribution, it can be said that in the 1940s and 1950s he was the most prominent figure on the soapbox, the speaker with the most authoritative voice. Yet when Shimkin wrote his *Contrary to Nature*, a history of cancer treatment and research, he did not mention Ochsner in the chapter on smoking and health.[14] Asked about the omission, he said: "There were many individuals who should have been included . . . but I was aiming for a reasonably sized book, and [to] reduce surgery, radiation and pathology to a minimum. Alton Ochsner was a pioneer in suspecting the cigarette–lung cancer link, although he performed no critical tests of his suspicion. I certainly did not intend to slight an old, respected and valued friend."[15]

Four years after his death, Merrell Dow Pharmaceuticals created the Alton Ochsner Award, to be presented annually to individuals and organizations for their efforts to help people stop smoking. The company produces a gum product designed to ease withdrawal stress.

14. Michael B. Shimkin, *Contrary to Nature* (Washington, D.C., 1977), *passim*.
15. Michael B. Shimkin to Harkey, n.d.

15 A Harvest of Fame

The years of fulfillment for Alton Ochsner may logically be dated from a midday in July, 1947, two months after his fifty-first birthday. He was having lunch at the Boston Club when members A. B. Paterson and Reuben Brown asked him to meet them privately upstairs when he had finished his meal. There, in keeping with the elaborate show of secrecy that covers Mardi Gras affairs, they told him that he had been selected as Rex, the King of Carnival, for 1948. Paterson was president of the School of Design, the official name of the Rex organization, and Brown was captain. It is the ultimate civic-social honor that New Orleans can bestow, and it was precedent-breaking. No medical practitioner ever before had reigned over the Mardi Gras festivities, and the number of outsiders who had received the accolade in the previous seventy-five years could be counted on the fingers of one hand. By New Orleans standards of the time, even though he had been in the city for twenty years, he still was a "Yankee." Yet despite the enmity of rival medical practitioners, Ochsner had won the admiration of the influential circles of his adopted city.

The news inaugurated a heady period of thirty-four years, ending only with his death, during which Ochsner enjoyed the rewards of his medical skills and his hard work. He still, almost to the last, labored overtime, but few men other than the most successful politicians, military heroes, and entertainment and sports superstars ever basked in such long-lasting rounds of applause. Life became a series of triumphs, election to prized society presidencies, honorary degrees, keys to cities, banquets, visiting professorships, consultations by ranking officials, vacations abroad, entertainment by millionaires. Nobody could call Ochsner a playboy, but his schedule was far from humdrum. Only rarely in his peripatetic days did he spend an unbroken week in New Orleans.

The Clinic was thriving. A few months before the Rex honor, the Foundation had settled into the hospital facilities at Camp Plauché. Ochsner's department of surgery at Tulane was recognized as a superior training center. His own star in the medical firmament was ascendant. And now he had demonstrated that his personality, tact, and aura of success could take him a long way in an environment that bore little resemblance to the Kimball of his boyhood.

No diary remains to record the occasion when Alton Ochsner, the medical scientist, began to take an interest in philosophy, politics, and causes. Probably he was led on by the discovery that many of his patients, respectful because of his ability to help them medically, could be influenced by his opinions. He guarded himself, however, against succumbing to the temptation to overestimate his powers because of his surgical successes. His oft-repeated explanation of why he could keep his head on his shoulders despite the flattery was to say that perhaps 85 percent of illnesses are self-limited, and the patient will get well no matter what the doctor does. Some will die in spite of treatment. Therefore, the practitioner can affect the outcome only in a small percentage of the cases seen.[1]

In any event, as Ochsner grew older he found himself publicly involved in election campaigns, civic movements, and most particularly, anti-Communist crusades. His background had not prepared him for this kind of activity, and in his naïveté he sometimes allowed himself to be used by promoters who took advantage of his name and fame. He was known on occasion to get carried away and make exaggerated, even ridiculous, claims. In the long run, his outside enthusiasms did nothing to enhance the reputation he had won in his profession.

Ochsner's years of fulfillment were marked by the severance of his active connection with the Tulane medical school. In a way, his foes did him in, but his departure was not really a defeat. He had reached the point in his career where he no longer needed to be identified as the Tulane chairman of surgery. He had achieved recognition in his own right. By that time, Tulane benefited as much or more from the affiliation than he did.

Ochsner said he told Paterson and Brown that he was overcome to be chosen as Rex, but would have to decline because he could not afford the costs involved. He had heard that an outlay of from fifteen thousand to fifty thousand dollars was required, and the amount was far beyond his resources. They explained that the Rex krewe paid all expenses except for

1. AO, interview, 1967. The theme stated here was a recurrent one in Ochsner's conversations.

modest gifts for the queen and court, which would not break him. Mardi Gras protocol dictated that he tell no one, not even Isabel, of his selection. During the following winter he obtained a special dispensation that enabled him to let Isabel in on the secret in order that she could arrange for Sis, who was at the Finch School in New York, to come home for the occasion.

Not one of the more than one hundred men who have ruled as King of Carnival—one chosen each year in recognition of his civic contributions—could have enjoyed his one-day reign more than Ochsner did. For as long as he lived, he could recount the experience in detail. Dressed in an elaborate costume, he rode on the king's float in a glittering parade through New Orleans streets. Thousands upon thousands—perhaps nearly half a million—spectators greeted him as he waved his scepter, dispensing a benediction to his "subjects." That night he presided over the pageantry of a Carnival ball.

The prim written histories of the Rex krewe do not mention an achievement of which Ochsner boasted. The parade route covers some five miles, and the king is on his float, in full public view, for five hours or longer, during which time he is toasted repeatedly with champagne. Through experience the krewe learned to provide Rex with two sets of tights and two pairs of boots, and to instruct him simply to let himself go when nature makes urgent calls: his robes would cover the evidence and a change would be waiting at the end of the line. "I resolved this would not happen to me," Ochsner said, "so I took no fluids at all after midnight and went on the float dry as a chip." He recalled that he drank nineteen toasts, including one in front of the home of Matas on St. Charles Avenue. He got back to the den with his costume dry. The histories also will not relate that, at a critical point in the pageantry of the Rex ball, the drawstring that held up his pants came loose. "If you will just wait a minute, I will pull up my royal breeches," he told the queen. And he did.[2]

The Carnival season always was a highlight of his year. Once, as a former Rex, Ochsner helped to entertain another former king, Edward, the duke of Windsor, who with the duchess visited New Orleans for Mardi Gras. On another occasion there were knowing grins on the faces of those in the medical community who were present at a ball when Ochsner and the surgeon Howard Mahorner, who was Rex in 1973,

2. Clint Bolton, "Carnival: From Kimball to Camelot," *New Orleans* (February, 1971), 51–65.

smilingly marched side-by-side during a procession of former kings: although the two once had worked together, they long since had become enemies.

For years, Ochsner would put on white tie and tails night after night to serve on the committees that helped carry out the ritual at balls. Most former kings are highly selective in accepting invitations to be committeemen, because a proliferation of krewes means that some groups lack social prestige. Ochsner, however, democratically responded to all who wanted him. In his last years, as senior surviving former king, he proposed the toast to each current Rex before the start of the parade.

Ochsner's first major civic award, evidence that he had earned the respect of New Orleanians, came with the *Times-Picayune* Loving Cup for 1945. The trophy is given annually by the leading newspaper to a citizen considered to have performed the greatest altruistic service for the community. Ochsner's recognition was for his calling the attention of the world to New Orleans as an important medical center. Matas was the winner for 1940. Ochsner served as president of International House, which promotes New Orleans as a world trading center, in 1962, and in 1968 received the Cunningham Award, offered by International House to the citizen of the United States who has done most to further the country's participation in international affairs. Ochsner was the long-time president of the Cordell Hull Foundation for International Education, named for the wartime secretary of state.

Ochsner's exit from his post as chairman of surgery at Tulane in 1956 came amid as much controversy as marked his entrance in 1927. Rufus Harris, who was president of the university at the time, said he was "sort of kicked out . . . which was an indecent thing to do. It was one of the dirtiest deals I ever saw in my life."[3] The forced resignation left Ochsner beset with contradictory sentiments. On the one hand, he resented what amounted to a dismissal; on the other, he remained on the faculty as a clinical professor of surgery, later accepted an honorary degree from Tulane, and, most significantly, supported what proved to be an unsuccessful effort to effect a merger of the medical school and the Alton Ochsner Medical Foundation. The ouster was engineered by Joseph Merrick Jones, president of the board of administrators. An overriding factor was the antipathy of the segment of the medical community that resented Ochsner's success.

3. Rufus C. Harris, interview, February, 1978.

What should not be overlooked, however, is the fact that Ochsner's presence was causing problems for Tulane, and that some of the development of the Ochsner institutions had come at the expense of the medical school. Ochsner himself had outgrown the chairman's job, and some of his allies in the Clinic had assumed roles in the functions of the school that understandably could cause Tulane administrators to feel they were losing control. The intertwining of Ochsner staff and Tulane faculty—thirty-five Clinic members were teaching at Tulane and a number of the school's faculty worked part-time at the Ochsner institutions—hurt the medical school's relations with the medical community. Harris, although no admirer of Jones's, emphasized that there was no mendacity in the latter's determination to get Ochsner out. He said Jones "just didn't know any better."

By the middle 1950s the medical school was having a financial crisis. The federal government was pouring millions of dollars into grants for health research, and Tulane's faculty was going after a big share. At one time a third of the faculty and more than half of the staff were paid in full or in part from grants. There were warnings from within of federal encroachment into medical education, and a fear that the school was getting away from its primary function of teaching. There came a realization that, to avoid an overdependence on federal grants, Tulane needed financial support from its practitioner alumni.[4] Harris said a few doctors convinced Jones that the alumni would be more generous if Ochsner were out of the picture.

Ochsner believed he was being undermined within the department of surgery by Ambrose H. Storck, who had been hired by the chairman but who became unfriendly after returning from World War II. Storck was on good terms with Jones. The Tulane medical dean, Maxwell E. Lapham, believed that Ochsner was more involved in the activities of the Clinic and Foundation than he was in the conduct of the surgery department. He suggested that Ochsner step aside in favor of a full-time chairman. Ochsner refused. When the five faculty members first began talking about forming a clinic, they discussed their plans with C. C. Bass, Lapham's predecessor. But nothing more was said after Lapham took office in 1940: although he had heard rumors, his first knowledge of the organization of the Clinic came from a newspaper story. President Harris got the news in the same way.

4. Duffy, *Tulane Medical Center*, 176.

Ochsner's divided allegiance surely was one of the reasons the board of administrators and the medical school authorities adopted, in January, 1955, a statement of policy saying that if "qualified and acceptable persons are available," in the future all appointments of department heads would be on a full-time basis. Two months later the administrators and executive faculty of the medical school invited Stanhope Bayne-Jones, former dean of the Yale University School of Medicine, to make a detailed study of the school and recommend measures for its future progress. He was a distant relative of Joseph Jones's. Ochsner later would describe Bayne-Jones as a hatchet man, and indeed he ultimately did deliver the chop that separated Ochsner from the chairmanship.

Bayne-Jones spent months in his investigation. In his report he cited benefits that the school had received from its close unofficial alliance with the Ochsner institutions, and also listed the problems, the chief one being the lack of a formal policy governing the relationship. He recommended a modified full-time status for department heads and chief associates. What he called for was the so-called geographical full-time arrangement, under which professors may have private practices, but must conduct them on campus. He also suggested that professors retain their fees up to a specified amount, all income above that to go into the school's coffers.[5]

The sequence of events in late 1955 is interesting. On November 27 the Commonwealth Fund announced that it had made a $750,000 grant to the medical school, and Jones said the amount would be matched by other contributions, the total proceeds being used to bring faculty salaries into line with those at other schools. On December 5, Bayne-Jones interviewed Ochsner. The discussion was in private. On December 7, Ochsner announced that he would resign the chairmanship as of June 30, 1956, but continue as a clinical professor of surgery. In his final report, Bayne-Jones said Ochsner recognized that "other demands prevented his giving his full-time to the department" and showed "a most generous appreciation of the need of a full-time chairman for surgery."

Ochsner said he spent as much or more time on his duties at Tulane as any other chairman, earlier or later, and his successor, his friend Oscar Creech, let it be known that he did not intend to put in any more hours than Ochsner had. Ochsner's departure was not an unfortunate development; it gave him more time for his other activities. Three decades after-

5. Stanhope Bayne-Jones, "Report of a Survey of the School of Medicine, Tulane University" (Washington, D.C., 1956), *passim.*

ward it is difficult to understand why he was so reluctant to relinquish a job that he had held for twenty-nine years and from which he already had derived all of the benefits, including prestige, that he could expect.

He said the deed was done "in a very underhanded way," adding, "the worst part of it was that Joe Jones tried to make out he was my friend. One night we went to his home for a cocktail party. He took Isabel and me out to the gate . . . and he said, 'Whatever happens, I want you to know I am your friend.' At that time I didn't know what was in the wind. He was telling me this and was just about ready to cut my throat. If he had said to me, 'Why, you old son of a bitch, you're not any good and we're going to get rid of you,' I would have said, 'Fine, Joe. That's all right.' He acted as my friend. I just can't forgive people like that."[6]

For a time Ochsner was cool toward Rufus Harris—the one rift in their long association—because he thought Harris had not come to his defense. Actually, Harris related, he considered resigning his presidency but was dissuaded by some members of the board of administrators who told him that the action would not help Ochsner's situation. Harris said Jones dominated the board. Harris explained that Jones regarded the presidency of the administrators as the equivalent of a corporate chairmanship, the chief executive, and did not hesitate to impinge on the authority of the university president. "Mr. Jones would say, 'He's so involved with his clinic and hospital he's not looking after the medical school.' 'Who the hell tells you he's not looking after the medical school?' I would reply. 'I'm the only one who could tell you that and I surely won't tell you that. The people in the medical school wouldn't tell you that. No one has seen any neglect in his department.' "[7] Harris was able to explain his position to Ochsner, and they remained friends.

In breaking the news to his family, Ochsner commented, "This is the best thing to do for everyone concerned. I know it is the best thing for me, and it is certainly the best thing for the Clinic, because I will now be able to devote all my activities to the Clinic and Foundation. I hope it will be the best thing for the university."

Ochsner continued as a clinical professor of surgery until he reached the mandatory retirement age in 1961, when the board of administrators and the executive faculty gave him the title of professor emeritus. He never would admit to any bitterness toward the school. "I have nothing against

6. AO, interview, June 14, 1978.
7. Rufus C. Harris, interview, February, 1978.

Tulane," he said. "You can't blame an institution because of some personalities. It's still a great institution." When in 1965 and 1966 there were
serious negotiations, partly financed by a $250,000 Commonwealth
Fund grant, for merging the Ochsner institutions and medical school,
Ochsner was an outspoken advocate of the proposal.[8] Opponents eventually prevailed. Ochsner's son John once was consulted about taking on
his father's old job of chairman of surgery at Tulane, but no deal was
struck.

In 1967 Ochsner received the Distinguished Service Award of the
American Medical Association, given annually to a doctor for his exceptional contributions to medicine. The two other practitioners considered
for the honor that year were close friends of Ochsner's, George Herrmann
and Owen Wangensteen. The award first was made in 1936, and Rudolph
Matas was the winner. Mike DeBakey was chosen in 1959. Ochsner had
died when, in 1983, his associate Merrill Hines became the recipient.

By 1947 Ochsner was selected as the first president of the Society for
Vascular Surgery, an elite organization that included among its members
Alfred Blalock of Baltimore, who had performed the first blue baby
operation—the repair of a congenital heart defect—on November 30,
1944. Other founders of the society included Ochsner's personal friends
Arthur W. Allen of Boston and Frederick A. Coller of Ann Arbor.

A. J. Ochsner would have been well pleased had he lived to know about
the full list of professional societies that elected Alton to their presiden-
cies. In addition to the Society for Vascular Surgery, they included the
International Society of Surgery, 1962–1963; Pan Pacific Surgical Association, 1961–1963; Interstate Postgraduate Medical Assembly of North
America, 1955–1956; International Society of Angiography (later the
International Cardiovascular Society), 1954–1956; American College of
Surgeons, 1951–1952; American Cancer Society, 1949–1950; American Association for Thoracic Surgery, 1947–1948; Southeastern Surgical
Association, 1944–1946; and Southern Surgical Association, 1944. He
also was the first president of the American Retired Physicians Association, 1976–1977.

He received honorary degrees from the Free University of Nicaragua,
University of Madrid, University of Athens, University of South Dakota,
Brigham Young University, University of Jacksonville (Florida), Tulane
University, Loyola University of the South, McNeese State University, and

8. Wilds, *Ochsner's,* 147–48.

William Carey College. A full accounting of encomiums such as honorary citizenships, honorary professorships, keys to the city, and the like can be summarized in the notation that they were conferred in Ireland, England, Greece, Japan, Nicaragua, Columbia, Honduras, Ecuador, Panama, and Venezuela, as well as in the United States. He got around.

Due perhaps to the influence of Rudolph Matas, Ochsner had an active dislike for the International College of Surgeons, a society with members in North and South America and Europe. Isidore Cohn, Matas' biographer, said Matas had "consuming" hatred for the international college, dating back to the early 1930s. Echoing Matas' sentiments, Ochsner complained that the college accepted nonsurgeon members and used political influence to require eminent surgeons in foreign countries to join its ranks. The international college became involved in a dispute with the American College of Surgeons over a move by the international to establish a new certification board to rival the American Board of Surgery. The American college contended another board was not necessary. Ochsner tried to discourage any doctor with Tulane connections from becoming affiliated with the international.

The strength of Matas' and Ochsner's feelings is reflected in an incident involving Frank Lahey, the founder of the clinic in Boston that is named for him. Lahey was invited to give a lecture at Tulane sponsored by the Nu Sigma Nu fraternity and bearing Matas' name. When Matas learned of the choice of speakers, he was angry, because Lahey also had accepted an invitation to appear at one of the congresses of the International College of Surgeons. Ochsner wrote to Lahey, a friend, suggesting that in view of Matas' feelings he either decline the invitation to Tulane or cancel his appearance at the international's congress. Lahey replied that Matas should not be so petty, and said his attendance at the congress did not mean that he was sponsoring the international. When Matas' step-grandson, Dr. Rudolph Landry, met Lahey at the airport, the Bostonian said he wanted to pay a courtesy call on Matas. Landry attempted to discourage the visit but Lahey was insistent. Landry asked Ochsner to come to the rescue. "I immediately went down to the hotel and told Dr. Lahey that he couldn't go by to see Dr. Matas because I knew what would happen to him if he did. Dr. Matas would have given a tongue-lashing which only a Latin such as Dr. Matas could do," Ochsner explained.[9]

Ochsner in 1956 turned down a Distinguished Service Award and

9. AO Recollection, Patients.

$500 honorarium from the American Society of Abdominal Surgeons. "I appreciate this very much, but, unfortunately, will not be able to accept," Ochsner said in a reply that met the minimum standard for civility, but barely. He did not explain his action. At the time, however, a group of abdominal surgeons was involved in a dispute with the American College of Surgeons over a plan to establish an examining board for stomach surgeons.

A. J. Ochsner was the first president of the Clinical Congress of Surgeons of North America, the association that became the American College of Surgeons, and Alton was seated as a trustee of the college at the early age of forty, fifteen years before he was elected president. He was on the firing line during the college's battles to establish an examining board of surgeons, to enforce standards for hospitals, and to wipe out ghost surgery and fee splitting. (Ghost surgery is the practice of bringing in a competent doctor to do an operation without the knowledge of the patient. Fee splitting is the custom of dividing the payment for an operation between the surgeon who does the job and the doctor who recommended the procedure to the patient.) Not surprisingly, Alton was an enthusiastic supporter of the college's stands all the way. He also was a member of a committee that worked out a change in the bylaws that permitted the initiation of the first black fellow.

Ochsner's early attitude toward involvement in such activities as campaigning for office seekers, endorsing proposed legislation, and seeking to influence public opinion may have been colored by his feelings about those doctors he regarded as medical politicians. "Unfortunately," he said, "there's too much politics in medicine." He complained that doctors who are the busiest do not have time to get involved in the affairs of the American Medical Association and the state and county societies that represent organized medicine. "The result is that the hierarchy in a society is usually controlled by people who don't have much to do, and who have the political desire to go on up," he continued. "The result also is that delegates to the state societies and AMA are individuals who have been in for a long period of time, and there is an advantage in knowing the ropes.

"But it's an inbreeding that's bad, and as a result organized medicine as such has gotten a very poor image in the United States." He called it a holier-than-thou image. The AMA, he contended, was wrong in opposing Medicare. The idea is good, he said, but those who can afford to pay for their medical care should do so. "I don't know why medical care is any more of an inalienable right than food," he commented. It worried him, he said, because physicians as a group had lost some of the respect felt by the public, although he believed that the individual physician still was well regarded. He blamed the "liberal" press for some of people's attitude toward organized medicine. "The press has been very cruel," he complained, in magnifying doctor deficiencies.

Ochsner said he himself had been derelict in not taking an active role in the politics of medicine. "I tried it in the beginning," he related, "and I was beating my head against a stone wall to such an extent that I felt 'what's the use,' so I gave up and just drifted, which was the wrong thing to do." He was not specific, and the statement is puzzling because the record of his early activities does not reflect ardent interest in the affairs of medical associations other than the specialty societies.

Once he concluded that practitioners should actively involve themselves in state and national politics, Ochsner went in headfirst, as he always did in any undertaking. Although his father may have had populist and Democratic inclinations in the distant past, there never was any doubt about Alton's philosophy. Every instinct was right-wing conservative, although he described himself as moderate. Some of his friends affiliated themselves in the 1960s with the activist, far-right John Birch Society, but Ochsner insisted he never joined up because "I thought it was a little bit too radical. I believe in the middle ground." When he moved to New Orleans he registered as a member of the Democratic party, not because he subscribed to the national platform or voted consistently for Democratic nominees, but because at that time, in one-party Louisiana, elections were decided in the Democratic primaries, and in order to vote in these a citizen had to be registered in the party. He changed his registration with some fanfare in 1969, when he became a Republican in order to help build up the GOP campaign in the state. "The thing that built this nation is the two-party system," he said, "and we've got to have it in the South." His move caused no surprise because he long since had been out front in supporting Republican candidates.

Unlike some political dabblers, Ochsner did not hide in the background to avoid the rough-and-ready exchanges of election campaigns. He marched into the fray as the publicly identified leader of electioneering staffs. Sometimes he picked the wrong horse. He was a campaign manager for David Treen in an unsuccessful attempt to unseat Democrat Hale Boggs as the United States representative from the Second District, but then helped Treen win his way into Congress when a redistricting took him out of contention with Boggs. Ochsner later worked for Treen in a losing race for governor of Louisiana. Finally, in 1980, he found himself holding the wrong pari-mutuel ticket when Treen became the first Republican since Reconstruction to be elected governor. Before Treen became a candidate, Ochsner had pledged his support to Democrat James E. Fitzmorris, who had ingratiated his way into the surgeon's favor. Ochsner tried in vain to persuade Treen not to run, telling him he would not win. Ochsner did not live long enough to see Treen complete his term. Treen readily forgave his old friend for his momentary defection and spoke at the memorial program after Ochsner's death.

Ochsner had to risk being spattered in the inevitable political mud-throwing. Once, a Democratic state representative, Edward F. LeBreton, Jr., called him "the most aggressive seeker and recipient of so-called federal handouts in the Second Congressional District," and credited Boggs with obtaining grants that helped make the Ochsner institutions successful.[10] Ochsner said Hill-Burton funds were obtained for the hospital by filing through customary state channels, and denied that Boggs was the man chiefly responsible for federal grants. He and the liberal Boggs jousted frequently over the years before Boggs was lost on an airplane flight in Alaska, not long before he was scheduled to become Speaker of the House of Representatives. Boggs always could disagree without being disagreeable, and he dealt respectfully with Ochsner. He was succeeded in the House by his widow, Lindy Boggs, who refused to allow the authors to scan Boggs-Ochsner letters. The other New Orleans congressman, F. Edward Hebert, was as conservative as Ochsner, and the two had no debates.

An indication of Ochsner's political views is given by his assessment of the administrations of Dwight D. Eisenhower, who certainly never made top grades on any liberal scorecard. "I think he was a very bad president," said Ochsner, "but I admired him as a man. He was trained as a military man and never should have been president." Ochsner at least was able to reject the extremist thought that Eisenhower was a willing tool of the Communist conspiracy.[11]

George W. Healy, Jr., late editor of the *Times-Picayune,* called Ochsner "the greatest public relations man I ever knew." On the basis of an episode involving Richard M. Nixon, Healy said Ochsner also was

10. *Times-Picayune,* October 23, 1968, Sec. 2, p. 20.
11. AO, interview, August 14, 1979.

pretty shrewd politically. It will be remembered that, after losing the 1960 presidential election to John F. Kennedy, Nixon ran for governor of California and again was beaten. He then held a press conference in which he told newsmen they wouldn't have Richard Nixon "to kick around any more." Seemingly, he was politically dead. Not long thereafter, Healy received a telephone call from Ochsner, who told him that Nixon was going to be in New Orleans and wanted to talk. They took the former vice-president to lunch on a Saturday, when few members were present at the Boston Club. Healy was an admirer of Nixon's, had been with him on a trip to Moscow, and had stood almost within touching distance during his widely publicized "kitchen debate" with Nikita Khruschev over the relative merits of democracy and communism.

Now Nixon wanted some advice. Should he try to recoup his political fortunes by getting back into the arena immediately? "I wasn't able to advise him as well as Al was," Healy recalled. "Al told him to go slow. Let the opposition make the mistakes that they were bound to do, and then make his move." Healy pointed out that Nixon did lie low for years, except to campaign for Barry Goldwater and quietly seek local Republican support.[12] Then, when the Vietnam War doomed Hubert Humphrey, Nixon took the Republican nomination and began his comeback. Ochsner enthusiastically supported Nixon.

More in sorrow than in disillusionment, Ochsner wrote to President Nixon on July 20, 1971, to say that the latter's decision to visit Red China "was indeed a shock to all of us who have been fighting communism throughout the years . . . although many believe and have proclaimed that this will be a great political advantage to you, and it may well be . . . I am convinced that this had nothing to do with your action. I know you honestly believe, as you stated, that this is the right thing to do. . . . Mr. President, we all admire you very much and have great confidence in your sincerity, integrity, motives, and ability, but I believe you have been badly advised."[13]

As the Watergate scandals were unfolding, Ochsner wrote Nixon on May 21, 1974, to say: "Jane [his second wife] and I realize what you and your family are going through at the present time when everyone is taking pot shots at you, but we are so pleased that you are standing firm. We know that you are going to win out in this thing in spite of all the vicious

12. George W. Healy, Jr., interview, July 26, 1977.
13. Alton Ochsner to President Richard M. Nixon, July 20, 1971, and May 21, 1974.

attacks being made to try to undermine you. I do not know of anyone else who has had to put up with what you have." In the end, the full disclosures shocked the forthright Ochsner. "I think Nixon let us down. He lied," the surgeon said. "I think Nixon was going down as our greatest president. But he should not have lied to the people when he said he didn't know anything about this. He should have said, 'Yes, this should not have been done. I do not approve of it, but it was done.'" He wrote to President Gerald Ford on September 10, 1974, to "congratulate you on the courageous stand that you took in giving full pardon to former President Richard Nixon. It was a splendid thing to do and will do more to end this Watergate controversy than anything else even though the liberal television people would like to keep it alive for a long period of time."[14]

Ochsner's name was for years the chief asset of the Information Council of the Americas, an association that claimed his interest because of its devotion to combatting communism in Latin America. He was one of the founders in 1961, along with Edward Scannell Butler, a young intelligence officer just out of the army, and A. E. Papele, dean of the law school at Loyola University in New Orleans. Ochsner served as president and later chairman of the board. His affiliation helped in fund raising, and he always found the time to participate in INCA activities planned by the promotion-minded Butler. In 1979 Butler reported that there were two thousand members "all over the globe," as well as twenty thousand supporters. But Butler also once said, "INCA is Dr. Alton Ochsner." INCA did not often appear in the news after Ochsner's death.

The council provided an outlet for Ochsner's anti-Communist zeal. He took part in the preparation of what INCA called "truth tapes," which were distributed to radio stations in Central and South America. The tapes were interviews with refugees from Cuba after the seizure of the government by Fidel Castro, the purpose being to expose Castro's Communist ties at a time before the fact had been established. One of the participants was Juanita Castro, Fidel's sister, who also appeared at a dinner in New Orleans at which Ochsner presided.

The tapes were sent to 175 radio stations in fifteen Latin countries. Ochsner's celebrated optimism in his medical practice carried over into his outside pursuits. He credited INCA tapes with turning the tide against Communist candidates in elections in Venezuela and Chile, and blamed a subsequent loss in Chile on the fact that INCA was concentrating its

14. Alton Ochsner to President Gerald Ford, September 10, 1974.

energies elsewhere and did not take part in the election campaign. It was not the scientist Ochsner who was speaking this time.

INCA subsequently staged a series of leadership conferences at which some three hundred college students were told how to prevent campus demonstrations, said by INCA to be Communist-inspired, that had erupted at colleges in the United States. "In the year 1970–1971 there were practically no campus disturbances," Ochsner said, "and we think it was due to the activities of INCA that this was the case."[15]

It was his connection with INCA that resulted in Ochsner believing, for a while in 1967, that he was about to be drawn into a fantasy that had New Orleans and the rest of the world agog. There is no evidence to support his supposition, but logic was making no headlines at the time. District Attorney Jim Garrison was about to bring man-about-town Clay Shaw to trial on charges that he was a conspirator in the assassination in Dallas of President Kennedy. The assassin, Lee Harvey Oswald, had been in New Orleans earlier, distributing pro-Castro pamphlets. He had engaged in a radio debate with INCA's Ed Butler. Mark Lane, who had written a book about the case and who subscribed to Garrison's theories, said in a New Orleans press conference that anti-Castro Cuban exiles had played a vital role in the assassination. It was anti-Castro Cubans who were making INCA's "truth tapes." Ochsner and Butler issued a statement: "The anti-Communist Cubans, many of whom cannot properly defend themselves in English, are being made scapegoats for the most twisted kind of illogical accusations and rumor. The temper of the times in New Orleans is getting dangerously close to that of the Crystalnight in Germany, when the massacre of Jews began."

Ochsner later said that Garrison "tried to indict me at the time he got after Clay Shaw." He said he understood the indictment would have been connected with Jack Ruby, who shot Oswald to death in the Dallas police station two days after the assassination. "I don't know who," Ochsner continued, "but someone made the statement that Ruby must have seen Dr. Ochsner because he had cancer of the lung, and Dr. Ochsner told him that he was not going to get well and had nothing to lose by shooting Oswald." Ochsner, of course, never saw Ruby in his life and there is no record of Ruby's being treated at the Ochsner institutions. Normally, Ochsner would have laughed at the ridiculous supposition, but a man was going to be tried for his life in New Orleans on evidence so thin that it took

15. AO Recollection, INCA.

a jury only an hour to acquit him. No indictment was returned against Ochsner, and he was spared the indignities heaped upon Clay Shaw.[16]

The subjects of communism and Russia could start Ochsner's imagination to racing. He liked to tell a story that begins at a meeting of the International Society of Surgery at Dublin in 1961. Ochsner was chairman of the nominating committee. "It was proposed that the next president of the society should be a Russian because a Russian had never been president," Ochsner related. "The majority of those present were very much opposed to a Russian because of the Communists, and I was violently opposed because of my anti-Communistic feelings." It was suggested that a European should not be elected, because it was Russia's turn and the choice of another man from the same continent would be an obvious slap in the face. "Finally, one of the members said, 'I think we should have an entirely new viewpoint.' He suggested that I be made president. I remonstrated that I was chairman of the committee, but they overruled me. You can imagine how embarrassing it was to me when I had to report to the meeting that I was the choice of my committee. It just goes to show that if one wants to be elected to something, it is a good thing to be chairman of the nominating committee. In this way one can have the inside track."

He said his activities against communism must have come to the attention of the Russian government. In 1975 the surgical society met in Moscow, and he decided to attend as a past president and honorary member as well. His friend, Moscow surgeon Boris Petrof, urged him to come. Then Ochsner received word from his travel agency that it could get no accommodations in Moscow. Ochsner informed Petrof, who replied that the Ochsners had a room at a leading hotel. "I stupidly sent this letter to the travel agency, and they came back immediately with a letter saying I did not have accommodations. I was the only one out of about six hundred who was not allowed to go to Moscow."

Of course, he commented, "I was very much relieved because I fear that there would have been an accident of some kind had I gone. It was the greatest compliment that they could have paid me, because it showed the Communists realized what I had been doing."[17]

While he made no pretense of knowing much about the operations of business firms and banks, Ochsner served as a director for an airline, two

16. AO, interview, August 14, 1979.
17. AO Recollection, Communists–INCA.

banks, and a company with interests in razors and motion picture enterprises. He took his duties seriously, traveling extensively to attend meetings and promoting his firms at every opportunity. During a stay in Guatemala as a guest of the government, he became friendly with Douglas Swim of Carmel, California. In 1962 Swim telephoned to offer a seat on the board of National Airlines, of which Swim was chairman. L. B. Maytag, Jr., of the washing machine family, had just purchased a majority of the airline's stock, was reorganizing the company, and wanted a director from New Orleans. Ochsner continued his membership until National was bought by Pan American Airways. The perquisites included free first-class seats for himself and wife, a boon for anyone who flew as often as he. He developed a friendship with "Bud" Maytag and was a regular on flights to Miami, National's headquarters. He insisted that the Ochsner institutions change travel agents when he learned that personnel were being booked on another airline when National flights were available. He set up a meeting for Maytag with the mayor and other New Orleans leaders when National was seeking support for a new route to the Northwest. He persuaded the airline to place resuscitation equipment aboard its planes for the protection of passengers.[18]

Beginning in 1971, Ochsner made frequent flights to Jacksonville, Florida, to attend meetings of directors of Florida National Banks of Florida, Inc. His seat on the board resulted from his friendship with Edward W. Ball, the legendary industrialist and financier who controlled the Alfred I. duPont Testamentary Trust. Ball's sister, Jessie, married duPont, a member of the Delaware family. After both died, Ball ran the empire that included a railroad, banks, a paper company, a petroleum conglomerate, and a million acres of land.

The manager of the Edgewater Gulf Hotel on the Mississippi Gulf Coast, one of the duPont properties, asked Ochsner to see Ball, who had a skin cancer on his arm. The next day the surgeon excised the growth and told Ball, "The next time you get one of these lesions, let me see it." Sometime afterward, the hotel manager telephoned and asked for an immediate appointment for Ball, who came in with a nonmalignant growth on his face. "I was in Amsterdam and I was shaving and I noticed it," Ball explained. "I didn't know there is a town in Florida named Amsterdam," Ochsner remarked. "There isn't," Ball said. "I was in Amsterdam, Holland, yesterday." Ochsner asked why the rush. "You

18. AO Recollection, Travels.

told me the next time I had one of these things to let you see it," said Ball. It was at about this time that Ball put Ochsner on the bank board.[19]

Ball died in the Ochsner hospital in 1981, at the age of ninety-three. Ochsner outlasted him by less than four months. As for Ochsner's contribution to the Florida banks, his comment was, "I was the only nincompoop on the board." He had served on the board of the National Bank of Commerce in Jefferson Parish for nine years before resigning to take the Florida directorship.

Ochsner's appointment to the board of Frawley Enterprises, Inc., in 1971 was made by Patrick J. ("Pat") Frawley, Jr., of Los Angeles, one of his associates in INCA. Even before this appointment, because of his friendship with Frawley, he had been invited to an anniversary dinner in Los Angeles that unexpectedly became one of the most important occasions in his life. But that is a story for a later chapter.

19. AO, interview, June 22, 1978.

16 Compassion, Conservatism, Contradictions

Alton Ochsner spent half a century earning acclaim, and the rest of his life relishing it. The transformation was complete, from the precocious but callow small-town boy to the skilled surgeon and urbane globe-trotter. His companions changed, from the lads who rode Shetland ponies with him and touched off Fourth of July fireworks to millionaire industrialists, the blue bloods of New Orleans society, and the elite of the medical profession. He attracted enemies as well as disciples. And throughout the years, he clung to the homespun virtues that brought success: hard work, forthrightness, a willingness to admit mistakes, compassion. He also was self-centered, inclined to be intolerant except where physical infirmities were involved, elitist, and a babe in the woods once he began to dabble in politics and movements. There were contradictions? Indeed.

The Ochsner of his prime was a handsome, well-groomed figure who battled ceaselessly to prevent his solid, five-foot-four frame from bursting through his self-imposed 160-pound barrier. The moustache that he cultivated upon his return from training in Europe in the hope that it would make him look mature had turned white, matching his hair. Until the very end, the twinkle in his dark eyes never faded. In the words of a friend, he looked "like a doctor ought to look." His physical presence bespoke self-assurance and success; his entrance into a crowded room turned heads. He made those in his company feel at ease, but did not invite familiarity. His bedside manner, exuding optimism, was no pose.

Still secret are the ingredients of the red "cocktail" that he sometimes prescribed for terminal carcinoma cases. "Take this four times a day and don't give up," was his instruction. "We'll save you yet." Misleading, perhaps, but are the last hours any easier if hope is gone? No wonder colleagues said he could coax patients to "walk to the grave." He was a "toucher," who very early learned the value of physical contact in establishing a bond. He included in almost every encounter with a patient a pat on the back, a squeeze of the hand, or a caressing feel of the forehead or cheek. He liked people.

His vitality was evident. He moved purposefully, with a sort of lope known to long-time associates as the "Ochsner walk," a gait shared with others in the family and so distinctive that a distant relative who did not know Alton's children once spotted John striding along a corridor and announced, "That's an Ochsner." Alton liked to dance, moving with a rhythmic bounce. He and Isabel were a graceful couple. Until he had knee problems in late years, he bounded up stairs instead of using elevators. Young interns and residents had to hustle to keep up with him as he made hospital rounds. Sometimes his entourage became a thundering herd on the stairways, alerting nurses that visitors were on the way. He advocated exercise, stipulating that there had to be enough exertion to cause one to puff if it were to be beneficial.

For a period he put himself through the rigors of the Canadian Air Force calisthenics regimen every morning. At the age of eighty, he created something of a stir when he told a newspaper reporter that he started every day by doing 105 push-ups. The announcement was viewed with some skepticism, but he was serious and willingly posed on his office floor for a wire service photographer. Even sons Akky and John had their doubts, and his second wife, Jane, was not convinced. But it was not like him to prevaricate, and the explanation accepted by most people was that he pushed up, all right, but not in the classic manner in which only the hands and toes touch the floor. There is no question but that the many thousands of hours he spent standing at an operating table developed strong legs and feet and a fairly fit body overall.

He admired and adapted himself to the ways of the South, but never acquired a Dixie drawl. He spoke with a clipped, nasal Midwestern twang. Anyone who has listened to the football telecasts of Ara Parseghian, the former head coach at Notre Dame University, could be excused for thinking that he was hearing Ochsner speak.

His well-developed sense of humor was titillated by the earthy stories emanating from operating rooms and nursing stations, and he saw to it that he had a fund of jokes to enliven his speeches. His best source was Mims Gage, who fed him the Cajun stories that he could recount with mimicry of the southwest Louisiana dialect. Later, his daughter Sis and his son Mims helped keep him supplied. His lofty status and imposing mien allowed him to get away with jokes that would be outrageous if told by others. Both of his wives on occasion wished they could vanish when he shocked an audience.

He liked to joke about sex, but when it came to personal conduct, Ochsner was fully as straitlaced as his generally conservative philosophy would indicate. He admitted being given the eye, but he was not responding. "It's usually the male's fault, and if he doesn't make advances it won't continue." Anyway, he added, forward moves by women "always had the adverse affect on me. When anybody did that, it just turned me off." He had only scorn for psychiatrists or psychologists who justified sexual relations with patients as being a form of therapy. And he saw sexual promiscuity resulting from the advent of the birth control pill as a communistic development likely to destroy the sanctity of the family. His own sexual drives continued into his eighties.

At work, except when he donned the green surgery regalia, he wore a crisp white doctor's gown. His name was stitched in script on the breast, but in inconspicuous letters: most of the hundreds of patients and visitors who milled through the corridors of the Clinic and hospital did not realize that the distinguished-looking figure they encountered was the man for whom the institutions were named. If recognized, he could have created a stir by striding through the fourth-floor waiting room en route to his Clinic office, but he almost always chose to take a less noticeable path behind the reception desk. He was careful to exchange greetings with nurses and other employees, pausing to chat with old-timers. He usually carried in his hand the percussion hammer used to test reflexes by tapping patients' knees.

One of his first questions as he entered the examining room to see a patient was, "Do you smoke?" If the answer was yes, the man or woman received a lecture warning that the consequences were likely to be dire. He never let up, and in the forty years that followed his discovery of a link between cigarettes and lung cancer, he delivered his message many thousands of times. As noted, after the age limitation barred him from operating, he continued to treat nonsurgical patients. More than one was surprised to find out that it was Ochsner himself who was performing a minor procedure on him, such as taking out stitches. His desk and a table behind him were cluttered with piles of papers, books, mementos, letters, and other work. Even Gertrude Forshag had only a general idea of what was there and where to look for it. His Boston bag—the satchel used by doctors to take instruments and medicines with them on house calls—

was a catchall into which he stuffed anything that he thought he might need sometime. "He'd come out to my office and say, 'Miss Forshag, where is the so-and-so?' I'd say, 'Look in the dead letter office.' I knew if something couldn't be found in its accustomed place, it would be stuffed into that bag."[1] He maintained an open-door policy throughout; not many people who sought to see him ever were turned away. Those who came went away with the impression that they had his undivided attention while they were with him.

His fatalistic Presbyterian belief was tested in the early 1930s when he was summoned to Shreveport to operate on an oil man who had been wounded in the head by a shotgun blast during a robbery attempt. The patient was near death when Ochsner was told that arrangements had been made to fly him to the bedside in a small airplane. "I had an aversion to private planes, but felt that this was a necessity because of the urgent emergency. I called Isabel to see if she would have any objection to my going up." He may have had vague hopes that his wife would rule that the flight was too dangerous, but she understood him to say that he was going by train, not plane, and told him to proceed. It was dark by the time the little craft reached Baton Rouge and encountered a severe storm that made an immediate landing necessary. There was no lighted airfield in the capital at the time. The pilot gunned the engine to attract the attention of people on the ground. Several motorists responded by shining their automobile headlights on the strip, and the plane was brought in successfully. The flight was resumed early the next morning, and the operation proved to be lifesaving.

"It was a harrowing experience," Ochsner recalled, deadpan. On another occasion he was being flown to Winnsboro, Louisiana, by Jimmy Wedell, a pioneer aviator and holder of many flying records, to operate on a patient who was gravely ill of an intestinal problem. Fog closed in, and again Ochsner came through an emergency landing at Baton Rouge.[2] The adventures must have convinced him that he was not destined to die in an airplane accident, because during the rest of his years he spent hundreds of hours aloft in all kinds of planes, airline, military, and private.

An occasional and not very proficient golfer, Ochsner spent more recreational time fishing, and once in a while he hunted, usually going after pheasants or quail. An unsuspected skill was revealed by his long-

1. Forshag, interview, November 17, 1956.
2. AO Recollection, Airplanes.

time friend, Owen H. Wangensteen, chairman of surgery at the University of Minnesota. During a visit to the Wangensteens at Prescott, Wisconsin, Ochsner was taken to a village dump that was overrun with rats. "Alton had a deadly aim with a slingshot," Wangensteen reported.[3]

By the 1950s Ochsner had contracted an incurable case of the wanderlust, the only relief being gained by boarding an airplane and flying off somewhere. He scheduled his operations and his teaching in two or three days a week in order that he could accept more of the flood of invitations to give speeches, conduct demonstrations, or participate in medical society conventions. The cost was no problem: when his expenses were not paid by his hosts, the Clinic took care of the bill. He was the best advertisement the Ochsner Medical Institutions had, and it was good business to afford him wide exposure.

Miss Forshag arranged his itineraries. Isabel, if she were not going with him, packed his suitcase, gave him whatever cash she thought he would need, and outlined to him what he was expected to do. In his more active years he watched his weight while in New Orleans by foregoing lunch. Once aloft or abroad, he forgot his diet and let his hearty appetite guide him. He was not shy about seeking invitations from friends in the cities he visited. David P. Boyd, a Lahey Clinic surgeon, told of meeting Ochsner at the airport in Boston and starting to drive him to the hotel where Boyd had made a reservation. "As we drove out Storrow Drive, I mentioned to him that I had these reservations. He immediately replied that he always stayed in a private home if he had the choice. I recall my wife's discomfiture when she met us at the door in her bathrobe."[4] Isabel wistfully told a friend she wished sometimes that she and her husband could be like ordinary tourists, stay in a hotel, and go sight-seeing. They missed a lot, she said, by being honored house guests.

Ochsner was not usually impressed by scenery. His daughter-in-law Mary Lou remembered a family trip in the Italian countryside: "We went through so fast you couldn't even see it." Once he reached his destination, he could appreciate a beautiful sight if somebody pointed it out to him. Even at that, Mary Lou noted, "He never had much time for the romantic."[5] In an automobile there were two pressure points, the accelerator and the horn. Ochsner always was in a hurry. Friends say the only faster driver than he was Mike DeBakey.

3. Owen Wangensteen to Harkey, April 4, 1978.
4. David P. Boyd to Harkey, February 23, 1978.
5. Mrs. John L. Ochsner, interview, June 2, 1977.

As much as he enjoyed the perquisites of fame, Ochsner did not forget that he was primarily a doctor, a healer. Frank A. Riddick, Jr., later medical director of the Ochsner Clinic, learned this after he joined the staff in 1961—a time when Ochsner's surgical career still was near its peak. As a junior member of the department of medicine, Riddick found himself on duty on New Year's Eve. A seriously ill patient who had been flown in from Central America was admitted to the hospital. Riddick diagnosed the problem as an obstructed bile duct and decided that surgical intervention was necessary. "The Clinic was closed and when I checked to see who was on call for surgery I discovered to my great surprise that Dr. Ochsner was the surgeon on call," Riddick recalled.

> With a great deal of trepidation I contacted him, explaining the situation, and asked that he come offer a surgical opinion on the patient. At that stage, having spent all my previous professional life in a cloistered medical school environment, where things tend to be delegated to the lowest member of the department, I was fearful that I might not be able to get any help. Dr. Ochsner showed up about half an hour later, went over the patient with me, and we agreed that immediate surgical intervention was indicated rather than delaying things because of the holiday. Dr. Ochsner spent most of that New Year's Eve operating on the patient who, needless to say, had a most successful outcome.[6]

Although as a surgeon he sometimes ventured into areas where the fainthearted did not go, Ochsner's basic approach to medicine, evolving from his rich experience, was cautious and conservative. He was grateful to have had the advantages of the discoveries in the golden age of medicine, yet he asserted, "I'm glad I got my training before we had antibiotics. I'm a better doctor as a result. We had to learn to treat the individual, to take advantage of his ability to get well." His advice to young doctors was: "Don't forget that you're treating people. You're not treating disease, but people." In his presidential address to the American College of Surgeons in 1952, he said, "While working for the 'benefit of humanity,' let us not forget that our work is also for the 'benefit of the patients,' the individual men and women who seek us out in their hours of trial and who need compassion and understanding as well as scientific care." On

6. Frank A. Riddick, Jr., interview, June 16, 1978.

another occasion he remarked, "It's surprising how much you can do by just talking to the patient."

"Anybody who gets rich in medicine is either doing too much or charging too much," he said. Alluding to unnecessary surgery, he observed, "A dishonest doctor is worse than a crook. If a person has been held up and robbed by a bandit, he knows that he has been victimized. But many times in medicine a patient becomes the victim of a dishonest doctor, and actually feels grateful to the doctor because he does not realize what has happened."

"There is no doubt," Ochsner emphasized, "that the general practitioner is the backbone of medicine." He also suggested that "we have too many specialists who become specialists before they become doctors. Doctors should be trained first in the general practice of medicine." And speaking as a founder of one of the big clinics, he cautioned, "I would hate to see a situation develop in which there would be only group practice. It is necessary to have individual practitioners and general practitioners."

Although he never felt a need for psychoanalysis, Ochsner supposed that his personality would have been described as aggressive, competitive, and perfectionist. "I don't tolerate anything short of perfect," he admitted. "I keep emphasizing to the young residents, as I did to the students, that medicine is an inexact science at best in contradistinction to mathematics, and it behooves us to make it as exact as possible." He had a maxim, "The successful physician is humble," and although that particular adjective might not occur to anyone trying to sum up his personality, the word *arrogant* would be much further from the truth. He told residents that a doctor "need never worry about feeling that a family or the patient would lose confidence if you ask for a consultation because then they know they can trust you. . . . Asking for consultation is not a sign of weakness; it's a sign of strength."

In old age, Ochsner talked about one of his strengths, the willingness to admit an error, the mark of honesty. "I often say the advantage that I have had for having lived as long as I have and having as much gray hair as I have, I made every mistake that could have been made but I hope to have profited by it." He did not have to cover up, to think of excuses. His enemies were disarmed, and he had a lesson to take to heart. Richard King, then a fellow, told of the day when he and other trainees were assisting Ochsner in a pneumonectomy. "Fellows, I always ligate and divide the azygos vein because in my early years I unfortunately opened one and lost a patient," he told those gathered around the table.[7] George H. Martin recalled a surgery residence conference at which he presented a case of large bowel intestinal obstruction in which he had done a colostomy. "I threw the X-rays up on the screen, and Dr. Ochsner said immediately, 'This man has a volvulus [a twisting of the intestine that causes blockage].' Of course, I had missed this completely and as I stood there in all my embarrassment he smiled and said, 'George, I've made every mistake a surgeon can make. But I've tried to profit by my mistakes, and I expect you to do the same.'"

By 1956 most of the mistakes were behind the surgeon. At a meeting of former Foundation fellows, one of the features was a session at which a series of chest case histories was presented by the chief surgical fellow and discussed by Ochsner and the medical department heads. As the findings and X-rays for each were given, each was discussed as to diagnosis and treatment. Rowland F. Zeigler picks up the story:

> Dr. Ochsner's opinions were never "perhaps" or "possibly," but were firm, positive and convincing—such as, "This patient must be operated upon," or "That is cancer of the lung," or "This case is not surgical."
>
> After all discussions and opinions, the chief resident arose to thank the participants for their advice, and then to everyone's surprise began what sounded like a farewell speech, thanking all for his happy and profitable years under their guidance. He concluded by saying, "I probably won't be around after today," and explained that the cases presented were not current, but were selected from the files for the past ten years. "And we know the answers," he said.
>
> There was a startled hush over the audience, a few of the discussants noticeably squirming and blushing. Dr. Ochsner smiled and remained cool and composed. When the summaries were given, he had been right in every instance! He batted 1.000 through this baited trap.[8]

Of course, the resident did not lose his job.

Ochsner's views were conservative but never reactionary so far as the practice of medicine was concerned. He was quite willing to accept organ

7. Richard King to Harkey, December 31, 1976.
8. Rowland F. Zeigler to Harkey, November 8, 1976.

transplants, and was pleased when his son John performed the first heart transplant in Louisiana. He predicted the eventual development of an artificial heart, but noted that the shortage of donor organs always would limit kidney, liver, and lung transplants. He was sanguine about the outlook for controlling cancer. "We already have controlled the infections, diabetes, pernicious anemia, and other diseases that once took a big toll," he said. "And as a result of research, cancer will cease to be too much of a factor."

Undoubtedly there were times when he "pulled the plug"—withheld heroic measures intended to prolong the lives of moribund, hopelessly ill patients. In an area so controversial, few doctors will discuss their own cases, but Ochsner did make his belief clear: "I think that one ought to be very careful about doing it. I see no reason for keeping a person alive who otherwise has no chance of recovery. It is terribly expensive and awfully hard on the family, and it is cruel to the patient. I think it is perfectly horrible just to keep them alive artificially. If there is a chance of recovery, then everything ought to be done. It ought to be explained to the family and all the possibilities discussed, and then it ought to be decided by several individuals, not just one."

His views on "socialized medicine," governmental intervention in the delivery and financing of care, were predictable. "If the liberal politicians continue to bait the voting public with promise of free medicine, the free enterprise system in the United States is in real jeopardy."

He admitted to an early prejudice against women in medicine because, he said, at the time, most women who underwent training abandoned practice when they married. "A waste," he concluded. But later, women continued in medicine after marriage, and he changed his mind. "I think women do awfully well in internal medicine, pediatrics, ophthalmology, pathology. Woman are smart, smarter than men." He was especially pleased with the career of one of his students, Grace Goldsmith, a nutritionist who became dean of the Tulane School of Public Health.

Although aware of the advantages offered by modern medical technology, he said too many physicians order laboratory tests before they even talk to a patient. "I fear we might be producing a group of highly sophisticated technicians rather than physicians." He felt that medical students were devoting too much of their time to the specialties at the expense of learning general medicine. Dermatologists, for instance, should be good doctors because "the skin is the mirror of the whole body, and they are in position to pick up signs of disease."

Because of his study of blood clots, Ochsner demanded that his surgical patients get out of bed and move around within hours of their operations. He knew that embolisms were likely to develop as a result of inactivity. He made his mother do scores of bicycling-type exercises as she was recuperating from the operation performed by Mims Gage.

His medical hero was Sir William Osler, the Canadian physician. "I thought Osler was the greatest man that ever walked," he remarked.

One of his favorite stories was of a dinner in Buenos Aires with Juan Perón while the latter still was the Argentine strong man. "As we were sitting after dinner, he turned to me and said, 'I like surgeons in government,' and I asked him why. He answered, 'Generals are no good, they order too much; lawyers are no good, they argue too much; engineers are no good, they can't make an opinion without using a slide rule; but surgeons are men of action.' "9 Ochsner always knew that he had chosen the right specialty, although he undoubtedly had the talent and temperament to have been outstanding in any branch of medicine—with the probable exception of psychiatry. In that field he would have empathized with patients, all right, but he never could have endured the protracted, contemplative sessions. He was a doer, a prime example of Perón's man of action.

His experience resulted in some firm ideas on surgery and surgeons. "Most of the time we didn't lose them to the knife; we failed to cure them before the knife," he remarked.

> I've often said I could take a good plumber—plumbers usually can use their hands well—and teach him within three months to do any surgical operation, but he wouldn't know when to do it or what to do. A surgeon is a doctor first and then a mechanic. . . . I like to differentiate between an operator and a surgeon. There are individuals who use their hands well but don't have the judgment. They may be very dexterous in doing a procedure, but I would rather trust a man who has a lot of judgment but is less dexterous and maybe a little slower. The technical side of surgery is by far the easiest to master. Surgical diagnosis, surgical judgment, and surgical pathology are the most difficult to learn and the most important to have. . . . I think surgeons are becoming more conservative all the time. In the final analysis, the surgeon should put himself in the place of his patient and make his decision on this basis. It is a good

9. AO Recollection, Duqué and Perón.

leveling influence if he does so. . . . A surgeon can have a zero mortality rate if he chooses only patients who don't have much wrong with them. The difference between the boys and the men [is] the individual who is willing to tackle the tough jobs and get them well, although he is going to have complications and lose a few because the risk is so much greater.

Bryan Bell, a New Orleans businessman who went to the Clinic to have a mole removed, was surprised when Ochsner entered the room and began preparing for the procedure. "Don't tell me that *you* are going to do this little job," Bell said.

"Why, yes," replied Ochsner, "Do you have any objection?"

"Of course not, but isn't this an excess of talent to apply to such a minor operation?"

"Bryan, the only minor operations are those done on somebody else." [10]

As a resident, Rowland Zeigler was helping his chief, Curtis Tyrone, perform a hysterectomy while Ochsner, already scrubbed, stood by to do a gall bladder operation on the patient when the others had finished. "Dr. Ochsner was standing at the foot of the table, resting his hands on the sterile drapes, undoubtedly with many problems on his mind, when Dr. Tyrone completed the inside work," Zeigler related. "Dr. Tyrone stepped back and peeled off his gloves, leaving me to close the incision, I thought. But he walked around behind me, pulled me away from the table, and said, 'Come on, Rowland, let's go. Al can close.' Dr. Ochsner was left with a first-year intern to close our wound before he could start on his own work. With a twinkle in his eye that seemed to say, 'Okay, fellows, you outfoxed me this time,' he quietly moved up, without saying a word, and started the closure." [11]

Gary Cooper flew all the way from the Bahamas to New Orleans for his first visit to Ochsner for treatment of his hernia. Ochsner sent him a bill for $10 for the examination. In 1945 a patient flew from California to obtain a second opinion from Ochsner about the desirability of surgery for a lung cancer. Ochsner saw him, concurred in the opinion that an operation was necessary, and wrote on the charge slip in the man's record that he should be charged $5 for the consultation. Merrill Hines, then Ochsner's surgical resident, added two zeros to the five. [12]

10. Bryan Bell, interview, July 9, 1977.
11. Zeigler, interview, November 8, 1976.
12. Hines, interview, 1985.

His devout mother could only have been disappointed in Ochsner's churchgoing habits as an adult. Perhaps once or twice a year Isabel could get him to the St. Charles Avenue Presbyterian Church for a Sunday morning service. He would look around the congregation, spot a friend, and murmur: "There's Edgar." He took the position that he had been to his share of services as a child, when he was required to be present for the full schedule of events at the Presbyterian church in Kimball. Apparently some of the early teachings did take hold. "I don't know what God is, but I believe in a Supreme Being," he said. "I think it is absolutely essential that we do. I've seen people who did not, and the people that do, they can stand almost anything. If you don't have faith, nothing means anything to you. I think that I don't know what God is, but I do know there is a Supreme Being and we have to believe in this. I do. I don't go to church regularly, but I try to lead the right sort of life."

He said he was worried over what he saw as an effort to de-emphasize religion, a movement that he described as Communist-inspired. He saw no real conflict between the religious experience and medical science. "I have seen people who have died for no reason at all because they just gave up," he explained. "Contrariwise, I have seen people who I was sure couldn't live two or three months go on indefinitely." He attributed the survivals to faith. His own experience bolstered his acceptance of a Presbyterian tenet that whatever happens is for the best. "I'm convinced that if you do the right thing, or try to do the right thing, it's going to turn out, even though at times it doesn't seem that it will." His background was all Protestant. But when he and Isabel had an audience with Pope John XXIII, he did not forget to inform the pontiff, "We have six grandchildren who are Catholics." Akky's children were reared in the denomination of their mother.

Ochsner espoused some of his philosophical ideas with almost religious fervor. One of these was the work ethic, the conviction that the greatest satisfaction life provides lies in labor. "The Joy of Working" was the title of his 1960 commencement address at his alma mater, the University of South Dakota. "I am greatly concerned," he said, "that we as a nation may be destined for a period when the gratification obtained from a sense of accomplishment, which is as great as any of the prerequisites for happiness, will be lost. There is an increasing tendency for people to want to do as little as possible, and the increasing demand for higher wages and shorter hours is not only depriving workers of the gratification of accomplishments but is also threatening the economy of our nation." No one could say that he did not set an example of industry. "If we don't stop we will become a welfare state," he commented. "If one kills the incentive for people to work, everything is gone."[13]

He identified himself with a citizens' campaign against criminal rackets in the New Orleans area, serving a term as president of the Metropolitan Crime Commission; his second wife, Jane, remarked, "If they ever find you in an alley dead, they'll know it is the Communists, the Mafia, or the tobacco people." The recurring theme of his conversations and his speeches was his intense dislike of communism. His advocacy of all things American was so well known that an incident in the Roosevelt Hotel one night was absurd to the point of being amusing. Mrs. Samuel Smallpage was attending a convention when she was told by her husband to go up to Room 782, where agents of the Federal Bureau of Investigation wanted to talk with her. She was puzzled, but did as directed. The agents quizzed her about her friendship with Ochsner and about his loyalty to his country. Later she learned the reason: the FBI had found out about the surgeon's secret trip to Buenos Aires to treat Juan Perón and had become curious about his politics.[14] Ochsner's patriotism was simply expressed: "There are a lot of things wrong with this nation, but God knows it's the best in the world. Don't destroy it."

Even fascism, in Ochsner's view, was not as evil as communism, although "of course, I hate the dictatorship part." He added, "But some of those countries have to have a dictator. Look at Cuba. They need a certain amount of dictatorship because when it comes right down to it, democracy is not the most efficient government in the world. The finest government is a benevolent dictatorship. But unfortunately, they don't remain benevolent very long." He said that when Mussolini came to power in Italy, "he was a very benevolent dictator. I was in Rome on the first anniversary of his coming into power. I'd been there before, and they'd steal anything. The rioting and the terrorism were simply horrible. He came into power and he instituted law and order and you could leave anything anywhere in Italy and it would be safe. It was just Utopia. But the trouble with dictators is that it goes to their head."

He was not inclined to be forgiving toward those on the other side of the political fence.

13. Alton Ochsner, "The Joy of Working," commencement address, University of South Dakota, June 6, 1960.

14. Mrs. Samuel M. Smallpage, interview, May 19, 1977.

I feel a liberal is an individual who is not much interested in the fiscal responsibility of this country, an individual who is more interested in getting votes than in standing up for the right thing. I'm very much concerned about a good many of the so-called liberals who think they are good Americans but are being influenced by individuals who are actually out-and-out leftists to the extent of destroying our economy and destroying our ecology under the guise of environmental protection. I am for environmental protection but not to the point of the destruction of the nation. All those demonstrating against nuclear energy are liberals. Most think they are good Americans, but they're being stimulated by individuals out to destroy the country. They don't have to destroy it from without if they can destroy it from within.

On a subject more closely connected with medicine—abortion—Ochsner's view offers no surprise. "I am opposed to abortion on request. I think abortion at times is necessary to save a woman's life, but that is the only time I think there should be an abortion."

Once he became an activist, he enjoyed it. He never lost his naïveté. After Isabel died, some Republican politicians approached him with the suggestion that he seek election as city councilman from an Uptown district where many voters shared his conservative views. It is true that there is a precedent in New Orleans for men and women in the top strata of society to become involved in government, usually in reform movements. Even so, the prospect of a surgeon of worldwide renown busying himself in the minutiae of city hall activities presented incongruities that were obvious, although not to Ochsner. He broke the news to John and Mary Lou when he went to dinner at their home. "Daddy, it's ridiculous," John told him. This was the wrong approach, because Ochsner's resolve always was strengthened when somebody opposed one of his ideas. Mary Lou fine-tuned her husband's argument. "Papa, it's ridiculous for you to step down like this," she said. "If you were running for United States senator it might be a little different, but for a man of your prestige to lower himself to that position is wrong." Besides, she said, if he ran he would spoil the chances of a qualified young Republican who wanted the job. "I'm sure if we had not spoken up, he would have run," John said later.[15]

15. John L. Ochsner, interview, July 14, 1977.

17 Losses Along the Way

The family converged at St. Onge, South Dakota, on July 11, 1926, to celebrate the fiftieth wedding anniversary of E. P. and Clara Ochsner. Alton, Isabel, and baby Akky had driven through the heat from Madison, Wisconsin, where Alton was on the medical school faculty at the University of Wisconsin. Alton's five sisters were there, along with their husbands and children. After a gala midday feast at the home of Pearl, Mrs. B. E. Colby, the adults were sitting around reminiscing when one of the nephews rushed in, frightened. Edward Hale Griswold, Genevieve's young son, had gone swimming in a pond, was in deep water, and could not stay afloat. The men ran to the pond and pulled the child out. Alton tried in vain to resuscitate him.[1]

As a practitioner, Alton had seen people die, of course, but this was his first experience with a personal tragedy. In the long lifetime ahead, he was destined to know sorrow and disappointment as well as joy and satisfaction. Among other woes, he would mourn all but one of his seven other family members—parents and sisters—who sat around the dinner table on that day. Ava Marie, Mrs. William Kaynor, was the last survivor of the eight who had shared happy days in Kimball in the long ago. When she died in 1983, she was a month past her ninety-sixth birthday, a testament again to the remarkable longevity of Alton's family.

Bitterness compounded grief for Ochsner in 1955 when his first grandson, Eugene Allen Davis, Jr., at age two and a half became one of fifty-two children who died as a result of inoculation with Salk poliomyelitis vaccine from a faulty batch. Akky remembered his father's anguish. "I was away in training," Akky related. "When I left he had dark hair. The next time I saw him he had white hair." The development of the Salk defense against the crippling, often-fatal disease had raised parents' hopes, and the vaccine was in great demand nationwide. Ochsner used his

1. AO Recollection, Sorrow.

influence to obtain a supply, and on a Wednesday 241 persons, including the children of Clinic doctors, were inoculated.

On Sunday little Davey became ill with what at first was thought to be influenza. But there had been some live virus in the faulty batch, and what the child had was polio. By Monday he was paralyzed, and on Tuesday he died. None of the others inoculated at the Clinic became seriously ill, but Daniel Trigg, a resident in pediatrics who was one of the physicians attending Davey, contracted polio and was left a cripple. He changed his specialty to pathology, which he could practice from a wheelchair. Whether his illness resulted from his contact with Davey is unclear.

Ochsner said he was resentful not toward the Cutter Laboratories, which produced the vaccine, but toward the National Polio Foundation. He complained that the foundation had staged a spectacular at the University of Michigan to announce the vaccine, instead of presenting the data in medical circles. He blamed this action at least partly on a malign allegiance to the memory of the late president Franklin D. Roosevelt, history's most prominent polio sufferer and, of course, political anathema to conservatives such as Ochsner: "The foundation wanted to glamorize Roosevelt, and a great play was made about [the vaccine]. Because of this there was a tremendous demand for it and there was a great urgency in producing large amounts of it. As a result they let down the bars in making it, and deaths occurred because the controls were not as good as before or since."[2]

Davey's parents—Sis and her husband, Allen Davis—filed suit against Cutter, a move that caused some hard feelings in the Clinic. Dean H. Echols and other doctors contended that Cutter was making a major effort toward the conquest of polio and should not be penalized for an unfortunate accident.[3] The Davises withdrew the court action, but a residue of resentment remained. Isabel stopped speaking to Echols. Ochsner said he was opposed to the suit because it would not bring Davey back.

In his late years, Ochsner suffered other bereavements. His nineteen-year-old grandson and namesake, Alton Ochsner III, a premedical student, died of a stroke. Alton III was the surgeon's last loss of a grandchild. After Ochsner's death, Allen Davis, by then divorced from Sis, was killed in an airplane accident in Florida, and Mims, at fifty-four and at the height of his career in urology, strangled on a piece of meat during a doctors' banquet at Savannah, Georgia, in 1985.

2. AO, interview, December 8–9, 1977.
3. Dean H. Echols, interview, 1977.

Along with the triumphs in the 1960s came troubles that threatened to blight the spirit that sustained Ochsner's soaring ambitions. One of his strengths always had been, in the words of his son John, an ability to "turn his back on things that he doesn't want to see." Now fate tested him with overwhelming developments from which he could not simply turn away. He survived, but with scars.

When Akky obtained his medical degree from Tulane, Alton arranged for him to begin graduate training under the elder Ochsner's close friend Fred Coller, chairman of surgery at the University of Michigan, and then to learn about heart surgery at Houston from Mike DeBakey and Denton E. Cooley. Alton plotted the same course for John. For a period the brothers were residents together under the man who once had been their baby-sitter. They made different impressions on DeBakey. Akky recalls complaining about some of the activities at Houston: "I was told to shut up. If I had not been the son of my father I might have been kicked out of the program."[4] On the other hand, DeBakey told John that, if he would stay with him for five years, he would arrange for him to be made chairman of surgery at some medical school. Later, when Ochsner and Merrill Hines went to Houston to recruit John for the Clinic, DeBakey asked how much the job would pay. He was told $16,000 a year. DeBakey said, "I'll pay him twice that to stay here, but of course he can go if he wishes."[5]

Meanwhile, Akky became a surgeon on the Ochsner staff in 1958. Open heart surgery for bypassing clogged blood vessels, a procedure of which DeBakey and Cooley were pioneers at Houston, was winning acceptance, and the Clinic wanted to be able to offer the operation as an alternative to conservative medical treatment. Alton never had made a secret of his hopes of bringing all three of his sons into the Clinic. He had dreamed of bequeathing his interest in the partnership directly to them. He yielded on the idea when, in 1957, the founders arranged to share ownership with the senior staff doctors, but even then a concession was made for the children of the five. The concession provided that offspring of the founders would be admitted to full partnership after one year on the staff, rather than having to wait five years as other doctors joining the Clinic had to do.

Under the circumstances, Akky perhaps could not be blamed for expecting that he would be somewhat favored. A period of transition was

4. Alton Ochsner, Jr., interview, July 16, 1977.
5. Hines, interview, 1985.

beginning in which the founders were handing over control of the Clinic to younger men. Akky believed that he was seen as a threat by others who feared he would capitalize on his relationship to Alton to win undue advantages, perhaps at their expense. Sometimes he did give the impression that he was throwing his weight around; for instance, by taking over his father's reserved parking space when Alton was away. Akky said he "got discouraged with the whole system of team practice because it hadn't been what I thought it would be. . . . You see, Clinic medicine is not federalization of medicine, but it is socialization of medicine. . . . If I came in late at the Clinic, I would be chewed out not by my daddy but by Julie Carnahan, the nurse. She treated you like you were a buck private and she was the top sergeant."

Akky, who considered himself to be one of the best-trained heart surgeons in the United States, was not getting the cases he had expected. In 1961 the Clinic management, eager for a share of bypass patients, hired John. As things turned out, it was a sad day for Alton Ochsner, who endorsed the action. Rivalry between the two brothers caused a break in the family. Later, Akky said that he had tried to work out an agreement with John. First he suggested that he do the adult heart surgery and John the pediatric operations. Then he proposed that they share cases equally. He quoted John as saying, "I want them all."[6] In denying that he made any such statement, John pointed out that patients were referred by the Clinic's cardiologists, who decided which surgeon they wanted to do the jobs.[7] In any event, Akky found himself with little heart work to do, while John was busy. Their bitterness became public when the brothers engaged in a yelling match one day in a hospital operating room.

Akky's frustrations were piling up in 1966, when Alton reached the age at which Clinic rules dictated he must retire as director of surgery. Apparently Akky still had hopes that he would take over the job, but when the board of management met, it was John who was named head of the department. By that time Alton no longer was a member of the board, but he attended the meeting at which the appointment was made and obviously acquiesced in the action. He did his best to stay uninvolved in the friction between his sons, but the doctors who were running the Clinic knew that, in any showdown involving the practice of surgery, he would favor John. Years later he would publicly proclaim John "the best surgeon I ever saw."

6. Alton Ochsner, Jr., interview, July 16, 1977.
7. John L. Ochsner, interview, July 14, 1977.

A crisis over Akky's status became inevitable, but in the meantime a far darker event intervened. Perhaps it was an instance of Alton's turning his back on something he did not want to see. His eyes were opened by an old friend. In December, 1965, Isabel accompanied her husband to Hot Springs, Virginia, for a meeting of the Southern Surgical Association. There they met Roy Rudolph, Alton's companion in the long-ago Chicago days. "I was shocked when I saw Isabel because she looked so bad," Rudolph said. "I immediately went to Alton and asked, 'What's the matter with Isabel?' 'Oh, nothing,' he replied. 'She's got a little cold on her chest.' I said, 'I don't believe that; she looks mighty bad to me. She's short of breath. I asked her to go for a walk and she wouldn't do it. You've got to promise me you'll have her checked. I'm worried about her.'"

Upon returning to New Orleans, Alton sent Isabel to the Clinic, where an examination revealed fluid in her chest. A few days later, in January, 1966, she entered the hospital for a tap that would permit examination of the fluid. Meanwhile, Alton went to Tupelo, Mississippi, to make a scheduled speech. At Tupelo he received a telephone call: there were cancer cells in the fluid. "God, the worst blow I ever had in my life," Alton recalled.

> I knew what the consequences were. If the cancer had already spread to the pleura, I knew there was no chance. Well, I was just absolutely shattered. The whole world dropped off. I came back home and they hadn't told her, so I went in with Dr. Hurst Hatch when he told her. She took it very stoically. "What does this mean?" she asked. Of course, I tried to make light of it. I said, "Well, it means that you've got cancer, dear, but they plan to give you radioactive phosphorous and let's hope that will cure it. It sometimes does." She said, "Well, we can't tell Sis. It will kill her." Well, I knew we couldn't keep it from Sis, so I told the boys and broke down and cried, and we told Sis and she went all to pieces. She and her mother were so close. Oh, God. I've never known any two so close.

Alton had known there was a scar on Isabel's right lung, the result of an old tubercular infection, but since it had not changed in years, he had not feared a malignancy. Now it was found that she had an adenocarcinoma that could not be treated surgically because it already had begun to spread. The wife of a world authority on lung cancer now had become a victim of "his" disease. Alton felt no solace in the fact that Isabel had been a nonsmoker.

Since Alton Ochsner, the surgeon, could do nothing himself to stem the inexorable progress of the cancer, he invoked the resources of medical science to prolong Isabel's life and make her comfortable. Radioactive phosphorous was injected into the pleural cavity to control the original lesion in the lower lung lobe. For one period of four or five months, she was in bed while undergoing a course of cobalt therapy. Alton knew he was grasping at straws when he sent off specimens of the pleural fluid to researchers at Detroit who were experimenting with a plan for taking cells from a tumor, culturing them, and producing a vaccine intended to immunize a patient against his own cancer. It was found that the tumor cells would grow, but so did red blood cells. The vaccine could not be used because it might cause Isabel to develop an immune reaction to her own blood cells that would destroy them.

The progress of the disease was marked by bone metastases to the skull, pelvis, and spine. These were treated with X-ray. A few months before the end, the metastasis to the spine caused so much pain that a specialist was flown from Chicago to do a cordotomy. He inserted a needle into the spine and destroyed nerves that conveyed the pain impulse. Alton was proud that Isabel withstood the entire ordeal "like a soldier." But the last two years of her life were full of misery.

There were happy times, too, as Isabel accompanied Alton on three trips to Europe, beginning in the summer that followed the discovery of her plight. They joined Vernon and Gertude Neuhaus, Texas friends, in a motor and air tour that took them to London, Stuttgart, Prague, Vienna, Athens, and Italy. Isabel even made a side trip with the Neuhauses to Budapest while Alton attended a meeting. Even in these circumstances, he kept a busy work schedule.

In the spring of 1967, they flew to London for a meeting of National Airlines directors, then went on to Paris to begin a motor tour of the French château country. Isabel was about to enter her last six months of life when she accompanied Alton to Vienna in September for a meeting of the International Surgical Society. From there they toured the Austrian Alps and then flew to Athens.

Not long after their return home, Isabel went into the Ochsner Foundation Hospital for her final stay. Alton knew the end was approaching. He was a regular in his office in the Clinic, only a short walk from Isabel's hospital room. He continued to see patients under an arrangement made when he formally retired in 1967. While he could not operate, he was allowed to treat those who wanted appointments, and to keep 95 percent of the fees. The income was welcomed because the pension paid by the Clinic to him and the other surviving founders was only $18,000 a year each. As concerned as he was over his wife's downhill course, he nevertheless retained his air of optimism and his zest for living.[8] He was given a new Cadillac by one of his grateful patients, and in his enthusiasm drove it onto the hospital grounds so Isabel could see it from her window.

Even had she not been dying, the last months would have been a trial for Isabel in her role as mother. Mims's marriage to "Paddy" (Corinne Cousins) was breaking up, and the family's first divorce was pending. As close as she was to her daughter, Isabel had to know that there also were growing strains in Sis's union with Allen. Allen served as a public relations representative for the Clinic and Foundation, but his income did not approach those of his father-in-law and brothers-in-law. Sis, with three sons to be educated, had gone to work as an interior decorator. Isabel's concern came out during a talk with John, who by that time was a highly successful surgeon, widely recognized as a worthy successor to Alton. Isabel asked John to promise that he would come to Sis's aid, financially, whenever she needed it. He assured her that he would. He came close to tears when Isabel told him, "I know my Johnny boy is not going to let anything happen to me."

A continuing worry was Akky's situation at the Clinic. As her firstborn and a sickly child, Akky had a special relationship with Isabel, who actively took his side in his difficulties with his brother John and with the Clinic management. Although Akky later said that Isabel advised him to resign from the staff when the dispute first flared, he made no move to leave after she became ill. Out of deference to her, the board of management took no action. Akky continued to work out of his office in the general surgery section, seeing the patients who were assigned to him under the routine scheduling procedures of the busy Clinic. His office was near his father's, as was John's. While Alton tried not to take sides, Isabel scolded Merrill Hines, medical director, chief executive, and management spokesman. "How little can you get?" she demanded.

Meanwhile, her condition deteriorated. On the morning of April 24, 1968, Alton arrived at the hospital and found her short of breath. "I

8. AO, interview, December 8–9, 1977.

realized that she was getting much worse," he said. He suggested that attendants give her oxygen, which relieved her, and then he summoned Sis, Akky, and Mims to the bedside. John was away at a meeting. By this time, Sis had become reconciled to the inevitability of her mother's death, and everybody was calm as the family had a last visit. After a couple of hours, Isabel said she was tired and wanted to sleep for a while. The others moved into an adjoining room. A half hour later, Isabel died. After forty-four years of marriage, Alton was alone.

Weeks before, Isabel had given Alton instructions about her funeral. The pallbearers whom she selected were her three sons, along with Allen Davis and two family friends, McDonald Stephens and Forres M. Collins. When the inventory of her estate was filed, it was revealed that Ochsner had not used his surgical talents and his renown to make himself a millionaire. The couple's total holdings, including assets inherited by Isabel, were listed at $651,883.03.

After he lost Isabel's support, Akky's days in the Clinic were numbered. The surgery department was overstaffed, senior men were available to do the nonheart operations, and John Ochsner and later Noel L. Mills handled the cardiac bypass cases. Akky resigned, deciding to make a new beginning in his career. He went into the private practice of surgery in the New Orleans area with considerable success, reportedly earning more than he would have at the Clinic.

While his grief over the loss of Isabel still was fresh, Alton bore the burden of the family conflict over Akky's departure. He insisted there was no estrangement, again turning his back on the obvious. "It hurt me to have Akky leave," he once commented. "He has to work twice as hard now in hospitals where there are no interns to help. He could have been an asset to the Clinic." Yet Akky expressed "great disappointment" over the fact that "from the time I left, Dad never did a thing for me. He put all of his efforts into pushing John." Previously, he explained, Alton had worked to get him into medical societies and toward advancing his career.

Akky said he felt that the changes stemmed from Alton's loyalty to the Clinic and Foundation. "Of course, he built this thing," he added. "It was his idea, and every brick in that place he raised money for, and everything he does is directed to the Clinic. I love him very much and I admire him but we're not as close as we were."[9] A residue of bitterness kept the family from ever again being as close-knit as it had been when Alton and Isabel

9. Alton Ochsner, Jr., interview, July 16, 1977.

would bring the clan together at Thanksgiving, Christmas, and other occasions. As the years passed, there was some thawing, and the Ochsners presented a proper, united face on occasions when it was expected.

Upon Isabel's death, Mrs. Robert Lee Slaughter gave Ochsner $10,000 for a trip to Europe with the children. John, Mary Lou, Allen, and Sis went with him. They stopped in London, Frankfurt, and Heidelberg, then rented a van for a tour of the Swiss Alps. Ochsner showed the others the church near Zurich where he and Isabel were wed, and he had reunions with two or three of the men with whom he had been associated during his training in Europe. The party visited Salzburg, Munich, and Vienna before flying home.

Now the most miserable period of Alton's life began. With the assistance of a housekeeper, he lived alone for a while in the huge home on Exposition Boulevard, then he and Mims were bachelors together after Mims's separation from Paddy. Alton learned how essential Isabel had been to his well-being. His self-reliance always had been taken for granted. It became evident that he must have the support of someone, necessarily a person with feminine intuition, and one willing to subordinate her own interests in order to help him carry on. The most likely prospect to take on Isabel's psychological role was Sis. Alton turned to her, and in so doing undoubtedly hastened the collapse of her already shaky marriage.

Allen, who of course owed his public relations jobs at the Clinic and Foundation to Ochsner, found himself a sort of combined companion, flunky, and nonmedical assistant to his father-in-law. He took care of some of the financial matters previously handled by Isabel, drove Alton to the airport, arranged for plumbers or roof repairers, and in general took details off Alton's hands and left him free to pursue his professional and social interests. Lonely and with no other place to turn, Ochsner was an almost daily guest at the Davis home, to which he had a key. It was Sis who saw him through his darkest hours as a widower. Allen said the relationship between father and daughter "was close to the point of interdependency that put everybody else at a disadvantage."

A sticking point was Ochsner's daily 7 A.M. telephone call to Sis. Always when he was in New Orleans and frequently when he was out of town came the ring, often awakening the household. No matter how late Allen and Sis had been out, they knew their number was being dialed sometime around sunup. Ochsner wanted to tell Sis his schedule for the day, inquire about her activities and her sons, or perhaps share a compliment that he had received. Seemingly, he needed the assurance that some-one cared about what he was doing. In any case, throughout his career he was oblivious to the annoyance felt by anyone being awakened at a bad time. Many hundreds of his patients learned that he made his hospital rounds early and was deaf to hints that he wait until after breakfast. In laying at least part of the blame for the breakup of Sis's marriage on Alton, Akky specifically cited the telephone calls as an irritant. Allen said they were a nuisance.[10] Sis could hardly be blamed for responding to what appeared to be cries for help from her grieving father. But she had her own problems, too. Allen, who described Isabel as a great lady, said his marriage would not have lasted as long as it did "if it had not been for her."

Within a twelve-month period in 1967 and 1968, Alton lost his surgical privileges and his wife. He made the adjustment to the sidelines without too much difficulty because he still had outside interests to keep him busy. Having Isabel taken away from him was another matter.

10. Allen Davis, interview, 1977.

18   Second Love at First Sight

A nd so the seventy-three-year-old man, lonely and miserable, slowly faded away down the path to the grave . . .

No. Not Alton Ochsner.

In the months after Isabel died in the spring of 1968, he kept more than busy. He maintained his Clinic office, presided over by the loyal Gertrude Forshag. He continued to see nonsurgical patients and, although his active connections with the Ochsner Medical Institutions were over, he nevertheless was an elder statesman whose counsel was valued. He traveled extensively to attend meetings and make speeches. He did some writing. The friends he and Isabel had acquired over the years continued to keep him active socially. He maintained, in fact, a schedule that would have exhausted the ordinary septuagenarian. Yet there was a void, an aching emptiness that robbed life of the joy it once had provided. Sis did her best to comfort and encourage him, but she was a daughter motivated by filial devotion, not a mate.

As chairman, Ochsner called a day-long meeting of the program committee of the Interstate Postgraduate Medical Assembly at Chicago on December 21, 1969. Soon after came an invitation from the children of Patrick J. and Geraldine Frawley to attend a dinner in Los Angeles on December 20, celebrating the Frawleys' twenty-fifth wedding anniversary. Frawley, an industrialist connected with Eversharp pencils, Schick razors, and other enterprises, and with interests in motion pictures, had won Ochsner's admiration and friendship with his anti-Communist activities. Both men were key figures in INCA. Ochsner also was fond of Gerry. He wanted to pay his respects to the Frawleys, but there was a problem. He was due in Chicago at 8 A.M. on the day after the dinner. He also had earlier commitments in New Orleans, and the only way he could be present was to fly to Los Angeles for arrival in the evening, go to the dinner, then board a midnight plane for Chicago.

Sis was concerned about this strenuous trip and urged her father to explain his dilemma and decline. Maybe a small voice whispered to Alton. Whatever the reason, he decided to go.[1]

In Los Angeles, Jane Kellogg Sturdy also had been invited by the Frawleys. Jane was an eye-catching blonde who would observe her fifty-sixth birthday on December 30. Her father's family, which had holdings in the Pullman sleeping car company, had migrated to California in the 1880s. They had established a showplace home on Coronado Island at a time when it was believed San Diego would be the dominant city that Los Angeles became. Jane's mother was eighteen when her family moved to Los Angeles from Chicago. Jane's maternal grandfather was secretary-treasurer of the Union Oil Company.

An only child, Jane grew up on the comfort and privileges of well-to-do Los Angeles. Her looks were the kind that bring motion picture offers, but she did not aspire to be an actress. She does believe she was the first child to sing for a broadcast over the first Los Angeles radio station. "The microphone did not go up and down, so they put me on a box and I stretched my neck to sing into the microphone, and I remember that as I was singing the box was slipping lower and I was stretching longer."

At the age of nineteen, she was married to Herbert Sturdy, eleven years her senior. He was an honor graduate of Yale University who became one of the leading corporate lawyers in Los Angeles and a power in the Yale Corporation. He also was one of the California Republicans who helped start Richard M. Nixon on the road to the White House. Jane shared her husband's conservative views. The couple built a home, Sturdywood, on Stone Canyon Road. They had two daughters, Sally and Nancy. Theirs was a happy marriage that lasted for thirty-six years until, on February 19, 1969, Sturdy died of cancer of the colon after undergoing long treatment at the Mayo Clinic.

In helping to prepare Jane for her husband's death, Donald Campbell of the Mayo staff had told her, "Your life is not over. You are a young woman." She responded, "Well, Don, it is for me." In the months afterward she played bridge with women friends and busied herself with family activities, but did not go out with men. She had been away from the social scene for nearly a year when the invitation from the Frawleys arrived. Her daughters did not want her to go to the dinner because it was

1. AO Recollection, Alton and Jane. Details of the romance and marriage of Alton Ochsner and Jane Sturdy are summarized in a lengthy memorandum prepared by Ira Harkey on the basis of interviews with the two.

her first Christmas season as a widow, and they feared she would find the occasion difficult. Jane delayed making a decision until the morning of the event, and then announced that she was going, even though she had no escort. As she was making an appointment with her hairdresser, Ochsner was getting ready in New Orleans to go to the airport to board a Los Angeles-bound plane.

When Ochsner's acceptance arrived, the Frawleys' first inclination was to seat him at their table. They decided, however, that he would enjoy meeting some new people, and assigned him to another table, between Mrs. Herbert Sturdy and Mrs. Hernando Cartwright, with whose husband Ochsner was acquainted. There was no matchmaking connivance in the arrangement. Later the actress Irene Dunne told Jane, "You know, I was sick the night you met Alton, and I just know I would have been seated next to him if I had been there."

When the 250 guests arrived at the Frawley home, they were handed cards assigning them to tables set up in the garden. Ochsner was met at the airport, taken to the home of a friend where he could don his dinner jacket, and delivered to the Frawleys. Jane was driven to the party by neighbors, Betty and Hal Ramser. At the reception in the home, Jane was busy greeting acquaintances whom she had not seen in months. Then dinner was announced, and the assemblage began moving to the garden. "There was nobody taking care of me," Jane discovered. "Everybody thought somebody else was taking care of me. I think the walk alone from the hall to the garden was the longest walk I ever made in my life. And there was Alton."

As Alton approached his seat, he found "the most gorgeous creature I ever saw in my life." He concluded that she must be a motion-picture star or the wife of a tycoon. On Jane's right was a man who had too many preprandial cocktails and who wept when Jane told him that Sturdy, whom he had known slightly, was dead. At Mrs. Cartwright's left was Conrad Hilton, to whom she turned her attention after Ochsner, in answer to her inquiry, said, "I'm just a country doctor." Soon Ochsner and Mrs. Sturdy were oblivious to the others. "The name is Jane," she told him and, at his request, wrote her address on her place card for him. In telling about the meeting, Ochsner did not say whether he suspected at the time that it might be as momentous in his life as the day, half a century earlier, when Isabel's sister asked him to hold her hand as she was being anesthetized in the Chicago hospital.

When dessert was served, Frawley came to the table and asked if

Ochsner would say a few words over the public address system. Ochsner did, noting that he and Frawley had been fighting communism together. Then he added, "I wanted everyone to know that this is one of the happiest times of my life." Remembering the moment, Jane smiled. "I knew he was saying this to me, so I sat there like a Cheshire cat." Ochsner was reminded that it was time for him to start to the airport, and he left without returning to the table.

"I loved him in two hours and went home and told my children I had met the man that I would spend my life with," Jane confided. That same night she took out one of her elaborate Christmas cards bearing a picture of her daughters, walked to a hotel next door, and mailed it to "Dr. Ochsner, Sr., Ochsner Clinic, New Orleans." The next night, on the plane from Chicago to New Orleans, Ochsner wrote a note to Jane, saying he hoped to see her again. Back at the Ochsner medical center, colleagues were greeted by a smiling "chief" who was more buoyant than they had seen him in many months.

Actually, the meeting at the Frawley dinner was not precisely first sight. Jane recalled when she and Alton were introducing themselves that she had shaken hands with him previously. Several years earlier Jane and Herbert Sturdy, in formal attire for a dinner dance at a Beverly Hills hotel, dropped in briefly at a reception where Alton was guest of honor. They were presented to the honored guest, had a cocktail, and were on their way again. Jane had forgotten the occasion until she met Alton again. As for Alton, he had no recollection of Jane, a circumstance that nettled her just a bit because she had been dazzling that night in a glittery white gown. She forgave him because she realized that he was distressed at the time over Isabel's illness.

On Christmas Day, Jane was going downstairs to have breakfast with her daughters and sons-in-law when a telephone call came from New Orleans, one of many that kept the lines busy during the next weeks. On December 30, which happened to be Jane's birthday, Ochsner called again. It was about this time that one of Jane's daughters told her, "Wipe that smile off your face. Remember, you're in mourning." Ochsner flew out for lunch with Jane and her mother. She drove him to the airport. "I think I should tell you how old I am," he began. "Oh, I know. I looked it up in *Who's Who*. We won't talk about that again." The December-October romance was only beginning when Jane decided she should make a few inquiries about Alton among doctors. She telephoned Donald Campbell at Mayo, saying, "I've met a nice man that I'm quite keen about. He wants to come see me. But I don't want to have him until I talk to you. Have you a pencil? He has a peculiar name and I will spell it for you. Look him up and see if it's all right to let him come see me. His name is A-l-t-o-n . . . " Campbell interrupted: "It isn't Alton Ochsner, is it? I don't know him personally but I certainly know of him. He's a very wonderful man. He's very much like Herbert, dedicated to his profession and people." Campbell then asked, "Jane, would you be willing to spend the rest of your life taking cigarettes out of strange mouths?" Jane's reply was, "I'd love to, Don." By the time Ochsner invited Jane to fly to New Orleans for Mardi Gras in February, they had decided they would be married in April.

Ochsner had been asked earlier by the Greek government to join eleven other doctors in Athens in February to study the country's educational system. The invitation included the wife of each doctor. Ochsner had arranged for Sis to go with him. They had plane reservations on Thursday, February 12, two days after Mardi Gras.

When Jane arrived in New Orleans, where she was the house guest of Sis and Allen Davis, she found Sis ill of influenza. "You think I didn't bring a germ with me?" Jane asked Sis. "I'm no fool. I'm just dying to get rid of you for that Greek trip." If Sis had known that Jane had a frock in her luggage that would be suitable for a bride, she might have been alerted by the remark, made in a bantering tone.

On Friday, Jane met Alton's family at dinner at the Exposition Boulevard home. On Saturday, Alton took her sightseeing up the River Road. On Sunday, they were guests at a luncheon, after which Alton left to attend a reception at which the Rex who would reign over Mardi Gras was introduced. Jane returned to the Davis home, where she found Sis still almost incapacitated.

"I'm going to marry your father Thursday," Jane announced.

"I think that's a marvelous idea," Sis responded. Allen's reaction was, "Oh, Jane, you can't do that to the chief."

A little later Alton called. "Janie," he said, "I'm down here at the King's Club and I just wanted to phone and tell you that I love you."

"Are you sitting down?" Jane asked.

"Should I be?"

"I think you had better."

"All right, I'm sitting down."

"Honey, you're marrying me on Thursday." After Alton's surprised gasp, Jane said, "You know, Sis really can't go to Greece."

Alton agreed. He said of Jane's plan, "That's wonderful." A problem about Jane's passport was solved when she put in a telephone call to the White House and asked to speak with Richard Nixon. The president was not available, but an aide made the arrangements. Jane's daughters, the Frawleys, and the Ramsers flew from California, and on the evening of Thursday, February 12, 1970, in the chapel of Trinity Episcopal Church, Mrs. Herbert Francis Sturdy became the wife of Dr. Alton Ochsner. They flew to New York and spent their wedding night in an airport hotel before beginning their flight to Athens the next morning.

Ochsner may have been blinded briefly by the dazzle of a whirlwind romance, an episode oddly at variance with his carefully planned, conventional life, but as usual he had made the right decision. He ended up with a devoted wife who brightened his last eleven years, who played her role in the closing act with the same sympathy and understanding that Isabel had provided earlier. Jane's part was more demanding because, in Ochsner's old age, impatience and sometimes petulance finally caught up with him. She was a lively, engaging, even ornamental companion in his travels, a gracious sharer of his social activities, and a hard-working homemaker who cooked and cleaned and kept a mother-hen watch over his well-being.

Jane had lost a husband who had been respected in the profession of law, and found one who was renowned in the world of medicine. She scored no financial coup by marrying; she was in comfortable circumstances already. But she left the loneliness of widowhood for a round of excitement with a mate who had won her heart. To an acquaintance who congratulated her upon acquiring a companion for her old age, she snorted, "I don't have a companion, I have a lover."

Jane redecorated the Exposition Boulevard house, which had been neglected while Alton was living there alone or with Mims. Before long Ochsner had resumed a pace about as strenuous as the one he had maintained before Isabel became ill. Jane fitted well into her niche. She accompanied her husband on most of his trips and won acceptance by Alton's out-of-town friends whom he saw at professional meetings. She found New Orleans social customs and attitudes different from those of Los Angeles, but her evident devotion to Alton and her tact disarmed most who might have regarded a successor to Isabel as an interloper. Like Isabel, she had to be ready to prepare dinner for as many as six when Alton would call after lunch and announce that he was bringing guests home. He liked to entertain. The approachable Jane soon was on a first-name basis with Alton's women employees, whose relationship with the more reserved Isabel had been rather formal.

Friendly and impulsive, Jane sometimes barged into situations in a way unexpected by Alton. There was the time when Gerry Frawley was a house guest, and Ochsner, scheduled to conduct one of his bull pen sessions at Charity Hospital, asked the two women if they would like to attend. A few days earlier he had finished a paper on ulcers and read it to Jane. Before they started for the hospital, Jane told him, "Now, Alton, I have heard those terrible stories about you in the bull pen. I don't want to sit there and be ashamed of you, and I hope you'll be on your best behavior."

In the hospital they saw a young doctor, and Jane remarked to Gerry that she hoped Ochsner did not choose him for the cross-examination, because "he's just so adorable-looking." A patient was wheeled into the amphitheater, and the blond youngster who had attracted Jane's attention was called upon to discuss the case. "Have you looked at the X-rays?" Ochsner asked.

"Yes, sir."

"What is the trouble here?"

"An ulcer, sir."

Ochsner started his interrogation. "Give me three causes of ulcers."

The young man said, "Nicotine. Cigarette smoking." The assembled students, conscious of Ochsner's crusade, started laughing.

"What is the second?"

"Stress."

"What is the third?"

The student stammered, "I'm sorry, Dr. Ochsner. I don't know."

Remembering the paper she had read a few days earlier, Jane leaned over the rail, cupped her hands over her mouth, and hissed, "Coffee."

Not everybody in the room heard her. Ochsner looked up, but made no response. He told the youth, "You're a pretty good student." He never mentioned the incident to Jane, who explained, "I tell you, I was so carried away that I was participating. I was in it with that boy. It was the first time in my life I ever did a thing like that." Isabel never did.[2]

Old age was beginning to bear down on Ochsner when Jane came into his life, and as he moved toward his eightieth birthday, time was taking its toll. He became increasingly short-tempered and impatient, secretive,

2. Jane Ochsner, interview, 1977.

and loath to discuss problems. His knowledge of his own financial affairs was so vague—since Isabel always had handled matters—that Jane ran across a $100,000 bond that he did not remember owning. Although it was not his fault, inept handling of Isabel's estate resulted in a reopening of probate and the imposition of $60,000 in additional inheritance tax. He was an easy mark for stock and bond salesmen, and once Jane had to bail him out when he was being dunned for payments on some transactions that he had made and forgotten. Since his name was on the sign outside the vast Jefferson Highway medical complex, most of the public assumed that he was a multimillionaire, and Isabel and then Jane had to be constantly on guard against attempts to overcharge him for goods and services and against schemes to cheat him. Yet there remained the appealing and refreshing aspect to this attitude toward money. As his eightieth birthday approached, Mrs. Slaughter consulted with John about sending him a gift. John said his father would not want a personal present, but would be grateful for a donation to the Ochsner Medical Foundation. When Alton opened the birthday card from Mrs. Slaughter, a check for $500,000 fell out—payable to the Foundation.

Jane, accustomed to being deferred to by Herbert Sturdy, inherited a second husband who had been crowned ruler of the household by Isabel. He made no gestures toward helping with the chores, living as a sort of honored guest even after the long-time housekeeper quit and left Jane to run things alone, with only occasional hired help.

As a young man he had been a speedy and aggressive automobile driver. As he grew older, his driving did not improve, and his boiling point got lower. When his eyesight faded, Jane insisted on taking the wheel herself, especially at night, and thereby let herself in for some verbal abuse, no matter who else was in the car. "For God's sake, why don't you go?" he would demand if she made a cautionary pause.

Friends noted that he seemed to enjoy belittling Jane in the company of others. Whether a latent streak of sadism was surfacing or whether he only was attracting attention to himself is not clear, but occasional examples occurred. Sometimes his wife knew how the students in the bull pen felt. He did not like to lose. Jane beat him in a Scrabble game soon after they were wed, and he never played again.

He did not achieve his successes without an appreciation of tact, and that is why one late-life lapse is memorable. In toasting the bride-to-be of a grandson, he welcomed her to "our distinguished family." A younger Alton Ochsner would have known better.

In his declining years, associates were taken aback by an exhibition of Ochsner's temper that they had never seen when he was younger. Trustees of the Foundation were discussing a proposal by the Schick Centers for the Control of Smoking and Weight to open an antismoking facility on the Ochsner campus. The centers were part of Pat Frawley's business empire. The idea of having a program for aggressively combatting cigarettes naturally appealed to Ochsner, and he heartily supported the plan. But internist William D. Davis, Jr., spoke out sharply against having an outside health activity on the Ochsner property. Ochsner grew increasingly angry as he listened to Davis' arguments. White-faced, he pointed a finger at Davis. "You are bullheaded, Bill," he exploded. "I can't believe you said it." Surprised by the vehemence, others at the meeting sat in uncomfortable silence. The proposal was rejected, although the Foundation later established its own smoking-aversion clinic.[3] Ochsner quit speaking to Davis for months, but it was inevitable that the long-time colleagues would be reconciled and the incident eventually forgotten.

The outburst was the reaction of an old man. In earlier days, at a Tulane senior banquet, students ganged up on Ochsner, sewed him in a hospital bag, jammed half a dozen lighted cigarettes between his lips, and rolled him around on the floor. The professor took it with a laugh.

Human frailties aside, Ochsner was a commanding figure who reached the eighty-five-year mark with his faculties intact and his zest for living hardly diminished. Jane's serene influence helped. Even his obsessive punctuality—he invariably reached an airport an hour before departure time—abated in the calm environment that she provided.

3. Thomas P. Gore II, interview, April, 1978.

19 "Do What You Have to Do"

In view of the genes handed down by his father and mother—and in line with his own sometimes-crude sense of humor—Alton Ochsner joked that he would live to be a hundred and then either go to the electric chair for rape or be shot in a whorehouse raid. As it turned out, extreme old age was cruel, bringing illness and injury, pain and perplexity. Not surprisingly, considering the habits of a lifetime, he refused to be downed by his ailments. Four months before his death, he attended a meeting in Paris. Two weeks before entering the hospital for his last stay, he was in Jacksonville for a bank directors' session.

His earlier medical history included the appendectomy performed by Mims Gage and a fistula operation by Merrill Hines. Ochsner's reputation for stoicism was enhanced by the fistula procedure. He was propped up on the stretcher, reading the morning newspaper, while he was being wheeled into the operating room at the Camp Plauché hospital. The next morning when Hines went to his bed to check on him, he was nowhere to be found. Hines telephoned his home and was informed that Ochsner had gone to Shreveport to present a paper.[1]

"I don't know whether it is just that he has so much on his mind and has so much to do that he ignores discomfort and what would ordinarily be a very painful condition, or whether he was just born with a high pain threshold," commented orthopedic surgeon A. William Dunn, who removed a damaged cartilage from one of Ochsner's arthritic knees. "I am inclined to believe that stoicism plays a large part." Ochsner was about eighty when he tore the cartilage, an injury Dunn believed occurred when he was bounding up the stairs. X-rays were made of both knees. "I have done many total knee replacements in patients with completely disabling pain in their knees, but whose disease was much less advanced than Dr.

---

1. Hines, interview, 1985.

Ochsner's," Dunn said.[2] Ochsner soon was climbing the stairs again, without a limp.

One morning in the early 1960s, he was doing push-ups as part of the Canadian Air Force exercises when he experienced a pain in the chest. He thought at first he had strained a muscle; when the pain worsened, he feared he had damaged his heart. X-rays revealed that he had crushed the eleventh dorsal vertebra. He had an electrically operated hospital bed set up in the living room of his home and spent two weeks flat on his back. With the aid of a dictating device, he used the time to prepare papers.

The physical problems mounted. The doctor who had devoted so much thought and effort to research on ulcers developed one of his own, a benign duodenal lesion. In December, 1979, he fell in the bathroom while dressing and crushed the body of the seventh dorsal vertebra. The pain was severe. Because of the ulcer, internist Chesley Hines did not want to prescribe aspirin, and ordered instead a combination of Tylenol and codeine. Ochsner was allergic to the Tylenol and became so ill "I thought I was going to die." Son John feared the fall had caused a head injury to his father, but a brain scan ruled this out. After about ten weeks the associated vertigo disappeared, but the back pain persisted for a year.

Ochsner was convinced that he had cancer of the stomach when, in the summer of 1980, he lost about twenty-five pounds as a result of anorexia, an aversion to eating. His mind was relieved only after exhaustive tests proved negative. The answer was found by William Arrowsmith, the Clinic's long-time whiz in internal medicine. He asked whether Ochsner had pain in the temples and difficulty in swallowing, because he suspected that the problem was temporal arteritis, inflammation of arteries leading to the head. Ochsner's answer was no to both questions. But he had an elevated sedimentation rate and anemia, and Arrowsmith suggested that the cause also might be polyarteritis rheumatica—inflammatory rheumatism. Arrowsmith said if this were true, there was a therapeutic test that would prove it. He prescribed five-milligram doses of the steroid prednisone. "I took one tablet and within an hour I felt well," Ochsner reported. He continued to take two tablets a day, as his symptoms disappeared and he gained weight. The relief was welcome, but the price was high, as will be seen. Only afterward did he realize that he did indeed have difficulty in swallowing in connection with the anorexia.[3]

2. A. William Dunn to Harkey, February 24, 1977.
3. AO Recollection, Health.

Meanwhile, the stout heart that had sustained Ochsner throughout a strenuous lifetime began to give way. The condition was diagnosed earlier, and Jane noticed the signs herself in 1977. A shortness of breath became evident as he pushed himself to take his customary brisk daily walks whether at home or away. As usual, he would not discuss his infirmities with his wife, who urged him to consult Clinic cardiologists. But he came home one day and told her, "I have what is known as an old man's heart. It is just giving out gradually." Cardiologist C. Lynn Skelton confirmed that he had an aortic valve stenosis, causing an insufficient flow of blood to the heart. The secretive Ochsner did not tell even Gertrude Forshag about the diagnosis. Jane worried about how she would handle an emergency, but was informed that no acute episode was likely.

By this time Jane had reduced the Ochsners' social schedule considerably, yet her husband still went to his office almost every working day. And his travel log for the first eight months of 1981 was not the kind that would be expected of an eighty-five-year-old man with a heart problem. In addition to the trip to Paris in May, he went to Jacksonville five times; Los Angeles twice; Washington twice; Puerto Rico; Stuart, Florida; Shreveport; Baton Rouge; Houston; and Tuskegee, Alabama. He and Jane planned to leave on Friday, September 4, on a flight to Athens, where he was to speak at a meeting of the International Cardiovascular Society, and then to go to Montreaux, Switzerland, for a convention of the International Society of Surgery. His Presbyterian luck ran out.

The last days of Alton Ochsner proved that age had not stifled the spirit of an optimistic activist. They also made a point about the revolution in medical care in which he was a ringleader: Wonders could be performed in an operating room. But when a patient's time had come, no miracles would save him.

On Sunday, August 30, he was as vigorous as he had been in a long time, looking forward to the trip to Europe. John, who was secretary of the cardiovascular society, also was scheduled to be in Athens, along with Mary Lou. Ochsner must have been ailing in his office on Tuesday, September 1, because he went to see Skelton. The cardiologist found he was in mild heart failure. Congestion had developed in the lungs because the heart was not up to pumping out the fluids in the normal way.

Skelton prescribed diuretics and told Ochsner to stay in bed at home and to cancel the flight to Greece. As he was leaving his office, not knowing of course that it was the last time ever, Ochsner turned to Miss Forshag. "You know, it's a good thing John will be in Greece. It would be too traumatic for him if he had to do a heart operation on me. But I've got a lot of faith in Noel Mills." The astounded secretary thus learned that her boss had the long-standing heart ailment.[4] Skelton telephoned John to alert him to the fact that "your dad's in poor shape."

When he reached home, Ochsner told Jane in a matter of fact way, "We're not going to Greece." She was thankful because she had wondered what she would do if her husband became critically ill in a foreign country. Ochsner was comfortable during the next couple of days and urged John to go on to Athens, since he was in charge of the program and was needed there. John concluded that there was no immediate emergency and that a decision about how to treat his father could await his return.

On Friday, September 4, when Jane took Alton's breakfast to his room, she found him seated on a bench at the foot of the bed, trembling. "This is only a lack of potassium. I've been taking diuretics," Ochsner explained. Within three or four minutes the shaking ceased, but he ate little of his breakfast. Jane knew something was wrong, for he always had a good appetite. "I want you to go to the hospital," she told him. "I don't want the responsibility of you over this Labor Day weekend."

Ochsner was furious. "Who's the doctor in this family?" he demanded. "We have to have it understood that you're not to practice medicine. I know when I should to go the hospital." In the course of a telephone conversation with Miss Forshag, Jane mentioned that she was having difficulties with her husband.

"You mustn't cross him at all; it would upset him more," the secretary advised. Then she quickly called Merrill Hines. Hines arranged for a hospital room and told Skelton what had happened. Skelton telephoned Ochsner, who announced, "Oh, Janie. Guess what. I'm going to the hospital."

He had never been to the Clinic or hospital any way but fully dressed, but this time he was wearing bedroom slippers as Jane helped him into the automobile. There was a flash of the old Ochsner as they arrived at the emergency room. Two women rolled out a wheelchair. "Oh, look how lucky I am to have these pretty girls take care of me," he said.

On Saturday his condition worsened, and tests revealed that he had experienced at least one severe heart attack. Jane believed it occurred at the time she found him trembling, although he did not complain of pain then. In the late afternoon he insisted that Jane go home and dress to

4. Forshag, interview, 1981.

attend a party being given by a neighbor. In the early evening Skelton called. "Dr. Ochsner is dying," he said. "I want you to come back out here as soon as you can." When she walked into the room, Ochsner wanted to know "What in the name of God are you doing here, honey? I sent you home." She told him "It was too lonesome," and he remarked, "Well, fine. I'm glad." That evening Skelton explained that heart surgery might be needed to save Ochsner's life. Heart catheterization would have to be done to pinpoint the problem.[5]

Noel Mills was summoned from his cabin near Picayune, Mississippi, where he had gone for the Labor Day weekend, and the other members of his surgical team were rounded up. If open-heart restorative surgery became necessary, Ochsner would be in good hands. Mills and John Ochsner had done hundreds of the procedures, and once had a series of more than three hundred consecutive cases without an operative death. If catheterization revealed that Ochsner's condition was the result of defective cardiac valves or arteries, his age would not automatically rule out reparative surgery. Older patients had been successfully operated upon at the hospital, although John Ochsner later estimated that perhaps three-quarters of the institutions performing open-heart surgery would have decided on the basis of his father's age alone that the procedure was contraindicated.

On Sunday, September 6, all the resources of the Ochsner medical institutions were concentrated on an effort to save the dying principal founder. In the operating theater where he had been the dominant figure for nearly twenty years, the attempt began with catheterization performed by Skelton and Thad F. Waites. Mills and his associates stood by, ready to roll him into an operating room and begin their task once the causes of the problem were known. Akky joined Jane. So did Mims, who had flown in from Florida, and Jane's daughter Sally, who had hurried from California. Sis had been summoned from London, but had not yet arrived.

Fully conscious, Ochsner knew why he was being catheterized. Before the procedure began, he told Mills that if surgery seemed indicated, he wanted it done. It was the last medical decision he ever made, and it was completely in character.[6] He never would have passively submitted to death. Jane, too, favored an operation. When she saw Mills in the corridor she asked, "Noel, can you operate? Please do." Mills cautioned,

5. Jane Ochsner, interview, 1981.
6. Hines, interview, 1981.

"Well, honey, he's eighty-five," whereupon she interjected, "Yes, but he really isn't eighty-five, only chronologically."

Cardiac catheterization involves introducing a tube into the blood vessels of the heart in order to inject dye. With X-ray pictures cardiologists can observe the course of the dye. This enables them to know which heart valves are working, which arteries are blocked. The procedure is done with a local anesthetic, and Ochsner could talk with the doctors, even watch the X-ray pictures on a screen.

Skelton and Waites had difficulty threading the catheter through an artery to reach the heart. First they tried to enter a blood vessel in the right groin area, and then the left. In both instances the path of the artery was so tortuous—a result of age—that they couldn't reach the heart. They told Ochsner they would have to go through the upper arm, and this time they obtained the pictures they wanted.

They found that the aortic valve was not working, and that because of arteriosclerosis—hardening of the arteries—one of the blood vessels was blocked. The condition was the type that made Ochsner a candidate for surgery. The valve could be replaced with a pig valve, and the occluded artery could be bypassed with a graft in order that the flow of blood to the heart could be resumed. Merrill Hines leaned over the patient and said, "Chief, they're going to operate."

"Do what you have to do, Merrill," came the reply.

By telephone from Athens, John concurred in the judgment of his two brothers and with Jane that the operation should be done. The family members who had been waiting outside were brought in to speak to Ochsner, then he was moved to the room where the surgery took place. The team went to work immediately. Present with Mills were two surgeon assistants, an anesthesiologist and assistant, a scrub nurse, two circulating nurses, and the two technicians who operated the heart-lung apparatus. Merrill Hines also scrubbed and was on hand to keep in touch with the family members waiting in the surgeons' lounge. Since it was Sunday, the surgical area was quiet.

In open-heart surgery, the heart is stilled while surgeons replace defective valves and install bypass grafts to restore the flow of blood around clogged-up vessels. The patient is sustained, meanwhile, on the heart-lung device that oxygenates the blood and takes the place of the heart in circulating it throughout the body. A critical moment comes when the repairs are completed and the heart once again must take over its function as the oxygenator is disconnected. In order to reach the heart, the surgeon must split the sternum, or breast bone, and spread the ribs to make an opening. Afterward the halves of the severed sternum are wired together; eventually, the bone knits.

Mills was increasingly optimistic as he proceeded with the operation. "It was one of the most pleasant days of my life," he remarked, "because I had the first team with me and we just clicked along and did the job and got a good result. It couldn't have gone better." He had no misgivings about Ochsner's heart once he opened the chest and saw that, except for the one occluded artery and the diseased valve, it looked exceptionally sound, considering Ochsner's age. Hines leaned over the anesthesiologist's shoulder to peer into the heart. "You see any gold down there?" a nurse asked. "This man's got a golden heart." When Mills called for the replacement pig's valve, the nurse held it up and remarked, "That's twenty-three hundred dollars itself." The substitute valve was installed and a graft bypass provided for the obstructed artery.

As Mills expected, the heartbeat was strong when the patient was taken off the oxygenator. "We were thrilled because we thought he would make it," the surgeon said. One difficulty was encountered. It did not seem to be significant at the time, but later would be recognized as ominous. "The sternum was almost melted away because of the steroid he had been taking," Mills recalled. "You could take your finger and break it off as if it were an eggshell." And inside the breast bone there was oozing from the marrow. The oozing finally was controlled by packing the area with gelfoam. Mills had to improvise and use reinforcing wires in order to close the sternum. "There was very little substance. I don't think in all my years I've seen a sternum as fragile as his." The prednisone had given Ochsner two years of relief from a potentially disabling ailment, but it had not been an unmixed blessing. Nevertheless, Mills was elated as he told the family how well the operation had gone and sent his patient to the intensive care unit.[7]

The cardiologist and heart surgeon had done their jobs. Now the key figure became an anesthesiologist, Robert J. Marino. In addition to their duties in surgery, anesthesiologists at Ochsner are the acute care physicians who coordinate the activities of the intensive care unit. The ICU is the last hope for the desperately ill, a facility equipped for continuous monitoring and for sustaining those who would die without the support of modern devices. At Ochsner, patients who have undergone open-heart

7. Noel L. Mills, interview, October 2, 1981.

operations are taken there instead of to the surgical recovery room, where others spend their first hours after surgery. The ICU is a bustling, brightly lighted area where doctors, nurses, and technicians outnumber patients. Ochsner was bedded in a central location, under constant watch. He was placed on a ventilator, an apparatus that takes over the breathing function by passing air into and out of the lungs through a tube inserted into the trachea.

It was in the ICU, not the operating room, that the critical, life-or-death battle was waged. Marino and his colleagues succeeded in stabilizing the cardiovascular status, bringing the heart output to acceptable levels. But while winning on one front, they were losing on another. Respiratory difficulties developed, the beginning of an overwhelming viral infection of the lungs and trachea. The virus was a form of herpes that causes a thickening of the tissues and prevents the exchange of oxygen and carbon dioxide. What two years of steroids did to Ochsner is questionable, but he was vulnerable to infection.

Anxiety intensified when the patient was slow to begin breathing on his own, off the ventilator. The family members—by now Sis had arrived—looked forward to removal of the tube as a sign that he was getting better. Keeping touch by telephone from Athens, John was told that things were progressing satisfactorily. But when, on the third postoperative day, he learned that his father still depended on the respirator, he headed home. "Of the many thousands of heart operations I have done," he said, "I can count on my two hands and two feet—no more than twenty—the number of patients who were still on the respirator on the third day."

Ochsner did reach a point where Marino felt it was safe to extubate (remove the tube), but some thirty hours afterward the patient was in such distress that it had to be replaced.[8] From then on, the road was downhill. Ochsner was conscious at this time. While the tube was in his throat, he could not talk but wrote messages on a slate board. He could speak faintly during the period when he was extubated. His last spoken words to Jane were: "Don't worry, honey. I'll make it."

Doctors tried to overcome the infection with drugs, but nothing worked. Marino was on the long-distance telephone to other medical centers asking about any new measures, as yet unreported, that could be tried. Finally, Ochsner lapsed into unconsciousness. He was moved from

8. Robert J. Marino, interview, December 2, 1981.

the spot where all eyes could be on him to a private cubicle. The time came for a decision. With ventilation, intravenous feeding, and drugs, he could be kept alive indefinitely, but as an insensate being—*vegetable* is the usual term—without hope. At a family conference it was decided to withhold extraordinary measures and allow the inevitable to occur. It was not technically an instance of pulling the plug. The ventilator was left on. Nobody doubted what Ochsner's own wishes would have been. He often insisted there was no reason to prolong life in hopeless cases. And he had been specific in a conversation with John: "Please don't ever let me get senile."

On Thursday, September 24, Jane asked Dr. Kenneth G. Pfifer, pastor of the St. Charles Avenue Presbyterian Church, to come to the hospital. As she and he were entering the ICU they encountered Mims, who said, "Daddy has a number of hours yet, Jane." They found Marino at the bedside.

"Jane, I want you to hold Alton's hand," Pfifer instructed. "I want to say a prayer." As he finished, a bell began ringing. "I looked up and his breathing had stopped," Jane related. The bell was part of the monitoring system, set to sound the alarm if the patient ceased breathing. Jane said that "something just made me go" to Alton's bedside that morning. Ochsner was the third of his family to die in this hospital that would not have existed except for his fame. Little Allen Davis was the first, Isabel the second.

Private funeral services, with only the family in attendance, were conducted at the St. Charles Avenue Presbyterian Church by Dr. Pfifer. Ochsner was buried beside Isabel in the Garden of Memories, a cemetery which permits only small markers, no monuments, on the graves.

The formal farewell, called a "Service of Tribute and Thanksgiving for the Life of Alton Ochsner," was said on Saturday, October 3, 1981, on the landscaped grounds of the Alton Ochsner Medical Institutions. A stage was set up alongside the fountain that is the centerpiece of the campus entrance, and chairs were provided for several hundred persons who turned out to pay their respects.

Governor David C. Treen read a message from President and Mrs. Ronald Reagan, who said they joined those assembled "to mourn the death of a man whose daring and indomitable spirit have brought hope and promise to our generation and generations to come." Ochsner was a friend of Mrs. Reagan's surgeon stepfather, Loyal Davis of Chicago.

Speakers of the service emphasized the various roles that Ochsner played. Governor Treen enumerated the achievements of The Patriot. Mike DeBakey, in discussing The Surgeon, recalled his apprenticeship under Ochsner. James D. Hardy, president of the American College of Surgeons, spoke of The Teacher, and C. Rollins Hanlon, executive director of the college, honored The Researcher. Richard W. Freeman, former chairman of the Alton Ochsner Medical Foundation, talked of The Civic Leader, and Merrill Hines, Ochsner's successor as president of the Foundation, of The Founder. Presiding at the ceremony were the two physicians who were chosen, with Ochsner's blessing, to lead the Ochsner institutions toward the half-century mark of their existence. They are George H. Porter III, president of the Foundation, and Frank A. Riddick, Jr., medical director of the Clinic.

In 1986 another ceremony was held at the site, this time for the unveiling of a bronze statue of Ochsner, a gift from one of his patients, Louis J. Roussel, New Orleans financier.

20 Legacy

A ghost has no place in the bustling, highly scientific environment of a modern medical center, and nobody has reported seeing a white-coated apparition floating through the corridors of the buildings on the Jefferson Highway campus. Nevertheless, years after his death, Alton Ochsner remains a presence in the institutions that bear his name—an influence still felt when decisions are made. The leaders who carry on acknowledge a sense that he is looking over their shoulders. "I think of him often," muses Dr. George Porter. "He left a legacy that always will be with us. He casts a big shadow." Dr. Frank Riddick says that he and other staff doctors consciously "strive to maintain the individualized and personalized approach to patients that Dr. Ochsner did so well."

By the time of his death, and with his endorsement, the institutions were committed to new strategies made necessary by the developments in the golden age of medicine. In 1981 the Clinic was planning satellite treatment centers designed to take Ochsner services to the neighborhoods where patients live, and by 1986 there were six such facilities in the metropolitan New Orleans area, and one as far away as Baton Rouge. Others in southern states were on the drawing board, and the Ochsner label was gaining wider exposure than ever before. The expansion was a response to increasing competition: too many doctors were trying to make a living. In the golden age a shortage had become a surplus.

Ochsner himself lived long enough to see the beginnings of major changes in the ways of financing health care. He and his associates founded a Clinic that was run on a fee-for-service basis; that is, a patient was billed after the fact for the treatment he received. In 1981 prepayment plans such as health maintenance organizations and preferred-provider organizations were establishing a beachhead, and more and more Americans turned to programs under which, for fixed amounts paid in advance, they were insured for whatever treatment and hospitalization they needed. The Ochsner institutions were among the pioneers to offer such arrangements in the New Orleans area, and since have marketed their services aggressively. The taboos against medical advertising no longer apply, and the Ochsner name is aired more widely than it ever was in Alton's lifetime.

Ochsner and his four fellow professors were forward-looking, certainly, but no seer could have forecast, back in 1940 and 1941, the form that the delivery of health care would take nearly fifty years later. Yet if somebody now were designing a medical center to take advantage of the opportunities offered in the late 1980s, the result probably would be a structure similar to that of the Ochsner institutions. Even posthumously, Ochsner's faith in his luck seems well placed.

The year 1986 was marked by a vigorous renewal of an uprising against cigarette smoking. The armed services cracked down with new restrictions, civilian smokers came under fire from advocates of a fume-free environment, and some cities banned smoking in public places. The American Medical Association pressed its drive for a ban on all cigarette advertising, already prohibited on the airwaves. Clearly, the tobacco industry was on the defensive to an extent unprecedented in the 1940s, when Ochsner's voice was the boldest warning of the health hazards.

And in 1987, the sixth year after his death, the New Orleans surgeon received credit from an authoritative source for his contributions to the cause. Walter S. Ross published a book, *Crusade: The Official History of the American Cancer Society,* in which he wrote: "Chest surgeons were the first in the country to detect a phenomenal increase in lung cancer. One, Dr. Alton Ochsner of New Orleans, was to have a particularly powerful effect in linking smoking with this trend in the United States." Ross gave an account of the meeting at which Ochsner's story about the Russian nobleman and his unfaithful wife helped persuade the board of directors of the cancer society to take a strong stand on the cigarette-cancer issue.

In the same year, the surgeon general of the United States Public Health Service, C. Everett Koop, hailed Ochsner as "one of the earliest and strongest foes of smoking. . . . He was very clear about the nature of the threat to health posed by cigarette smoking more than forty years ago." Koop added, "In the course of those forty years science and government have proven that Dr. Alton Ochsner was absolutely right."[1]

1. C. Everett Koop, address at symposium on smoking, New Orleans, February 27, 1987.

In 1986 Dr. Oscar Auerbach of the Veterans Administration Medical Center in East Orange, New Jersey, received the first Alton Ochsner Award Relating Smoking and Health, winning the $15,000 honorarium provided by Merrell Dow Pharmaceuticals, Inc. George Porter made the presentation at a convocation of the American College of Chest Physicians at San Francisco. Auerbach was a member of the committee that in 1964 drafted the first surgeon general's report pointing to the health hazards of smoking. In accepting the award, Auerbach noted that in 1964 "very few people were aware" of the harmful effects of cigarettes. In 1986, he added, there are "very few people who will say that cigarette smoking does *not* cause lung cancer and emphysema."[2]

The development that would have pleased Alton most also occurred in 1987. All of the facilities of the Ochsner Medical Institutions, home campus as well as satellites, officially became "smoke free." A drastic ban on smoking by patients, visitors, and employees took effect. The only exceptions applied to a few patients in the psychiatric area of the hospital and to guests who could smoke in the privacy of their own rooms in designated sections of the Brent House hotel. Otherwise, tobacco could not be used in the buildings or on the grounds of any Ochsner property. In announcing the policy, Porter and Riddick said the institutions had a special obligation to discourage smoking because Ochsner was a pioneer in linking cigarettes and lung cancer. They cited a statement made by Ochsner in 1954: "Every type of smoking carries a deadly risk. Tobacco is a loaded weapon. Time pulls the trigger."

The genes that Ochsner liked to think were shared with Paracelsus still were dominant in the third generation of his own brood, as well as in the second. Eight years after his death, sons Akky and John still were at the height of their medical careers, and six grandchildren either already were practicing or were in the various stages of training.

Akky, busy as a general surgeon in New Orleans, inherited his father's activist leanings and took a leading role in the conservative causes that Alton espoused. Akky's daughter Jessica Coller was in the private practice of dermatology in New Orleans. His daughter Isabel was practicing emergency medicine in the same city. The other living children of Akky and Barbara Mequet are Mequet Ochsner Smith, mother of three; Cecely; and Mary Lyons.

John, who held down his father's post as chief of surgery at the

2. Oscar Auerbach, at presentation ceremony in San Francisco, September 23, 1986.

Ochsner Clinic, was one of the country's leading heart surgeons and an officer in international professional societies. John and Mary Lou Hannon are the parents of John Lockwood, Jr. ("Lock"), an orthopedic surgeon at Ochsner, and Katherine Isabel, who was practicing ophthalmology at Louisville. Other children of John and Mary Lou are Joby Hannon and Frank Hannon.

The son of Mims and Corinne Cousins, Mims Gage Ochsner, Jr., was a medical officer in the United States Navy, stationed in the Philippines. His sister, Corinne Cousins, completed premedical training at Tulsa and was planning to enter medical school. The other children of Mims and Corinne are Laura Howard and Alexandra. The daughter of Mims and Rise Delmar, Skye Mims, was in school in California, where her mother, formerly on the Clinic staff, was practicing ophthalmology.

Sis, now Mrs. John Pelham Mann, wife of a retired British industrial executive, was living in New Canaan, Connecticut. None of the three sons of Sis and Allen Davis chose a medical career. Alton Ochsner Davis was an architect in New Haven, Connecticut; Allen Pinkerton Davis, a stock broker in New Orleans; Stephen Lockwood Davis, a travel agency proprietor in Hammond, Louisiana.

After Alton's death, Jane moved back to California to take up life again near her daughters, settling in Pasadena. Sally, Mrs. James L. Stewart, lived on Taluca Lake in the San Fernando Valley. Nancy, Mrs. Henry T. DeNero, lived in Pasadena with her husband and two children, Karen and John, Alton's only step-grandchildren.

Late in 1988 the number of patients registered at the Ochsner Medical Institutions went over the one million mark. Alton would have greeted the development, unheard of among other independent southern medical centers, with unconcealed pride. The patient list continued to expand at an unprecedented rate. There was the making of a dynasty in a family with so many members involved in medicine. All in all, it appeared that Alton Ochsner would be remembered for a long time to come. He would have relished that, and furthermore would not have been in the least surprised.

Bibliography

BOOKS

Bickner, Mrs. Donald W., Mrs. John W. Lytle, and Mrs. Ervin C. Petula, eds. *Echoes of the Past*. Kimball, S.D., 1980.

Caldwell, Guy A. *Early History of the Ochsner Medical Center*. Springfield, Ill., 1965.

Davis, Loyal. *Fellowship of Surgeons*. Chicago. 1960.

Duffy, John. *The Tulane University Medical Center*. Baton Rouge, 1984.

Durant, Will. *The Reformation*. Vol. VI of Durant, *The Story of Civilization*. New York, 1957.

Dyer, John P. *Tulane: The Biography of a University*. New York, 1966.

Lyons, Albert S., and R. Joseph Petrucelli II. *Medicine: An Illustrated History*. New York, 1978.

Major, Ralph H. *A History of Medicine*. Vol. II of 2 vols. Springfield, Ill., 1954.

Shimkin, Michael B. *Contrary to Nature*. Washington, D.C., 1977.

Wilds, John. *Crises, Clashes, and Cures*. New Orleans, 1978.

——. *Ochsner's: An Informal History of the South's Largest Private Medical Center*. Baton Rouge, 1985.

ARTICLES

Bolton, Clint. "Carnival: From Kimball to Camelot." *New Orleans* (February, 1971), 51–65.

Creech, Oscar, J. P. Woodhall, and Alton Ochsner. "The Necessity for Tracheotomy in the Treatment of Tetanus to Prevent Lethal Respiratory Complications." *Surgery*, XXXI (1951), 62–73.

Gray, Paul. "In Celebration of Life." *Time*, May 14, 1979, pp. 86–94.

Knowles, John H. "The Struggle to Stay Healthy," *Time*, August 9, 1976, pp. 60–62.

Mahorner, Howard R., and Alton Ochsner. "The Use of Leeches in the Treatment of Phlebitis and the Prevention of Pulmonary Embolism." *Annals of Surgery*, CVIII (1933), 408–21.

Meade, William H., and Alton Ochsner. "Spool Cotton as a Suture Material." *Journal of the American Medical Association*, CXIII (1939), 2230–31.

Ochsner, Alton. "Acute Intestinal Obstruction." *Southern Medical Journal*, XXIV (1931), 93–97.

———. "Die Bluttransfusion nach Percy." *Klin Wchnscher*, XXXVI (1923), 697–712.

———. "Judgment, Accuracy and Honesty in Medical Reporting." *Mississippi Valley Medical Journal*, LXXXI (1959), 45–47.

———. "Lobectomy or Pneumonectomy." *Surgical Clinics of North America*, XLVI (1966), 1255–64.

———. "My Experience in Introducing Blood Transfusions into Europe." *Medical Tribune*, August 28, 1974, p. 19.

———. "On the Role of Vitamins C and E in Medicine." *Executive Health* (1974), 1–6.

———. "Prognosis of Malignant Melanoma as Influenced by Therapy." *Arizona Medicine*, CLV (1962), 539–45.

———. "Rudolph Matas: Scientist, Scholar and Humanist." *Journal of Cardiovascular Surgery*, III (1962), 3–11.

———. "Surgical Treatment of Pulmonary Tuberculosis." *International Surgical Digest*, XII (1931), 321–28.

———. "The Treatment of Acute Empyema." *International Surgical Digest*, XI (1931), 67–74.

Ochsner, Alton, and W. B. Ayers. "Case of Epignathus." *Surgery*, XXXI (1951), 560–64.

Ochsner, Alton, and John Blalock. "Carcinoma of the Stomach: Need for Earlier Diagnosis and More Adequate Therapy." *Journal of the Florida Medical Association*, XLII (1955), 99–107.

Ochsner, Alton, and Michael DeBakey. "Primary Pulmonary Malignancy." *Surgery, Gynecology and Obstetrics*, LXVIII (1939), 433–51.

———. "The Role of Vasospasm in Thrombophlebitis and Its Treatment by Novocain Block of the Sympathetics." *Tri-State Medical Journal* (1941), 2654–56.

———. "The Surgical Treatment of Coronary Disease." *Surgery*, II (1937), 428–56.

———. "Thrombophlebitis and Phlebothrombosis." *Southern Surgeon*, VIII (1939), 269–90.

Ochsner, Alton, I. M. Gage, R. A. Cutting, and Earl Garside. "Relative Values of Heat and Cold on Experimentally Produced Peritonitis." *Proceedings of the Society for Experimental Biology and Medicine*, XXVII (1927), 220–22.

Ochsner, Alton, Mims Gage, and Kiyoshi Hosoi. "Treatment of Peptic Ulcer

Based on Physiological Principles." *Surgery, Gynecology and Obstetrics,* LXII (1936), 257–74.

Ochsner, Alton, M. Meyer, and Karl Nather. "Der Parietale Inspiratorische Ventilpneumothorax, Der Exspirations-Ventiltroikart." *Deutsche Ztschr. f Chir,* CLXXXVIII (1924), 13–75.

Ochsner, Alton, and Ambrose Storck. "The Prevention of Peritoneal Adhesions by Papain." *Annals of Surgery,* CIV (1936), 736–47.

NEWSPAPERS

Brule County (Kimball, S.D.) *News,* July 3, 1980.
Kimball (S.D.) *Star,* date missing.
New Orleans *Daily States,* May 4, 1896.
New Orleans *Times-Picayune,* 1927–81.

MATERIALS IN THE ALTON OCHSNER PAPERS, HISTORIC NEW ORLEANS COLLECTION, NEW ORLEANS, LOUISIANA

Letters

Alway, J. Douglas, to Geoffrey I. W. Cottam, February 22, 1974.
Boyd, David P., to Ira Harkey, February 23, 1978.
Charbonnet, L. Sidney, Jr., to Ira Harkey, January 22, 1977.
Cole, Warren H., to Ira Harkey, November 5, 1976.
Cottam, Geoffrey I. W., to Ira Harkey, August, 1977.
Dunn, A. William, to Ira Harkey, February 24, 1977.
Fousek, Mrs. George, to Ira Harkey, July 8, 1977.
Graham, Evarts A., to Alton Ochsner, February 5, 1957.
King, Richard, to Ira Harkey, December 31, 1976.
Matas, Rudolph, to Lincoln Davis, April 25, 1929.
Ochsner, Alton, to Geoffrey I. W. Cottam, June 29, 1918.
Ochsner to family, December 3, 1922, November 18, 1924.
Ochsner to Evarts A. Graham, February 19, 1957.
Ochsner to President Gerald Ford, September 10, 1974.
Ochsner to President Richard M. Nixon, July 20, 1971, May 21, 1974.
Peterson, Marvin G., to Ira Harkey, February 3, 1977.
Shimkin, Michael B., to Ira Harkey, n.d.
Wangensteen, Owen, to Ira Harkey, April 4, 1978.
Wilson, Julius Lane, to Ira Harkey, February 26, 1977.
Zeigler, Rowland F., to Ira Harkey, November 8, 1976.

Interviews by the Authors

Beacham, Woodard, D., 1980
Bell, Bryan, 1977
Bradford, Joseph K., 1976
Caldwell, Guy A., 1979
Carnahan, Julie M., 1977
Charbonnet, L. Sidney, Jr., 1977
Clark, Mrs. Russell, 1977
Cummins, Harold V., Jr., 1978
Davis, Eugene Allen, 1977
DeCamp, Paul T., 1978
Echols, Dean H., 1977
Forshag, Gertrude, 1976–87
Gage, Mrs. Mims, 1977
Garside, Earl, 1977
Gillis, Mrs. Gary, 1977
Gore, Thomas P., II, 1978
Hanley, Patrick H., 1978
Harris, Rufus C., 1978
Healy, George W., Jr., 1977
Hines, Merrill O., 1976–87
Kaynor, Ava Marie Ochsner, 1976
Kittredge, Willoughby E., 1985
Krementz, Edward T., 1980
LeJeune, Francis E., 1977
LeJeune, Mrs. Francis E., 1977
Loria, Frank L., 1978
Mann, Mrs. Isabel (Sis) Ochsner, 1977
Marino, Robert J, 1981
Mayerson, Hyman S., 1978
Mills, Noel L., 1981
Ochsner, Alton, 1950–81
Ochsner, Alton, Jr., 1977
Ochsner, Mrs. Jane Sturdy, 1977–81
Ochsner, John L., 1977
Ochsner, Mrs. John L., 1977
Ochsner, Mims Gage, 1977
Ochsner, Seymour, 1978
Porter, George H., III, 1978–87
Riddick, Frank A., Jr., 1978–87
Schramel, Robert J., 1980
Smallpage, Mrs. Samuel M., 1977

Tyrone, Curtis H., 1977
Weed, John C., 1979
Weiss, Thomas E., 1979
Zieman, John A., 1986

Miscellaneous

Bayne-Jones, Stanhope. "Report of a Survey of the School of Medicine, Tulane University." Washington, D.C., 1956.

Mayo, William J. "Memoir: Albert J. Ochsner." Augustana Hospital School of Nursing publication. N.d.

Ochsner, Alton. "Peculiar Individuals Whom I Have Aided Without Apparent Success." New Orleans. N.d.

Index